Not As Bad As The Truth

Also by David Pawson:

Jesus Baptises in One Holy Spirit
Once Saved, Always Saved?
The Challenge of Islam to Christians
The Normal Christian Birth
The Road to Hell
When Jesus Returns
Word and Spirit Together

Not As Bad
As The Truth

Memoirs of an
Unorthodox Evangelical

David Pawson

Hodder & Stoughton
LONDON SYDNEY AUCKLAND

Copyright © 2006 by David Pawson

First published in Great Britain in 2006

The right of David Pawson to be identified as the Author
of the Work has been asserted by him in accordance with the
Copyright, Designs and Patents Act 1988.

1

British Library Cataloguing in Publication Data
A record for this book is available from the British Library

ISBN 0 340 86427 3

Printed and bound in Great Britain by
Bookmarque Ltd, Croydon, Surrey

The paper and board used in this paperback are natural recyclable products
made from wood grown in sustainable forests. The manufacturing processes
conform to the environmental regulations of the country of origin.

Hodder & Stoughton
A Division of Hodder Headline Ltd
338 Euston Road
London NW1 3BH
www.madaboutbooks.com

I would like to dedicate this book to all those who with selfless and sacrificial service have distributed my teaching material, opening up doors for a worldwide ministry, among whom are:

Jim and Linden Harris – UK and overseas
Peter and Bev Bettson (retired) – Australia
John and Jean Spall – Australia
Nelson Garcia (deceased) – Philippines
Bob Harvey – United States
Chung Sieu Leng – Malaysia
Johan Carstens – Africa
Rudi Hafliger – Switzerland
John Dunning – New Zealand
Kim Tan – Spanish and Chinese languages
De Wet Ferreira – South Africa
De Wet Swanepoel – South Africa
Varian Watson – Canada

Many others have also circulated tapes and for them all I thank the Lord.

Contents

Foreword
by Sir Cliff Richard OBE

All of us, I guess, meet people during our journey through life who touch or influence us in a way that leaves a lasting impression. For me, David Pawson was just such a person.

During the 1970s and early 1980s, I remember so vividly sitting, Sunday by Sunday, in the back row of Millmead Baptist church in Guildford, enthralled by David's preaching. I was a young and hungry Christian, still puzzled and unsure about many aspects of theology and doctrine. I was no academic and many sermons I listened to in those early days left me untaught and unmoved. But at Millmead I was fed. In his book, David explains that his preaching intention was 'to make Scripture real and relevant'. I know of no one who did that with more effect. I would learn and understand more in a forty-five-minute David Pawson sermon than from any other teaching source. In his inimitable, low-key and chatty style, David spoke right into my heart – everything always so real and relevant and personal. Parables that I thought I knew leapt into life with fresh meaning and dusty passages that seemed obscure and difficult became exciting and pertinent.

I was baptised during a Sunday evening service at Millmead, and it was David who baptised me.

We are influenced so much by the people we meet. I am so grateful that, for a relatively short period in my life, I had the privilege of listening to, learning from, and being inspired by one of God's great servants and communicators.

Foreword
by Jennifer Rees-Larcombe

There are two things that will always remind me of my illustrious relation, sparrows and beards! Because I've always felt sad when I find a dead bird I thought it was hardly surprising that the Almighty should also be concerned when a sparrow dies and falls to the ground. Then one day I was riveted as I listened to one of David's tapes on Matthew 10.

'When Jesus talks about sparrows "falling to the ground", his words could just as easily be translated "hops" to the ground.' At that time I spent most of my life in a wheelchair and had plenty of time to watch the sparrows in my garden hedge. Each one hopped to the ground to peck about in the dust a thousand times a day. Multiply that the world over and it suddenly dawned on me just how amazing God's love for us really is! This realisation was enhanced by another of David's tapes where he said that the phrase 'Seek the Lord's face' could also be translated 'Stroke the Lord's beard'. Through David's 'giveaway' remark I glimpsed the degree of intimacy that the

Creator of the universe wanted to enjoy with me – personally.

David has kept his personal life very well hidden throughout more than half a century, preferring people to concentrate on the message rather than the messenger but, at long last, in this book he has stepped out of the shadows. I hope that as you come to know the messenger as I have known him, you will find his message even more powerful.

For years I've waited eagerly for this book! I guessed it would be fascinating and, like the Queen of Sheba, I have not been disappointed. As far as I am concerned David Pawson is the greatest Bible Teacher of our time. Like the Master he has served for so many years, he has a way of taking complicated concepts that are far beyond the comprehension of ordinary minds and in a few simple words make them totally intelligible. Dusty old minor prophets have become real people to me as I have listened over many years to David's tapes; his knowledge of background history and his imaginative way 'of reading between the lines' have indeed 'unlocked' the Bible for me, along with many thousands of others the whole world over.

Because David has taken a controversial, hard-line approach to such things as divorce and remarriage, 'Leadership is Male' and his opposition to the concept of 'Once saved always saved', people who only know him through his sermons and books could well have developed a mental photo-fit picture of him as a harsh, Old Testament type prophet. Because he is my cousin (his uncle was my grandfather) I know that this is far from the truth. Yes, he most certainly is a fearless and outspoken prophet who never shrinks from facing unpopular subjects most of us prefer to ignore, but the man inside all that has one of the kindest hearts I have ever encountered. During my life I have hit some very dark times but David was willing to travel hundreds of miles out of his way, and carve valuable time from his tightly packed schedule, to visit me during those black moments, and his love and encouragement coupled with his wise advice have been invaluable.

Prologue
'It Always Happens to David'

This was one of those 'family sayings' that dogged me for many years. I think it originated with my mother, who said it with some amusement. My two sisters picked it up, with a slight undertone of resentment.

It just happened that my life has been full of unusual and unexpected events, most of which I have not sought. I have a habit of 'falling on my feet'. Opportunities have come my way. Coincidences have been common.

This can be illustrated by experiences of flying, which has played a major role in my life, especially when I was a chaplain in the Royal Air Force.

My very first flight was in a twin-engine, four-seater, second-hand plane bought for £3,800 and destined to be the first used by the Missionary Aviation Fellowship. I was sixteen and saw an announcement of a national tour to raise interest and support, including a 'limited number of free flights'. I was the first to arrive at Newcastle airport (then just a field and a shed), but to my dismay over two hundred joined me with the same hope. The plane finally landed and four smart young men in blue uniform, all of whom had served in World War II, emerged. Many were disappointed when told that the pilot would give only three of us the advertised free flight. Names were put in a cap. Guess whose was the first picked out! I am still in touch with the pilot alongside whom I sat during that thrilling experience.

On another occasion, I was allocated a very cramped 'economy' seat for a very long flight and was not looking forward to the tedious discomfort. While waiting for take-off, a groundcrew man in dungarees and a fluorescent jacket walked down the aisle, came straight to me and told me to pick up my hand luggage and follow him. Meekly obeying this complete stranger, I found myself led forward to an empty first-class seat. He left without another word. Was he an angel? He certainly had shining raiment!

I had been on a preaching tour of Australia and my next engagement was in India, a convention in Hyderabad run by Bakt Singh. I could just make it by transferring flights at Bangkok in Thailand. But the flight from Sydney was delayed and I missed my connection. I was stranded late at night, with no flights until the next day, which would not get me to India in time. I pleaded with the girl at the desk to find some way to get me there overnight and a nearby official overheard, muttered in her ear, then asked me if I'd mind not having any meal on the way. Puzzled, I said I'd put up with anything if they could get me there. It appeared that a brand new 747 was being delivered from the Boeing factory in Seattle, USA, to Delhi for Indian Airways and was refuelling at Bangkok. The shining monster duly landed and I was ushered on board. The huge cabin was dimly lit and deserted. From getting on to getting off I saw no one. I slept a bit and woke up wondering where I was. I was tempted to go upstairs and see the pilot but thought he might not know he had a stowaway and my sudden appearance might give him a heart attack – so I stayed put. Anyway, I made it.

Coincidence or providence? Lucky or led? My final example,

out of many others, points to the Lord's hand upon my journeys.

I was going to New Zealand for five weeks' ministry, covering most of the North and South islands and not relishing the travelling involved, by car, train or whatever. Landing at Auckland, my wife and I were met by a young man in smart white uniform who informed us he was our pilot during our stay! Obeying a prompting of the Spirit, he had mortgaged his house, bought a twin-engined, nine-seater plane 'to fly visiting ministers'. He had been a ski pilot, flying skiers to the Southern Alps around Mt Cook and could test the firmness of the snow with the plane skis. He flew us when and where we wanted and we became so blasé about our air taxi that when we took off from Nelson, the air traffic controller came on the radio to tell us I'd left my coat and case on the field. We arrived home feeling we'd had a holiday! The Lord honoured Wade's sacrificial obedience – he became the Prime Minister's personal pilot and now has a fleet of planes.

So now, perhaps, you can understand why my family teased me with 'It always happens to David'. Looking back over seventy-five years, I have had a most interesting life and would not wish to have exchanged it with anyone else.

I hope you will find it interesting as well. But I would not have written these memoirs for that reason alone, especially since I have now reached my 'anecdotage'. Indeed, for years I have resisted the very thought of an autobiography, with its suggestion of self-importance. However, increasing pressure from others came to a climax when I shared my experience of preaching with 600 men in Westminster Chapel. Their response to my testimony was quite extraordinary and showed me that sharing my story could help others to serve the Lord.

So I hope these pages will be instructive and inspiring as well as interesting.

Those who have received my annual newsletter, read the prologues in some of my books or simply listened to tapes will already be familiar with much written here. At least those glimpses are put together in a whole picture. Incidentally, my book *The Road to Hell* was advertised in a national Australian magazine under the headline 'Read David Pawson's autobiography'! I guess the reviewer had only read the introduction. Anyway, here's the real thing.

I wish to thank Jennifer Rees-Larcombe, daughter of my cousin Jean Rees, and (Sir) Cliff Richard, both ardent tape listeners, for their Forewords. And Ivan Wimbles, who laboriously transformed my handwritten manuscript into a form acceptable to the publisher. Above all, my wife, who intensely disliked the idea of such publicised egotism but who has loyally accepted it.

May you, the reader, share the enjoyment I have had in recalling and recording the goodness and mercy (the Good Shepherd's sheepdogs) that have followed me all the days of my life.

1

Family Trees

It was like looking into a mirror. I was reading the description of a man called Pawson who lived and died in the fifteenth century, sent to me by someone devoted to research into ancestry. To my amazement each detail of temperament and appearance fitted me exactly, even down to my nose (which 'runs' in the family). I have often wondered how much we are influenced by our genes. Here was an answer.

Such knowledge enables us to blame our forbears for our faults and weaknesses and excuse ourselves. And, of course, I can trace the undesirable traits in my nature to my most notorious ancestor, who bore the name of Adam. Nevertheless, I know that what I am is the result of the choices I have made and that God is justified in holding me responsible for what I have done with my heredity and environment.

It is both customary and instructive for biographies to begin with some account of preceding generations on both sides of an individual's family tree. So here goes, on the courtesy principle of 'ladies first'.

Mother came from the Scottish clan of 'Sinclair', whose

territory was the north-east tip around John o'Groats. Their motto was: 'Commit thy work to God'. One tradition claimed that the pure bloodline had been tainted by sailors in the Spanish Armada shipwrecked nearby and could be used to 'explain' violent outbursts of temper.

Halfway up the stairs in my boyhood home hung a full-length portrait of the most illustrious, Sir John Sinclair, famed for his agricultural research, for which he coined the word 'statistics'. He was resplendent in a vivid red jacket with appropriate tartan embellishment and a mysterious large bulge under his left armpit, which led to much speculation. Passing it so frequently, I was imbued with a sense of history.

My grandfather, another John Sinclair, and his brother Robert tramped south, crossed the border and settled in Newcastle upon Tyne, to make their fortune in tobacco manufacture, one in cigarettes (Craven 'A'), the other in pipes. When John retired he built an impressive granite and timber hunting lodge in Allendale, with a magnificent view of the Northumberland moors and the occasional derelict 'chimney' of former lead mining and smelting. Here my mother was born, fifteen years after her brothers and sister, virtually brought up as an only child. One brother, Harold, was killed in World War I and his little sister was convinced God had the same name, praying: 'Our Father, which art in heaven, Harold be Thy Name . . .'

Since there was no Church of Scotland anywhere near, the family attended a Methodist chapel as the next best thing. At one stage, the minister was the Rev. Samuel Pawson, my great uncle. One Sunday his young nephew, Cecil, was the preacher. He began with the memorable assertion that 'life is a long, straight road full of twistings and turnings'.

One young lady in the congregation, Miss Jean Sinclair, was captivated. It was love at first sight. Throughout their married life together, she always wrote a love-letter on each wedding anniversary, addressed to 'my preacher man'. She proved to be quite a remarkable helpmeet bringing 'a happiness no one can possibly describe and without which I cannot conceive how impoverished my life and experience would have been' (I'm quoting from my father's autobiography, *Hand to the Plough*, Denham House Press, 1973).

But her family did not approve, considering that she was marrying 'beneath' her, as they put it in those days (it was Lady Astor who said that 'all women do'). She was taken to Menton on the French Riviera to forget her infatuation but confided to her diary that as soon as she returned she was determined to marry Cecil Pawson. She did, though only her mother attended the ceremony.

Before turning to Father's side of the family, I must mention Mother's brother, who played an indirect role in my conversion. On his occasional later visits I was always in awe of him. He had inherited the cigarette business, my grandfather having died before I was born, and eventually reached the top of the Imperial Tobacco Company in London, driving to work in a carriage and pair (of horses) from his Hampstead home.

However, there was a spiritual side to him. As a young man, he had tried out every denomination to see which came nearest to his 'ideal' of New Testament practice, settling for one of the many varieties of the 'Brethren' (called 'the Glantons' after the Northumberland village where they began). He even wrote a book about the prophecies in Daniel and Revelation, as an ardent 'Dispensationalist', following Nelson Darby's innovative interpretation of Scripture. He was clearly wary of my father's Methodist affiliations and convictions, even though Methodism then was not as 'liberal' as it has since become.

He had seven children, three sons and four daughters. One of the latter, Lois, married Andrew Gray, head of Pickering and Inglis, leading Christian publishers in Glasgow. Another, Jean, married the leading British evangelist in the post-war years, Tom Rees (more of him later). His son Keith devours my tapes to this day.

So much for my Scottish ancestry. Now for the English.

I had always assumed that 'Pawson' was a contraction of 'Paul's son', like Poulson and even Polson. On a visit to Poland, I was amused to be called 'Mr Peacock'. When I asked why, they told me that in their language *paw* (pronounced 'pav' not 'por') was the name of that marvellous bird. On returning home, I discovered that the Anglo–Saxon *paw* had this same meaning. I always say I'd rather be descended from a peacock than a monkey. However, it does imply vanity!

The name is comparatively rare, though it has been borne by a famous footballer, a chocolate shop in Bournemouth and a stone quarry in Yorkshire. That county is their original home, centred in Wakefield. The tribal motto is '*Favente Deo*' (God favours).

Most Pawsons have been farmers and/or preachers. My father liked to claim direct descent from John Pawson, one of John Wesley's earliest and best-known colleagues in the eighteenth-century revival that reputedly saved England from the French revolution. I have his published letters on my shelf. Certainly Methodism was the strongest strand on my father's side of the family.

His father, David Ledger Pawson, was a Methodist minister, as much an evangelist as a pastor. His biography was entitled *Harvesting for God*, but all its dialogue is in the 'Geordie' language of Tyneside, since his best-known ministry was in the industrial region of Newcastle upon Tyne, just above the Vickers Armstrong engineering works and off the 'Scotswood Road' of ballad fame. His 'People's Hall' mission has long since disappeared, but the solid stone manse, in which my father spent much of his boyhood, still stands in Rye Hill. Tuberculosis of the throat interrupted my grandfather's dynamic preaching but he recovered in the healing air of Davos, Switzerland. He died when I was only four, so I hardly knew him. But he too had a goatee beard (I never thought of that until years after I had mine). When asked to sign an autograph album, he always added either 'He whose sermon is a godly life will never preach too long' or 'When the outlook is bad, try the uplook'.

When my father left school, his headmaster told him: 'Well, Pawson, you're not brilliant, but you're a slogger, and if you'll keep it up, you'll get there.' And get there he did, confounding his relatives-in-law. My mother's intuition had picked a winner. He became a household name to many, for quite different reasons.

He chose agriculture for his career, but without having any land he pursued it academically. Starting as a student in King's College, Newcastle, then part of Durham University, he moved steadily up the ladder through reader and lecturer to doctor and professor, with a chair in crop husbandry. He worked in the same room throughout and was given it for life on retirement. He directed the faculty's experimental farm at Cockle Park, near Morpeth, becoming widely known for improving grassland with an application of basic slag, a by-product of the steel industry. He wrote definitive books about people like Robert Bakewell, the pioneer animal breeder, and was made a Fellow of the Royal Society in Edinburgh. During World War II he was in charge of all Northumberland farms and was awarded the MBE for his record in county food production, though disappointed to receive it by registered post due to King George VI's indisposition.

But his major fame lay elsewhere, in his work as a lay preacher. He became known throughout the north-east of England and further afield. He always 'preached for a verdict' and kept a book of all those who responded to his appeals for conversion or rededication. I have it now, with its 12,000 names and addresses. He became known nationally and internationally when he was appointed Vice-President of the Methodist Conference, the highest office a layman can hold in that denomination. His book on 'Personal Evangelism' led to his inclusion in a volume of *Heroes* by William Barclay, the famous Scottish divine.

So my parents' marriage was a most unusual combination of background and potential – and a very public one. I was their second child.

2

Father to the Man

I was helped into the world by a heavy cast-iron garden roller. I was late arriving and my impatient mother tried pulling it backwards and forwards over the grass behind our house. This desperate measure succeeded and I aroused the whole household at 5.30 a.m. the next morning on Tuesday 25 February 1930. She wrote in her diary, 'Tuesday's child is full of grace', perhaps intuitively guessing how much I would need to be (I have since understood 'grace' to be the undeserved favour of God, not an irresistible force). One of my boyhood's assigned tasks was to cut and roll our lawns, so I became well acquainted with the monster that ushered me on to the world's stage!

Shortly thereafter I was christened by one of my grandfathers and named after both – John (the 'beloved disciple' of the New Testament) and David (the Old Testament king, whose name means 'beloved'). So I was twice 'beloved', by both parents and, as I discovered later, by Jesus and his Father. For some reason, never explained, I was also circumcised, though much later it gave me a feeling of identity with God's chosen people Israel. I was always called by my second name, which creates some difficulties in contemporary society. Airlines insist on booking me in as 'John' and my bank began to refuse cheques made out to 'David Pawson' without the 'J'. But I prefer 'David', and if I changed now people would wonder where I'd gone to or speculate about my motives for switching.

So there I was, with an older sister already and a younger sister to follow. I did not think much of this arrangement, neither having the authority of the first-born nor getting the attention of the last-born. Yet the pattern would be repeated in my own three children.

The traditional upbringing of children on my mother's side had been care by a nanny in a nursery for the first few years, followed by private infant and primary schools and then being packed off to boarding school well before reaching teens. This was to be applied to my elder sister Helen and myself, but not to my younger sister Ruth, who seemed to be my parents' favourite. She was kept at home the whole of her childhood, even during the war, when Helen and I became 'evacuees'. I was jealous of her and fear I took it out on her when I returned home. I think I would not have been so resentful had I known then that she would only live to the age of thirty-six. She and my mother both contracted Hodgkin's disease, a cancer of the lymphatic glands, at the same time, though it is not contagious. A medical friend told me in confidence that their difference in age would radically affect the prognosis. He gave my sister eighteen months and my mother seven years and was incredibly accurate.

'Nanny', the adult who figured most prominently in my early years, was from the large family on a Northumberland farm near Capheaton where I would later be an evacuee for part of the war. I have vivid memories of her kind, gentle and caring nature. I can see her face and hear her voice even now. She was a rock of security in the unstable years of the thirties.

All the more surprising, then, that I suffered dreadful nightmares, waking the whole family with my screams, though

I could never recall their contents. Decades later I was chatting with a Dutch friend, who was an experienced counsellor, using gifts of the Spirit to diagnose problems. Out of the blue he said he detected a strand of fearfulness in my make-up (of which I was already aware) and said it had been planted in me by 'a nanny who was terrified of her responsibilities'. I protested that he could not be more mistaken, that mine had been outstandingly cool and competent. I looked out an album of photographs of my early years. Working backwards, I showed him every picture of a relaxed boy, and then a baby, with an equally relaxed guardian, which puzzled him. Then, suddenly, there was a change. I was held by a young girl staring into the camera with frightened eyes, looking as if she was about to drop me. I had no memory of her, nor had I ever been told about her, so I have no idea who she was. It was clearly a mistaken appointment, of the 'she'll have to go' kind. Thus can a baby be affected for life. I have always been a poor sleeper, especially before and after public speaking, particularly on Sundays. But my nightmares these days consist of such horrors as arriving at the wrong church (miles from where I ought to be), on the wrong date (always after the proper one), with the wrong topic notes (or unable to find the right ones), at the wrong time (always late) and in the wrong clothes (if any). I wake up in a cold sweat, soon breathing a prayer of thanksgiving on finding it had not happened. I often think of the vicar who dreamt he was preaching in St Paul's Cathedral and woke up to find he really was!

I'm afraid I'm jumping around between the past and present, which may irritate readers who prefer a strictly chronological account. But the title of this chapter gives a clue to my thinking. Whoever said 'The boy is father to the man' was expressing a profound insight. So back to my boyhood.

I have already mentioned the social disparity between my parents' backgrounds. I became aware of this quite early through contact with my grandmothers and other relatives. A tiny doubt about my own identity was accentuated by the unusual circumstances of the neighbourhood where we lived.

A property developer had purchased a long, sloping strip of land between two much older roads (Grainger Park and Bentinck) in the West End of Newcastle and intended to develop a new one (Dunholme) as a semi-private, rather exclusive estate of detached houses with quite large gardens. He began with a tennis club and there was only one house next to it when my parents purchased the next two plots and erected identical, architect-designed Georgian-style houses, one for themselves and the other for my retired paternal grandparents and an epileptic son who still lived with them and needed my father's constant attention. After one more house had been built, the developer went bankrupt and sold out to another with quite different ideas. He crammed the rest of the road with over seventy much smaller semi-detached houses of a standard design, which quickly sold to quite a different clientele. Even the garages limited them to smaller cars, whereas ours held a maroon, twenty-horsepower Vauxhall limousine. We were the only family with living-in domestic staff. I became acutely aware of the gulf that had to be crossed to build relationships with neighbours and this was only successful with a limited number.

Though we were surrounded by the 'Geordie' accent of Tyneside, some examples quite strong, I never really picked it up, even though I loved its musical sound. I can put it on and enjoy re-telling the sermon of a preacher who said: 'And Joshua tarned tiv 'is troops and said: Haway, lads, grab your baits [lunchpacks], we're gan across the Jordan in the mornin.' But I did pick up the short 'a's (dance instead of damce, Newcastle instead of Newcarstle). I've finished up with a real mixture of dialects.

Most of the houses opposite ours were occupied by older couples who had saved up enough over the years to purchase their own nest. There were few children in the immediate vicinity and all of them were girls. So my playmates were my sisters Helen and Ruth and my neighbours Doreen, Pat and

Margaret. This five-to-one ratio made for games of doctors and nurses rather than cowboys and Indians. Indeed, my father forbade me any toys like guns and soldiers. So my aggressive instincts had to be sublimated into teasing rather than wrestling, a habit that is still with me (amateur psychoanalysts are going to have a field day with these memoirs!).

I have never been able to decide whether my childhood experience of society has been a help or a hindrance. Negatively, it has left me with an uncertainty about where I fit in and how I ought to behave, causing me to be somewhat ill at ease in social settings at any level. Positively, I think it has given me something of a 'classless' nature which can adapt and appeal to most levels, an asset essential to my later career. Those who know me can decide which has been uppermost.

Home is usually a greater influence than neighbourhood, so let me return to 'Overdale', my parents' home for their entire married life. They were exceptionally busy people, involved in a multitude of activities.

Mother was very creative and highly organised, addicted to gadgets (as I am). She was a keen amateur photographer, entering competitions. Her most valued material possession was a state-of-the-art Leica camera, to which was later added one of the early hand-held cine movie cameras. We were her reluctant models, especially for the dreaded 'Christmas photo', sent far and wide every year, with at least one glum face every time. She wrote plays, producing and performing in them. She also wrote poems and tales for children illustrated by posed photographs of guess who. She did quite a lot of public speaking, mainly at women's and missionary meetings. She ran a 'Girls' League', raising support for missionaries, largely by making and selling hand-painted jewellery. She enjoyed cooking, with her beloved 'Aga', which was a bosom friend (should I say bottom friend) to the whole family in winter (those who are acquainted with one will understand).

Father's weekdays were also packed full. In addition to all his university work, he used much of his spare time for evangelistic and pastoral pursuits. Every Tuesday evening was devoted to a 'class meeting' for men, at first in the house, later on church premises. He kept this up for over forty years, producing, among other fruits, a steady stream of candidates for the Methodist ministry. Every Saturday evening was given to what is now called 'counselling', attracting all sorts of people: Catholics and Jews, jailbirds and police, employers and the unemployed. Many of the latter came to our back door during those hard days, begging for a bit of food or money. Mother usually set them weeding the extensive crazy paving in the garden, to give them a scrap of self-respect by 'earning' what was given.

One unusual feature of home life needs to be mentioned, which may or may not have influenced my later life. Our guest bedroom was in constant use – by famous preachers! In Newcastle central YMCA, a 'Midday Service' was held every Tuesday, to which well-known preachers of many denominations were invited. Invariably they stayed with us and our home became known as 'The Preachers' Inn'. So I became acquainted with a galaxy of big names in the thirties, forties and fifties. Top of the list were the three Methodist Doctors from London, Leslie Weatherhead (said to 'love the people'), Will Sangster (said to 'love the Lord') and Donald, later Lord, Soper (said to 'love an argument'). All these were to play a part in shaping my ministry in years to come but, like the others, left little impression on me as a boy. Among the others were James Stewart and James Black from Scotland, Alan Redpath, Martyn Lloyd-Jones, Townley Lord, Norman Dunning (whose great nephew distributes my tapes in New Zealand), S.W. Hughes (who had carrot juice for breakfast and swam every day, so I joined him) and many more, some from overseas, like Toyohiko Kagawa from Japan and Martin Niemuller from Germany. But I was never taken to hear them preach so only saw them in a domestic setting, where not all of them were as inspiring and impressive! Mother took movie films of them all for a series she called 'Preachers out of the Pulpit'. I have an old suitcase full of 9.5mm black and white spools and 16mm colour ones. It is ironic that I had such contact with so many preaching giants before I had any interest in or inclination to the calling myself. Only God knows if they had any subconscious influence. There was certainly no conscious impact. Indeed, they constituted yet another distracting interruption of family life.

However, there was one day a week which was more or less kept for the family, namely Sunday; that is, apart from Father's many preaching engagements, though most of these were near enough for him to return home between morning and evening services. It should have been a day to look forward to, but his sabbatarian convictions cast a shadow over it. To say that I dreaded its arrival would be an exaggeration. Dreary seems a more appropriate word to describe a day combining what we couldn't do with what we had to do.

Toys were put away. Games were abandoned, though Mother invented 'Scripture Lotto', a kind of Bible bingo, to fill the gap. Bicycles were taboo, as were cameras; Mother loyally accepted prohibition of the latter, so I have no photos of myself in my 'Sunday best'. School uniforms and leisure wear gave way to formal dress appropriate to our divine appointments. We dressed up 'for the Lord', though I'm not convinced that the current habit of dressing down for ourselves at the weekend is a sign of spiritual progress.

We walked to church on Sunday morning, the car staying in the garage, though that restriction was relaxed when my parents got older. I was made to sit through the whole service, though other children soon left for their own activity. When Father was with us he put his left arm around me for the sermon, more, I suspect, to keep me from fidgeting than a show of affection.

Sunday lunch was always the best meal of the week, invariably roast beef and Yorkshire pudding, followed by apple tart with custard and cheese (another Yorkshire 'pudding'). But even these gastronomic delights for the body came with a discipline for the soul. The repast was always followed by 'family prayers', for which we all knelt on the floor by our chairs. Father's fluent petitions and intercessions were as long in scale as they were wide in scope. I can still feel the protests of my knees and elbows.

My parents had a well-earned nap in the afternoon while we walked to Sunday School. I looked forward to being an adult! On one Sunday in my early teens, I announced to my mother that I was not going to Sunday School ever again. She took it surprisingly well, suggesting that I went to the evening service instead. I did and found to my delight a three-sided gallery full of young people, over half girls. I kept going, though my motives were social rather than spiritual.

Sunday evening was spent quietly, which means that going to bed was almost a welcome relief. My parents listened to the BBC radio, particularly to the Palm Court Orchestra from Bournemouth (or was it Eastbourne?). Apparently, their music was sufficiently 'spiritual' even if it wasn't specifically 'sacred'. Or were we winding down for 'secular' Mondays? One serial play made a deep impression on me, not *Dick Barton: Special Agent* or Valentyne Dyall, the 'Man in Black', but a contemporary dramatisation of the life of Christ, *The Man Born to be King* by Dorothy L. Sayers, better known for her detective stories. There were protests from those who thought apostles with Cockney accents bordered on the blasphemous, but for this young listener Jesus came out of the stained glass window and into the living-room.

Holidays were not exempt from this schedule. We would drive to our resort on a Saturday (I suffered car sickness on most journeys but thankfully grew out of it). The next day while others made for boats and beaches in casual clothes, we went in the opposite direction in our Sunday best, making for the nearest chapel for services and Sunday School. Since we returned on a Saturday, a week's holiday boiled down to five days' fun.

But holidays were special. For one thing we had our parents' undivided attention. And they chose the most delightful destinations. Apart from visiting my grandmother's town of Allendale, with its river valley and moors to explore, we had two favourite places.

One was Seahouses on the coast of Northumberland. We would rent a house or bungalow on the sea front, looking south to the fishing harbour, north to the superb beach, with its rock pools and towering (to us) sand dunes, stretching all the way to the magnificent castle at Banburgh and east to the Farne Islands. We would sail out to them in blue and white fishing cobles to see the seals and birds, as well as the reef where the *Forfarshire* was wrecked and the heroic rescue of the crew by Grace Darling and her father. Many of the boats had religious names, like *John Wesley* and *Glad Tidings*. There was also a fishermen's choir who enlivened Sunday worship in the Methodist church. I disgraced myself and embarrassed my family by whispering quite loudly to my mother: 'There's a man in the front row with the biggest nose in the whole world.' Tact has never been my strong point.

The holiday highlight was often a trip to Holy Island, crossing at low tide, splashing through the water in a rusting Ford Model 'A' saloon, guided by a row of tall stakes, some of which had little ladders and a tiny platform for luckless pilgrims trapped by the incoming currents. Here I became acquainted with Celtic Christianity, brought from Ireland to the island of Iona off Scotland, by St Columba and from there to Northumberland by St Aidan and on to Durham by St Cuthbert (known as 'Cuddy' by his devoted converts). I was fascinated and later held a grudge against the Abbess of Whitby who presided over the council that decreed England should accept the Catholic (i.e. Roman) version of the faith, rather than the Celtic, a tragic decision with fateful consequences. In my twenties I lived and worked in the Iona Community under the inspiring leadership of Dr (later 'Lord') George MacLeod. I never forgot one of his sermons on 'The God who walks'.

Our other favourite resort was the village of Kippford, near Dalbeattie, in south-west Scotland in the county of Kirkudbrightshire (pronounced 'Kirkoobreeshire' but meaning 'the church of Cuthbert shire', so we were still within the influence of the Celtic saints). The small family hotel, 'The Pines', overlooked a tidal inlet of the Solway Firth full of small boats and had a nine-hole golf course behind, where I made my first attempt to master the sport which Mark Twain called 'a good walk spoiled'. There was a wonderful walk over hills and through woods to Rockliffe Bay and Rough Island, reached by a causeway at low tide. A little further away were the endless sands near Colvend, where my uncle had a holiday home and a stable with horses. A ride across the wide beach when the tide was far out was both inspiring and invigorating.

I know that 'nostalgia isn't what it used to be' but I love sentimental trips to these places, filled with memories of some of the happiest days of my early life. Which brings me to the final strand of my childhood which needs to be recorded, namely, my education. School days are supposed to be the happiest days of your life, but mine were the exception that proves the rule, partly due to the fact that they were rudely interrupted by a German dictator called Adolf Hitler, who precipitated World War II without any consideration for my welfare. I was in the Allendale Methodist Chapel where my parents first set eyes on each other when war was announced at 11 a.m. on 3 September 1939, which happened to be their wedding anniversary. We used to tease them every year afterwards by saying that this was the date 'when war broke out'.

The result was that my basic education was completed in five schools in six locations. When I was four I was enrolled in a small private academy in the next road, run by a Miss Skelton, whose appearance matched her name. She was a strong disciplinarian and a superb teacher. By five I was dabbling in French, and when I moved to another school at seven I astonished my new headmaster with my mathematical skill. I scored 98 in a 110-word spelling test; it should have been 99, because I wrote 'broach' instead of 'brooch', thinking of subjects rather than ornaments.

This was at the Newcastle Preparatory School, at the other side of the city. I changed trams in the centre, outside a sweet shop, which sold the most delicious fudge (then called Italian Cream) and I became a life-long addict (though I abhor the beige rubber blocks often sold today). School uniform included the refined torture of a stiff Eton collar with studs and a black cap with three concentric circles of gold ribbon, earning us the nickname of 'Ringworms' from other schools nearby.

The headmaster believed in applying the board of education to the seat of learning. He was a firm believer in corporal punishment, but only with a definite end in view! We would listen outside his door to the 'thwack' of the cane, followed by a howl of pain and slink away thinking 'there but for the grace of God, go I'. Few of us escaped 'the Persuader', wielded by an ex-sergeant-major in the gymnasium; it was a strip of rubber tyre tread, which left a stinging pattern on the palm of the hand. We were easily 'persuaded' to climb ropes and walk horizontal bars. He taught us to swim by lining us up naked at the edge of the pool and pushing us in. The first stroke we learned was a frantic doggy paddle. He did, however, have a pole with a big net to fish out the drowning.

When war broke out the school was evacuated to a country house in North Northumberland. Since the disrupted tend to become disruptive, discipline became a major problem and canings very common. I wonder now if the staff were simply not able to cope with a day school that had suddenly become a boarding school. Most of us were miserable and in every letter home I begged my parents to make other arrangements, preferably with them.

Their response was to send me to Nanny's farm for a few months while they looked around for a 'proper' boarding school. Through the winter of 1939 I cycled three miles to a village school in Capheaton. Here another much more serious war had broken out, between village children and evacuees. I had to rescue my mangled bike from ditches. But I loved life on the farm, with its toilet in the orchard, baths in a tin tub in front of the kitchen fire and candles at night. Very romantic!

All too soon my elder sister and I were packed off to Methodist boarding schools, both now moved from potential bombing zones. Helen went to Hunmanby Hall from Filey, then in Bassenthwaite Hall near Keswick, and I went to Ashville College from Harrogate, then in Bowness Hydro near Windermere. Though we were both in the beautiful Lake District, we only saw each other when our parents and another family rented a boarding house in Ambleside for the summer vacation.

Life in the former spa hotel was thoroughly routine and my memories focus on a few events which relieved the tedium.

We were all given numbers (mine was 120), as if we were prisoners rather than pupils. Perhaps that explains why boys regularly ran away, in carefully planned escapes, first noticed when a number at roll call was met with silence and grins on the faces of those who had aided and abetted. But there were few successful 'home runs', most being apprehended on the platform of Oxenholme station near Kendall. They were brought back in disgrace, but we welcomed them as returning heroes. I never tried it.

My greatest misdemeanour followed a birthday present from a friend – of a small tin of luminous paint. Our dormitory bedroom had a wall covered with a heavily flowered paper, which I now realise was a William Morris design. I set to and carefully picked out a large area of leaves. At night they glowed pale green and gave a wonderful impression of a tropical forest. I was quite proud of my handiwork, until a housemaster burst in late one night to tell us to stop talking. He stared in utter astonishment. I will draw a veil over the immediate consequence but the ultimate result was that my end-of-term report to my parents was accompanied by a hefty bill for redecoration. Years later, I was invited to preach at an 'Old Boys' weekend. I went to the Harrogate campus I had never seen, to be greeted by the headmaster, assistant head in my time, with 'Ah, Pawson. Wallpaper!' Why do teachers have such good memories for our bad deeds? At least he didn't call me '120'.

At one stage there was a spate of bullying by a gang of senior boys. I was made to spend a cold and precarious night on the roof tiles and learned that the best defence was to keep a low profile. It came to an abrupt end with a number of expulsions.

The most exciting event was when we went looking for a German pilot, who had escaped from the Swanwick Christian Conference Centre, then a POW (Prisoner of War) camp for enemy officers. He was reported to be hiding in Grizedale Forest, on the opposite side of Lake Windermere. It was our chance to be directly involved in the war, but if the truth were told, we were scared stiff of finding him. Von Werra was the only one to make it back to Germany, via Canada and America, taking with him invaluable knowledge of British interrogation methods.

Apart from the delights of weekly visits to our tuck boxes or the tuck shop, I can recollect little else and nothing of educational significance.

Later in the war I returned home and spent the last years of my education at Dame Allen's Grammar School in Newcastle. I never found out anything about her but guess she had some Christian convictions, for the school tradition included a holiday on Ascension Day (always on a Thursday). But this was not an unmixed blessing, since we had to attend a morning service in St Nicholas Cathedral. I had not the slightest idea what it was all about, little dreaming that I would one day write a book on the very topic, entitled *Where is Jesus now – and what is he doing?*

The school staff was a mixed bunch, many younger ones having 'gone off to fight'. Some had been hauled back out of retirement, others were exempt from military service and there was a preponderance of women. But I do not blame them for the fact that my academic career, which had begun with such precocious promise, had now lapsed into mediocrity. Nor could I lay it at the door of frequent changes of school. The basic problem was that I was not very motivated. School was something to get through.

I did manage a handful of passes in the 'School Certificate' examination, enough to qualify for university. It is ironic that 'Scripture Knowledge' was one of my poorest marks. But then the lanky young vicar who taught us was far more enthusiastic about cricket, which was an obsession with him.

So I left school at sixteen, with little distinction, but knowing what I wanted to do with the rest of my life. I wanted to be a farmer. Agriculture was in my blood on both sides of the family and visits to Nanny's farm had increased the desire. I did not then know of my earthly father's plans to make this a practical possibility, much less my heavenly Father's very different intention.

I had a 'gap' year before I could enter college to study the theory of farming, so it was decided that I should gain more practical experience. Through my father's contacts, I found work on two farms, for six months in Northumberland and another six in Yorkshire.

My boyhood was over. The transition to manhood would be abrupt and traumatic.

3

From Plough to Pulpit

At sixteen, my entry into the adult working world was, quite literally, a rude awakening. Most industries have their own 'initiation rites' to humiliate apprentices and agriculture is no exception. My 'induction' had three parts.

Part one was to put me on a 'dry' cow to learn to milk. I pushed, pulled and squeezed for forty-five minutes without any result, while they told me it was a knack which would suddenly come 'like riding a bike'! The cow seemed to enjoy my efforts, but I didn't.

Part two was to bury a still-born calf. They told me local bye-laws demanded a grave twelve feet deep and selected a patch of sticky clay for the internment. Hours later I was up to my chin when the farmer passed by and asked if I was trying to escape to Australia.

Part three was to strip me and hold me down while my genitals were smothered in tractor oil and massaged! I had no idea what they were trying to do, so they soon gave up and left me to clean up the mess as best I could.

I was on a large 'mixed' (arable and livestock) farm in mid-

Northumberland, not far from the coast. I got 'digs' in one of the worker's homes overlooking the magnificent ruins of Warkworth Castle. We had to rise at 4 a.m. to cycle three or four miles to work, milking ninety cows before breakfast. After that I washed and sterilised the machines and utensils. Before the evening milking we did other jobs.

One of my first was to give sight to newborn lambs. Cheviot babies sometimes had dropped eyelids. The cure was to take a needle and thread and sew the eyelid to the eyebrow, until the muscle took over and the thread rotted. I often think that was not unlike my later calling!

I learned to build corn sheaves into stacks, scrape bristles off a slaughtered pig with boiling water and put rings in bulls' noses. I looked after some young prize bulls worth a fortune and my worst moment was one morning when I found a number dead and others dying in seizures. The farmer was beside himself and I trembled for my future. The symptoms suggested lead poisoning, but there were no accessible pipes or paint. Eventually we did an autopsy and found a stomach full of damaged airgun slugs. The farmer had given an airgun to his youngest son for his birthday, who had then shot at so many birds in the barn that the corn was filled with lead, which we had threshed and ground for feed. I was so relieved that I was not directly to blame.

The severe winter of 1947 cut us off with deep snowdrifts. We dug a way out for a tractor and sledge, returning with sacks full of loaves of bread. We had to tip all milk produced down the drain, but kept the cream for ourselves (I've been an addict ever since).

Social life was limited. On Saturday nights we would pile into the farm's Morris truck and head for a village hall where there was a 'hop'. I didn't drink and couldn't dance (forever apologising for treading on toes) but I enjoyed the mixed company. The highlight was our Kern (Harvest) Supper when we cleared and cleaned the upper floor of the barn, sprinkling the wood with soap powder to make it slippery, ready for the overnight feast and ball for all the workers and their families. We also attended activities of the YFC (Young Farmers' Club), where I took my first tentative steps in public speaking in their regular debates, totally unaware that this would take over my life.

I spent the second half of this 'gap' year, before going to university, on another farm in North Yorkshire which nestled under the cone-shaped peak of Roseberry Topping, near the charming village of Great Ayton ('Canny Yatton'), home of Captain Cook, whose monument stood on the hills above and whose cottage was dismantled, shipped to Australia and rebuilt in Melbourne. Many years later I looked out of a hotel window in that city and there it was, with its stone walls and roof of red pantiles; it made me feel quite homesick. The village was famous for its Quaker school facing the green and for a fish-and-chip shop called 'Dirty Mary's' (I never discovered whether the adjective referred to the proprietor, the premises or the product but the latter was delicious, depending, of course, on which newspaper it was served in).

I had changed from brown and white Ayrshires to black and white Fresians, but otherwise it was a regular 'mixed' farm.

Here I learned that farming can be tedious. One job was 'looking'. Armed with a long-handled, narrow-bladed hoe we walked up and down the cornfield spiking weeds to prevent their seeds contaminating the harvest. Even a small field seemed like a huge prairie. Nowadays, herbicide sprays have eliminated such drudgery. I attribute my ruddy complexion, which still makes me look healthy, to this particular task, involving days in the sun, wind and rain.

I also learned that farming can be dangerous. Indeed, it is the most dangerous livelihood, even more dangerous than coal-mining. Many fatalities come from machinery, particularly tractors overturning on a steep slope, others from livestock, particularly bulls and horses. We had one or two incidents which could have been very serious but which turned out to be very humorous.

A cow with mastitis had been quarantined in a very dark loose box and was milked by hand by a pensioner called 'Enery, who liked to help where he could. A newly purchased bull arrived and was temporarily housed in the loose box, the cow taken elsewhere. We were all working in the field when we saw 'Enery arrive with bucket and stool. We yelled a warning but he was very deaf. We ran over but arrived just as he came out, muttering: 'Ee, I don't know what's wrong with t'auld thing today; she won't let me near 'er.' We had expected to be carrying his corpse out but perhaps the beast had been too astonished by the attempt to milk him to do more than stand still in amazement.

When a round haystack was completed, the top was pinned down by a heavy metal spike, a kind of Iron Age sword. One of these was inadvertently left leaning against a rick, point upwards. A worker slid down the side. The spike entered the seat of his dungarees, went up the back and emerged between the collar and his neck. He was not even scratched but had been within millimetres of sharing the same fate as a victim of Vladimir the Impaler.

Then there was the time when we were chasing a visiting boy around the buildings. He escaped us by running up the stairs to the granary over the cowshed, which had three compartments separated by partitions, each with a large door. We thought we'd got him, for there was no other exit. But there was. In the end was a door with a crane for lifting sacks from trailers and trucks in the cobbled yard many feet below. To our horror, our quarry opened this last door and ran through without hesitation. We could not see his face as he fell but it must have had an expression seen in many children's cartoons at the cinema. Fortunately, he fell on a pile of straw that had been carelessly left there, shaken but unhurt.

There are moral as well as physical dangers on a farm, even though the idyllic countryside looks devoid of temptation. I loved working with animals and machines, but I was also working with people. And I was in transition from boyhood to manhood, at a stage when one is particularly vulnerable to the pressure of peers. I became chronically aware of how sheltered my upbringing had been and was now exposed to four unfamiliar adult weaknesses – smoking, swearing, drink and sex.

Smoking was not a real problem. I had given that up at the age of ten, on the same day I had taken it up. Four of us had gone into the bushes and consumed a whole packet. We were sick as dogs and never wanted tobacco again. I was once preaching in Derby's City Hall and mentioned this incident. A Methodist minister on the platform behind me leapt to his feet and shouted: 'I was with you!' Be sure your sins will find you out. I now tell men that smoking won't take you to hell but it will make you smell as if you've already been there.

Swearing was more of a pressure. I was hearing a whole new vocabulary of blasphemy and obscenity. Most 'bad language' degrades the two most 'sacred' relationships in life: man with God and man with woman. Of the three most common words, 'bloody' is a contraction of 'by our Lady' (Mary), while 'hell' and the F-word are self-explanatory. Surrounded by such talk, it is surprisingly easy to slip into it, especially when angry or frustrated. I only lapsed occasionally, but that was more due to my upbringing than my conscience.

Alcohol tended to pass me by. Like most Methodists in those days, my family were strictly teetotal and a keen Sunday School teacher had planted a deep fear of 'demon drink' in my soul, with horrific stories of its effects. And I was now witnessing first-hand what silly behaviour resulted from the loss of self-control, plus I didn't like the taste. I am no longer teetotal in principle, though I rarely drink alcohol.

Sex, however, was a different matter. Dirty jokes and boasted exploits implied a contempt for virginity. This outward pressure coincided with a new awareness of inward urges. I felt inferior and anxious. And girls were available. There were some World War II 'land-girls' working with us and others dropped in from nearby villages. I took one into the hayloft, but after a kiss and a cuddle I didn't know what to do next and she didn't take any initiative. On discovering our 'nest', the lads gleefully welcomed me to the ranks of the fallen. I was too ashamed to tell them nothing had really happened! On another occasion a girl came into my bedroom, lay on the bed and calmly announced that she was not wearing any underclothes. In my naivety I failed to see the point of this seemingly irrelevant remark and she left disappointed. Then there was an older girl who did domestic work in the farmhouse. She was an outrageous flirt and tease. When she got you alone her hands were all over you but she would never let you touch her in any way. She kept that for a tall, fair-haired, blue-eyed German boy, a prisoner of war working with us while he awaited repatriation to his home country.

So I remained relatively unscathed, but this comparative innocence could not have been maintained indefinitely. My spiritual state was in decline and could not have resisted such temptations much longer.

I had kept up church attendance in the earlier months of this year in farming, cycling quite a few miles to the nearest Methodist church. This involved two problems. First, I believed I was committing sin by riding a bike on the 'Lord's Day', which at least gave me something to confess when I got there. Second, since cows don't observe the sabbath, I had been up early to milk them and invariably fell asleep during the sermon, especially if the preacher spoke in a dull drone. But the main reason why regular attendance became intermittent and then occasional was that I didn't see any relevance or receive any benefit, not yet having a personal relationship with the One being worshipped.

Without realising it, I was reaching a crucial stage in life. I was not making any conscious decisions about my direction. It was more a case of drifting with an ebbing tide. But a choice would soon have to be made if this was to change. The narrow road to life was fading behind me and the broad way to destruction beckoned ahead. Which was it to be? That question was answered in September 1947 quite unexpectedly.

I must now tell you about a man called Tom Rees, who married my cousin, another Jean Sinclair like her aunt my mother (one of father's ardent love-letters was opened by the wrong 'Jean' when they were staying together, greatly perplexing her!). Tom was descended from a Welsh station master who gave Bibles to all passengers leaving Carmarthen; they were collected up at Swansea and returned on the next train back.

Tom and his brother were keen evangelists, though Dick, as an ordained Anglican, worked mainly within his denomination. Tom was probably the best-known evangelist in Britain immediately after the war, though he also spent half the year in America, which helped to cover expenses. During the winter, he held a monthly rally in London, packing the Royal Albert Hall, which he modestly called his 'little mission hall in Kensington'. He had been very impressed with the results of outdoor camps for young people across the Atlantic, but thought that for an 'English' version a country house would be more fitting. So he raised funds to purchase 'Hildenborough Hall', near Tonbridge in Kent. Over a hundred young people came to stay each week.

My parents were invited to host one week, father to be the guest speaker. They invited me to accompany them and I looked forward to making more social contacts, little dreaming I was to experience a radical change. What led to it was not the morning and evening 'meetings' but encounters with the other guests, who had something I hadn't got. By the end of the week I realised it was Someone. I met two ex-Battle of Britain fighter pilots, decorated for their exploits flying Spitfires. That such heroes could be convinced Christians was an eye-opener. Then I met young men and women who had suffered for their faith, some having been physically beaten by parents. Yet they were joyful, in spite of (or because of?) their troubles, which had simply strengthened their relationship with 'the Lord'. This was different from my parents' influence. These were my peers.

At the 'testimony' session on the last evening in the lounge, I was first on my feet. To this day I have no recollection of what I said. But one thing I was quite sure about. I was no longer trying to depend on the second-hand faith of my parents. I now had a faith of my own, which has kept me until today. I could now call Jesus Christ my own Lord and Saviour. It was a turning-point.

I received no counselling afterwards, not even a comment. Maybe they did not think my father's son would need any. Maybe I had not made it clear enough that this was my very first profession of faith. Whatever the reason, I was setting out on the Christian life without a proper start and the full resources available.

With the hindsight of more biblical knowledge and theological insight, I'm not even sure how to define this crucial event, or even describe it. Some simplistic evangelicals would call it my 'conversion', the day when I was 'born again'. I'm not so sure.

I have since written a book called *The Normal Christian Birth*, now referred to as a classic. In it I said that there is nothing in the New Testament to suggest that the second birth is instantaneous but that it is, like the first birth, a process that takes time, long or short, and is not complete until four essential elements are present – repenting towards God, believing in Jesus, being baptised in water and receiving the Holy Spirit. In my case, it would take another seventeen years to gain these four foundational features of initiation into the Kingdom of God. Such a long 'labour' or 'delivery' was far from normal, but probably average ('normal' being what should be, 'average' what generally is).

There was little repentance in my case, certainly no confession of sins (which is always specific in Scripture, never general). I was more conscious of being saved from future sins that might have been committed than past sins that had been. Like many, I only applied 'sin' as the world uses that word, for blatant immorality, rather than more subtle and more dangerous things like pride and self-centredness, even ingratitude. I had never doubted the existence of God but was well on the way to godless living.

Baptism never came up. Then, had it done so, I'm sure I would have been told that all that had been taken care of when I was a baby.

In regard to receiving the Holy Spirit I was left in complete ignorance about it and him. In the Christian circles I had known and would now get to know, 'receiving' was exclusively applied to the second, not the third, person of the Trinity (in spite of the verb being exclusively transferred from Jesus while he was still on earth to the Holy Spirit after his return to heaven).

But I was absolutely sure I was now a believer myself and a 'disciple' of Jesus (a learner, apprentice, follower: the most frequent description in the New Testament). I went back to the farm a different person. I sang choruses to the cows while I milked them. A magazine called *Farmers' Weekly* published an article claiming that relayed music in the cowshed significantly raised milk yields. I wanted to write and say that I had pioneered that improvement. Had I known about the effect I was having, I could have taken out a patent for the discovery.

Just one month later, my circumstances changed quite radically. I left the farm and enrolled as a university student to gain a B.Sc. (Agric.) degree. I found myself sitting at a desk again, in King's College, Newcastle, then still part of Durham University. I went there because tuition was free for children of staff. Of course it meant living at home again, though I was no longer a boy, which demanded some adjustment.

Subjects for the first year were general, like botany and zoology. Part of the latter was a course of lectures on evolution. One fellow student, a leader in the Christian Union, openly heckled the lecturer, who silenced his opponent by confessing to being 'a practising Christian'. I failed in chemistry but was able to retake it, successfully, after some personal tuition.

Second and third years were much more practical, applied rather than pure science. Twenty-one subjects included accounting, engineering and veterinary skills, but we majored on crop and animal 'husbandry', an archaic word for 'looking after'. I'm surprised it has not been revived by the environmentalists, but I suspect it would offend the feminists (life was rather simpler before political correctness invaded our culture). My father concentrated on the 'crop' side and always ended with a lecture on the relation between faith in the Creator and use of creation, attendance at which was voluntary but usually of the same number.

I did not take much part in the extra-curricular activities of the students but was elected to represent our faculty on the SRC (Students' Representative Council). Here I had my first encounter with a real live Communist. Turning his back on a family fortune made in shoe manufacture, he was totally devoted to his political ideology and ambition. I remember feeling challenged about the level of my own dedication as a Christian.

But my Christian life was rapidly developing, more in the context of home than college. The reality of my recently found faith led to an ever-growing urge to share it with believers and unbelievers alike – in other words, an increasing desire for fellowship and evangelism. This was expressed at first in an 'unofficial' way, outside church and denomination, but later moved into such 'official' channels. The first phase was marked by relationships with two of Father's converts and their many friends.

Peter was a young farmer, living in an old mill with his elderly aunt, twelve miles from Newcastle in the village of Milbourne and scratching a living from a few acres. He had a magnetic personality and adventurous spirit, so drew young people all around him like flies to jam. He had a transport collection, including an HRD Vincent 'Black Shadow' 1000cc motorbike (which I once borrowed to 'do the ton', i.e. exceed 100 mph, which scared me stiff), a huge Humber armoured car (without the gun) and an ex-US army 'jeep'. He could drive a steamroller (which a careless council left outside his gate one night with steam up) and learned to fly on a DH (de Havilland) Tiger Moth (I flew with him in the rear open cockpit, which put the wind up me in more ways than one). My first Harvest Festival service was in one of his fields, a tractor seat serving as my pulpit. And his jeep served the same purpose when we spoke together at open-air meetings, outside cinemas to the people queuing to get in or to crowds on the seafront at Whitley Bay.

Jack was an older man, living in the mining village of Wheatley Hill, in County Durham. An ex-bookmaker, he now worked at the local pit as 'check-weighman', weighing the tubs of coal as they came to the surface to make sure the men below got their deserved bonuses. He lived in a tiny council house, which always had a blazing fire in the living-room (mineworkers got a good allowance of free coal, regularly dumped in the street outside). Seated by the fire was his elderly father, whom everybody called 'Grand-da', invariably reading a Family Bible. I asked him once if he'd read it right through and, if so, how many times. He simply replied that he was on his eighteenth way through and, when I further asked him why he did this, an equally simple but sincere answer came: 'I don't want to miss anything.'

Jack had also gathered many young people around him and his dramatic conversion led to theirs. At first they met in his house but soon had to use public premises (club rather than church) for over a hundred. Wisely he linked them with wider youth organisations, two in particular. One was just coming to the country from America, YFC (Youth for Christ). They also linked up with OCW (Order for Christian Witness), a British movement founded and led by Dr Donald Soper (later Lord Soper) of Kingsway Hall in London, who spoke every Sunday at

Hyde Park Corner (I went to hear him there on his ninetieth birthday, still going strong). Every year he held a 'campaign' (same as a US 'crusade') with hundreds of young people on the 'team' and with emphasis on getting out of churches and into the world. I went to two of these, to the 'Lower Western Valley' in South Wales, centred on Risca and Crosskeys, and Cannock Chase in the Midlands.

So my early preaching was in pubs and working men's clubs or in the street. Soper was a master of the open-air meeting and taught us the basic technique of gathering a crowd, namely: never speak loud enough for the people at the back to hear. The result was that they pressed in closer to hear what was being said and more curious passers-by took their place. He encouraged heckling to arouse interest and was brilliant at repartee. A classic example was:

'What shape is your soul?'

'Oblong. Next question.'

'Where is the soul in the body?'

'Where the music is in the organ.'

Both answers were profoundly true to Hebrew thinking, where 'soul' is a breathing body (hence, 'SOS' = save our breathing bodies), rather than the Greek separation of body and soul. The Bible teaches the resurrection of the body, not the immortality of the soul.

Dear me, I've started preaching in this book already! But during this time I was developing an appetite for Christian books, which was to become a lifetime's obsession. I now have over three tons, according to our last furniture remover, filling two rooms in the house and a garden shed. They are a blessing to me and a bane to my wife! I divide them into three categories: those I have read, those I intend to read and those I will probably never read but was tempted to buy. I began with Leslie Weatherhead's classic, *The Transforming Friendship*. The prologue alone brought thousands face to face with Jesus. When he stayed in our home I proudly showed him my shelf full of his books.

Alas, his later writings became rather liberal and even sceptical (*The Christian Agnostic*).

I now went to hear the preachers who lodged in our home. One who had been a hero when playing rugby on Tyneside came back to conduct a crusade in the City Hall. Alan Redpath made a huge impression, not least because of his physical frame. He had developed shoulders for the scrum by pushing against a brick wall for hours at a time but was now equally disciplined and determined to share his faith. The City Hall witnessed another evangelistic rally, addressed by a young lanky American with a shock of fair hair, and a name nobody had heard of (Billy Graham!) on his first ever visit to these shores, sponsored by Youth for Christ.

All this Christian activity fell into what I have called 'unofficial channels'. However, alongside this I was getting involved in 'official' (i.e. denominational) ways. Living at home again, I was attending the same church I had always known: Dilston Road Methodist, head of the north-west 'circuit' of Newcastle churches.

The first step was to become a member. I attended membership classes. We began with about ten applicants, but this number gradually dwindled until I, even I only, was left, at which point I was 'welcomed into membership' (in case I also left?). I was soon wanting to get from pew to pulpit, so was given a 'Note to preach', enabling me to accompany an 'Accredited Local Preacher' (a layman attached to the circuit), take part in leading the service and 'give a word' under supervision. I was soon 'on probation', taking services on my own.

For some reason, I suffered chronic nerves in front of silent congregations, where I had been so bold in pubs. I suffered diarrhoea before and after and dry throat during (I called the latter 'Pharaoh's plague of frogs'). I drained every glass of water in the pulpit, some of which were an interesting study in pond life. I remember reaching under for a glass when my fingers encountered warm fur. Glancing down I saw a sleeping cat on the shelf.

My treatment of a text was somewhat bizarre. I was using the Authorised (King James) Version at first and did not then realise that Elizabethan words could have very different meanings (for example 'let' and 'prevent' have actually swapped significance since then). On one occasion I gave out my text, 'Ye are a peculiar people' (1 Pet. 2:9), and proceeded to enlarge on the theme that the church is full of weirdos and eccentrics and by the grace of God can and should cope with them. I marvel that they did not stone me!

I was beginning to get known as a preacher outside the 'circuit' and accepted invitations to preach more widely in the counties of Northumberland and Durham. The only snag was that I could not go anywhere my father had not already been, leading to comments like: 'Isn't he like his father' or, more likely, 'He's not up to his father'. I hated these comparisons and longed for the day when I could get out from under his shadow. That did not come until I left the Methodist Church altogether, over a decade later.

In spite of my nerves, I enjoyed preaching. It was becoming a passion. In a subtle way I felt I was made for this. I began to live for the next opportunity to share what I was discovering in God's Word, which I was studying more than ever before, and not just because of the written and oral examinations required of Methodist lay preachers. Studying Scripture was an exciting voyage of discovery. I had been bored with history at school but now it had become 'His story', altogether fascinating.

I was becoming schizophrenic about my future. I still wanted to be a farmer and was no less interested in my student studies. But I also wanted to be a preacher. Could I be both, as some of my Pawson ancestors had been? But that would mean confining preaching to my spare time, which farmers don't have much of. I was being torn two ways. However, now I knew such difficult choices were not mine to make. It was up to my Lord to decide which it was to be.

It may be helpful at this stage to describe the principles of 'guidance' which were worked out then and were to govern the rest of my life. Starting from the meaning of 'Lord', which could be roughly translated as 'Boss', I believe it is his responsibility to tell me what to do, not mine to try and 'read' his mind. What earthly boss would come to you on a Monday morning and say: 'Guess what I want you to do this week.' If he wants you to tackle a different task, it's his job to come and tell you. If he doesn't, you assume (rightly) that he wants you to carry on with what you are already doing. That is exactly how I have been with my 'Boss'. Too many Christians leave a task or situation before they have clearly heard about the next, announcing that they are 'seeking the Lord's will' about the future, often resulting in confusion and panic. Itchy feet are not necessarily a divine call! So I have promised the Lord that I will, by his grace and strength, always do what he tells me to do, go where he tells me to go and say what he tells me to say, regardless of cost or consequence provided, of course, that he does his part and tells me clearly. He has the incentive to do this, knowing that he has an obedient servant, and I have the incentive to obey, knowing his yoke is easy and his burden is light. His service truly is perfect freedom.

I put it to him – farmer, preacher, both or either? Very shortly after, I had two clear 'words' from him through others. Peter, my best friend at college, was having coffee with me when he stared at me for what seemed ages and finally said: 'You know, David, you'll finish up in a pulpit rather than behind a plough.' That was not clear enough for me and I remembered the scriptural requirement of at least two witnesses. Later, walking through Newcastle, I bumped into a Methodist minister, who had been at our home church, but was now retired (I could take you to the very spot where we met). His first words to me were: 'David, why aren't you in the ministry?' That was clear enough!

The first step was to go to our present minister, the 'superintendent' of the circuit, and tell him of my desire and intention to offer for the Methodist ministry (I had no knowledge of or contact with any other denomination, so never even considered another, at that stage). By this time, we had a very colourful character in the manse, an ex-Army chaplain who still used his rank title 'Major' and wore his uniform for the first few months. He was very deaf, from military bombardments, and wore a large hearing aid attached to his belt, with headphones. Used to giving orders, he had galvanised the church into activity and packed the auditorium with unusual pulpit presentations. When I shared my ambitions with him, he sharply told me to go away, complete my degree and come back in a year's time. Years later I found out he didn't support my application at all. I suspect it was partly due to my having escaped two years' 'National Service' in the forces, farming being a 'reserved occupation' and full-time students being exempt. If he recommended me for clergy training, I would never have to face military discipline. However, I persisted with my application and another minister, then Chairman of the District (Methodist equivalent of 'bishop'), interviewed me and gave me his backing.

Just weeks later, my father called me into his study to tell me he had begun negotiations to rent a small farm for me to take over when I reached the age of twenty-one. I was touched by his foresight but had to tell him that my heavenly Father had beaten him to it by a few weeks and called me to the ministry. He was far from disappointed and I suspected I was fulfilling his secret wish for me.

My degree course in agriculture completed, my 'candidature' for the ministry now went ahead. But it would be a year before I could begin training, so I had a second 'gap-year' to fill. To my complete surprise, I was to begin full-time ministry long before I expected to and in a location I had never even thought about. How that came about I will keep until later.

4

Finding My Feet

The family was breaking up. My two sisters and I were leaving home and going our separate ways. The elder, Helen, took a course in Domestic Science (I called it 'Silence') and became first Housekeeper at Tom Rees' Hildenborough Hall and then Manageress for Methodist Holiday Homes. The younger, Ruth, headed for London and the British Broadcasting Corporation, where she was soon helping to produce the *Radio Times*.

However, our diverging careers were to converge again in a most unexpected way. Both of them met and married Methodist ministers! It must be unusual for all siblings in a family to find themselves employed by the same organisation, on the same salary and living in other people's houses with other people's furniture. This gave us much in common for some years.

I think my father was 'humbly proud' (one of his favourite phrases) of having populated so many Methodist manses, both from his men's class and now his family. He regarded the Methodist ministry as the noblest vocation of all, perhaps because this had never opened up for himself. It must have been a great disappointment to him that only one of his three 'sons' stayed the course to retirement. Ruth's husband gave up active ministry, even before her premature death, and I later left Methodism for the Baptist ministry.

In 1950 I was still a bachelor, 'footloose and fancy free' and I could not 'candidate' for the Methodist ministry for another twelve months. I thought I would use this 'gap year' to gain some pastoral experience, just as I had used an earlier one to work on farms. So I made an offer to the Methodist Home Mission Department to serve them 'anywhere in Britain'. I was shattered when they told me they were sending me to the Shetland Islands, which were as far away as possible! I could not even have placed them on a map. Vague memories of school atlases saw them in a box in the Firth of Forth, or somewhere else off the East coast of Scotland. But I soon found myself leaving Leith, the port of Edinburgh, on a coal-fired steamship, SS *Magnus*, sailing due north for days, calling at Aberdeen and Kirkwall in the Orkneys, passing Fair Isle and still further on. We seemed to be making for the North Pole, but stopped just short of the Arctic Circle. My travels for the Lord had begun.

My first impression of these islands was one of desolation. Rolling moors devoid of all trees. Towering cliffs covered with birds. A few scattered 'croft' cottages, some of them empty and even in ruins. It was a relief to enter a bay and see the 'capital' town of Lerwick, with its harbour and steep alleyways up the hill on which it was built. The Methodist church and the manse next door, where I was to be based, were at the top, exposed to the legendary gales. Our dustbin used to cross the road without touching it.

The Chairman thought I had been sent as a shorthand typist to deal with his correspondence. Since I had neither skill, he soon gave up trying to dictate letters to me and assigned me to the pastoral care of four churches in the north of the mainland. I had taken a BSA Bantam, my first and only motorbike, with me. It was a mistake. Riding the lonely one-track roads with passing places was quite hazardous even in the long summer days. But the short winter days brought darkness, gales and ice to contend with. I felt I was more off than on it and the climax came when a speeding car drove me into a peat bog on a hairpin bend. The driver was the Chief Constable full of profuse apologies! From then on I felt safe from the law but no longer safe on a bike. I sold it and bought a Ford 8 van for £30, which had been used to sell fish. You could tell that with your eyes shut and for the first few weeks housewives would come to the door with a large dish when I made pastoral visits. When Dr Sangster, the Methodist President, visited Shetland and realised this was our transport he remarked: 'I would never have guessed it was second-hand. I thought it was home-made.'

There was economic distress then, long before oil was discovered in the North Sea. The islands were being depopulated as young people went south to find work. In one of my churches I took one christening, no weddings and nineteen funerals in a year. The herring fishing was in decline. Tuberculosis was a problem. Deserted crofts could be bought for a song, which later would sell as holiday homes for oilmen.

One fifth of the population belonged to the Methodist chapels, more than any other denomination. A Shetlander in the British Army had been converted through Methodist fellow soldiers. Wounded at Waterloo, he returned home and began an extraordinary revival in the early nineteenth century. Over a hundred years later its legacy was still there. In one of my villages we had a minor echo of that revival and the chapel, without a house in sight, filled up again. In another I had a youth group and I urged them to evangelise others; they began to giggle and finally stopped me with: 'But we're all here!' In a third lived a large 'Viking' lady who ran a little chapel at the water's edge. She would stand outside in all weathers pulling a bell-rope to call worshippers together. If no one came, she would say to me: 'We're here and the Lord's here, so let's start.' I would pick out the hymn tunes with one finger on a decrepit harmonium, even take the offertory from her and preach to a congregation of one.

It was 'with angels and archangels' that both of us magnified his holy name. Isa must be enjoying being with them now.

Wesleyan 'class meetings' had long since died out but 'class tickets' were still written out and given out personally, which at least ensured that I visited every member every three months. This meant consuming endless 'bannocks' (large dry floury scones), washed down with thick tea (brewed in an aluminium teapot on the peat fire). I once made a cup of tea for an elderly lady in bed who spat it out with: 'That's so weak it needs helping out of the pot.'

The people were more Scandinavian than Scottish, as was their dialect. My knock on a door would be greeted with: 'Cum trow, hoo ist dee?' (Come through, how are you?), changing from 'dee' to 'du' when you were accepted as a friend. I had many boat trips but never on a fishing vessel. Fishermen were very superstitious, refusing to go to sea with a pig or a parson on board! Theirs was a dangerous vocation and some villages were full of widows in black. Funerals were for men only and gravestones were often laid flat, to save putting them up again after gales. Summer evenings were adorned with the aurora borealis (northern lights), which were called 'The Pretty Dancers' as the pink and green bands flitted over our heads.

I flew south twice, in converted Dakotas from World War II, to 'candidate' for the Methodist ministry, once to preach a 'trial sermon' in Paisley Central Hall and once for a final interview and medical examination. I must have been nervous about the latter and had to visit the toilet just beforehand. When handed a flask and told to produce a sample, I could do absolutely nothing about it, however hard I tried. A fellow applicant took pity on me and kindly shared his with me. Fortunately he proved to be quite healthy! I learned that I had been listed for training at Cambridge.

The year had passed so quickly. I had come to love the people and the place. I had learned far more than I had taught. I had gained confidence in caring for churches, particularly in preaching, little dreaming that this would be undermined in college. As I drove south from Aberdeen, awestruck by trees meeting overhead, I was already feeling homesick for 'Ultima Thule' (the island's ancient name). I had left part of my heart there, though I've never been back to find it.

Cambridge is a beautiful city, with its magnificent buildings, green open spaces and river banks. Life there could be idyllic. Many times I punted up the river through the meadows to Grantchester, where the church clock always stood at 'ten to three'. In those days we had to wear gowns most of the time, particularly after dark when proctors and their two 'bulldogs' (men actually) roamed the streets looking for rebel students. This made us very conscious of the social tension between 'town and gown'.

Wesley House was in Jesus Lane, next door to Jesus College. I never did get used to crowds watching the 'bumps' (boat races on the Cam) and yelling: 'Come on, Jesus!' Our college was known by other Methodist colleges as 'a stud farm for theological race-horses'. All of the students already had degrees and could therefore get a BA Theology in just twenty-one months from start to finish, changing it into an MA a short while later, for a small fee. However, one had to sleep a requisite number of nights within the city boundary to qualify, even staying during vacations to 'sleep nights'.

While we had a few lectures and tutorials from our own staff of two (named Flew and Flemington), most of our studies were in the School of Divinity, with students and scholars of other denominations. Among the latter was C.H. Dodd, then chairing the translators of the New English Bible. He went to the wholesale butchers at Smithfield Market in London with six alternative renderings for 'the fatted calf' in the parable of the prodigal son, to see which would be best understood today; they told him they were used to 'the fatted calf'! Another was John A.T. Robinson, who later became notorious as the Bishop of Woolwich, author of the radical, even heretical, book *Honest to*

God, which was a bestseller, largely due to media coverage. But his lectures on Romans were a superb grounding in Paul's gospel. When he later returned to academic life, which he should never have left, he recovered his confidence in Scripture.

But my faith in God's Word was coming under pressure. It seemed as if we were being taught to read the Bible with a pair of scissors. Genesis was not written by Moses but compiled from four sources – J, E, D and P. The prophet Isaiah had met his death by being stuffed into a hollow tree trunk and sawn in half; now his prophecy was cut into three, adding Deutero- (second) and Trito- (third) Isaiahs. The gospels, likewise, were analysed and dissected, one 'source' called 'Q' (from the German word *Quelle*, meaning 'source'), since no one knew where or what it was. Paul didn't write all the letters that bore his name. Added to the 'Lower Criticism' (a valid attempt to recover the original text) was 'Higher Criticism', mainly German in origin (judging the truth of Scripture by human reason and scientific philosophy, questioning such 'supernatural' elements as miracle and prophecy).

Our feet were kept on the ground by going out at weekends to preach in churches within reach, by bike, bus or train. One of my first 'appointments' was in a village near Peterborough, where my great-uncle had once been the minister. An elderly man met me at the door and led me through the chapel to the vestry, asking me if I'd like a cup of tea after the service, before cycling back. I said I would, upon which he pointed to a cast-iron, pot-bellied stove with a pipe chimney, which heated the building and said: 'When you begin to preach, you'll see me put a kettle on that for your tea. We have an understanding here that when it boils the preacher winds up his sermon.' I inquired how long it usually took and was told exactly twenty-two minutes. Then, with a wink he added: 'Mind you, for some of the preachers we get here, I only half fill the kettle!' Since it was my first visit, I got the full allowance.

There was a famous and flourishing Christian Union in the

university: CICCU (Cambridge Inter-Collegiate Christian Union). Had I joined up with that, I might have averted a looming crisis. But we were discouraged from doing so and urged to give our limited spare time to 'METHSOC', the Methodist Society, within which each of us led a weekly fellowship group, in which most discussion was simply pooling our ignorance. I was therefore not to discover 'evangelicals' until much later.

There was a growing gulf between my studies and my sermons. I was living on material I had delivered in Shetland and rapidly using it up. By my second year I found myself unable to produce anything new. My first 'Trial Sermon', preached before fellow students and staff to be judged by them afterwards, had been a triumph but the second was a disaster. I was losing confidence in preaching, both message and method.

I passed my exams and got quite a good degree (a 'Two-One', just below a 'First'). But I felt hopelessly unready to face the practical demands of pastoral ministry, the very thought of which brought on feelings of panic, which I shared with no one. In desperation I thought of a way out of the dilemma. I would apply to stay on at college for a post-graduate year to pursue my own studies. To my amazement, this was accepted. Looking back, I believe the Lord was being exceptionally kind and patient, knowing I needed this breathing space to prepare for what lay ahead.

I was free to set my own agenda, to choose what subjects to study, lectures to attend and books to read. I ranged from philosophy and psychology to writing a paper on 'What really happened on the Day of Pentecost in Acts 2', coming to the conclusion that it was too far away and too long ago for anyone to be sure! Even the scholars I looked up couldn't agree.

In my rather diffused reading, I came across two books which rekindled my faith and restored my confidence. I've met one author on earth and look forward to thanking the other in heaven. They were the right books at the right time.

One was *Christ and Time*, by a Swiss theologian, Oscar Cullman. The Greek philosophy underlying our Western culture had left an impression that God was outside time, eternal meant timeless. Now I began to think like a Hebrew. God was working out his purpose inside time (and space), the living God who was, is and will be. For the first time I saw the Bible as a whole story and was caught up in the breathless wonder of the divine plan to redeem the universe as well as the people in it. I had something to preach again, this time much bigger than anything I'd done before.

The other was *The Household of God* by a bishop in the recently united 'Church of South India', Lesslie Newbiggin. This gave me a much larger understanding of the Church than the denominational tradition I had grown up in. He predicted that the Pentecostal/charismatic stream would become as large and influential as the catholic/sacramental and the evangelical/biblical and that all three together were needed to accomplish a mission to the end of the earth and the end of the age.

With a deeper view of the Bible and a larger view of the Church, I began to be more confident about the future. I was more relaxed and took up gliding as an antidote to hours spent in my study. I threw myself into the life of a church near the airport, where I could minister to 'normal' people again, outside the hothouse environment of the academic world. I began to look forward to my first 'stationing', as the Methodist Conference called the placing of ministers. Through a former college friend's father an invitation came from the Walton on Thames circuit of churches, which I accepted.

By Methodist standards it was a small 'circuit', five churches and two ministers. The 'Superintendent' looked after Walton and Weybridge, the rather posh part, and I was assigned to Chertsey, Addlestone and Shepperton. I saw very little of him since he preferred to concentrate on his end and left me to my own devices.

They found me lodgings with two older ladies, spinsters and

spiritualists. Neither they nor I persuaded the other to change religions! Their garden was full of nasturtiums and I made the mistake of saying their leaves could be eaten as salad. Guess what became a regular item in my diet!

I lived in Chertsey, a sleepy little town known for its lock on the Thames and its curfew bell in St Paul's Parish Church rung every night at 6 p.m. If you've heard the song 'Hang on the bell, Nelly, hang on the bell – Your poor lover's locked in a cold prison cell', you'll know the story. A reprieve was on its way from London for her young man but he was due to hang at 6 p.m. She stopped the bell ringing with her body.

With only three churches I was able to manipulate the preachers' quarterly 'Plan' to fit in a few short series of sermons. One of my first was on 'Salvation' with six parts – from sin, by grace, through faith, with assurance, to holiness, for eternity. I was already more of a teacher than a preacher. And I soon noticed the cumulative effect of such continuity in the pulpit. The congregations began to grow; interest and expectancy also rose steadily. In one church we had to re-open a gallery which had been closed for years. It was a pointer to the future.

But within months I felt I was stagnating, or at least coming to a plateau. Ministry was becoming routine. I was surviving in a denominational system that left little room for change, experiment or ventures of faith. I was learning nothing from anyone else, only meeting my colleague once a quarter to 'make the Plan' of preachers for the next three months. I was in a cul-de-sac.

The fact is that I was feeling lonely and bored. I bought a decrepit 1928 Austin 7 saloon and rebuilt it, painting it in a neighbour's garage. I called her (not 'it') Dorcas, after the woman in Acts who was 'full of good works'. I used to drive over to Guildford to watch the new cathedral being built, little dreaming that I would one day take part in 'renewal' events in that very building, dedicated to the Holy Spirit.

And there were a few colourful incidents that relieved the

monotony. One was at a funeral. The landlord of a nearby pub had died and, since his grandmother had been a Methodist, the undertaker came to me. I expected a godless congregation of his customers and was not disappointed. I decided to risk all and 'roast them over the pit', as a sermon on hell was crudely described in those days. While I was still preaching, the deceased's brother left his pew and charged up the aisle towards the pulpit. He was big and burly and I thought he was going to lay me out cold for implying his brother had gone to the wrong place. Instead, he came into the pulpit, shook me warmly by the hand and said: 'Damn fine sermon, padre!' I realised he had prepared for the occasion with a little liquid courage, told him I hadn't finished yet and suggested he return to his seat for the rest. He went quite meekly. I realised then what a delicate balance is required when burying an unbeliever. Say too little and the mourners get false comfort. Say too much and they are offended – at least if they are sober!

5

Arabia via Yorkshire

I must begin by explaining that Methodism is deeply indebted to one family by the name of Rank. Joseph Rank made a huge fortune with flour-mills in Hull and left it in a benevolent trust, which financed many a church building or project. His son, J. Arthur Rank, dominated the British cinema. As well as adult films, especially comedy, he made children's films for Saturday Morning Clubs and religious films for use in evangelism. He also taught a Sunday School class for many years.

The Home Mission Department had come up with an idea that combined the resources of father and son. They proposed sending out evangelistic units composed of a mobile cinema van (projecting films through a translucent screen at the back) pulling a caravan in which two ministers would live. Most of the men were straight out of college, since there were few with pastoral experience who were still bachelors. Hence an invitation to me.

I leapt at the opportunity and was linked up with Roy as my colleague. We soon found ourselves being taught to handle electric generators and full-size 'arc' projectors. Then we set off for our assigned area, the South Yorkshire coalfields around Doncaster, using Methodist churches as a base.

Moving from one location to another was quite a palaver, since I still had my Austin 7 and he had a Lambretta scooter. I would drive the large Fordson van and caravan to each new site, followed by Roy, and then ride back on the scooter so that I could collect Dorcas. Roy was very easy to get on with, readily accepting my leadership, and he could cook an excellent full English breakfast. Most other meals we received from local church members. We met miners at the coal-face, sometimes wriggling through impossibly narrow seams, and at the gates when they came off work, heading for the clubs and pubs. Little did we guess that most of these pits would be closed down in a few years' time. 'King' Arthur Scargill was not yet in the public eye.

To be honest, I don't think the project was a great success, if that is measured by the number of conversions of non-churchgoers. Those trained for pastoral ministry rarely make good evangelists (except in Pentecostal circles, where too many evangelists are trying to be pastors!). There are different gifts and callings. We found ourselves doing less outside and more inside the churches, seeking to inspire and instruct them to reach out, by taking them afresh through the basics of the gospel. I think the same thing happened with other teams and the whole experiment faded into oblivion quite quickly.

But it was an invaluable experience for us. Constantly meeting new people, tackling new situations and trying fresh approaches made us adaptable and adventurous. For myself I was now quite sure that I was a teacher (fifth in the Ephesians 4 list of gifts), whether in a pastoral or evangelistic context. It brings a real sense of freedom to know where you 'fit' in the body of Christ. It saves all the frustrating effort to try and be what the Lord neither wanted nor intended you to be and enables you to focus time and energy on what he has.

At one time we had crossed the border into Lincolnshire and

held two missions in and around the town of Scunthorpe. In the village of Gunness I met the young lady who is now my wife (but I'm keeping that story for later). My little car came in very useful then; who could go courting in a large truck? I announced our engagement at our final rally in Doncaster, packed with people from the whole region.

Perhaps my preoccupation with this new and more permanent partnership partly explains why, after that evening, Roy and I have never been in touch again, though we had lived and worked together for twelve months. I cannot recall any tension between us, much less a wrong word, largely due to his gentle and accepting nature. But we had remained working colleagues and never became bosom pals.

Our 'contract' was only for one year, so we had both wondered where we would be going next. The Chairman of the Manchester District wanted me to go and see a new church on a vast council housing estate. My grandfather had had a distinguished ministry there, in the Oxford Hall. From the start I knew it was not the place for me. Returning on the train, I had an extraordinary presentiment that a letter was waiting for me on the caravan floor that would tell me the next phase of my ministry. Sure enough, there was a blue envelope with a crest on the flap. It was from a Group Captain Hopkins telling me that there was a vacancy for a chaplain in the Royal Air Force. Nine ministers had already applied but he wanted to add my name to the list. I had never been in the armed services, nor did I relish the idea at all. I remember searching the caravan to see if there was another letter, offering me a choice. But this was the only one. I had no option but to agree.

Within days I was seated on a solitary chair being questioned by a row of officers. It would have been very daunting had not the NCO (Non-Commissioned Officer), who directed us into the room one by one, whispered in my ear: 'Imagine them all in their underwear, Sir.' I shall always be grateful for his advice. Visualising them all in string vests, I lost all my nerves and relaxed. So I got the job, though I was the only one who didn't really want it!

From there I was whisked to the CME (Central Medical Establishment) for a thorough examination. I hate such things, which rob one of all dignity and self-respect. Looking back, I can laugh at it, especially at two incidents. My hearing was roughly tested by words said at decreasing volume which I was to repeat as long as I could hear them. I duly said, 'Fish', then 'Chips', but the third, in barely a whisper, was an obscenity and I said I couldn't repeat it because I was going to be a chaplain. He laughed, said, 'You're OK!' and signed the sheet. Later I walked into a cubicle stark naked, to face a doctor writing at a desk. He looked up and said: 'Ah Padre, come on in.' That was the popular title for a chaplain and I wondered how he knew. Did I have a pale ring round my neck from wearing a dog collar? I shared this later with a pilot also being examined; he grinned and said: 'At least he didn't call you Rabbi!'

A visit to Moss Bros' second-hand uniform department fitted me out for the rank of Flight Lieutenant. Most chaplains went first to an OTU (Officer Training Unit). I was posted straight away to Cosford, near Wolverhampton. With 2000 boy entrants in their teens it was more like a boarding school. Mornings began on a huge parade ground, complete with band and prayers. Fortunately, I was under the tuition of a senior chaplain for a few weeks to 'learn the ropes'. He told me that on the first morning I should stand among some bushes behind the flagpole and watch him take the prayers. But he slept in! The Commanding Officer arrived, saw me and snapped: 'You on duty, Padre?' 'No, sir, I've just arrived and have no idea what to do.' 'Then get out there and say some prayers.' I ambled out, having never marched in my life, and met up with a tall, elegant gentleman who had no chevrons on his upper arm or stripes on the lower arms. I assumed he must be very important so saluted him and with a look of surprise he returned it. He was the Station Warrant Officer, a number of ranks below me. I did an about turn and tripped. All this endeared me to the boys but left me in a cold sweat. I bribed a Flight Sergeant with cigarettes to drill me in my office until I could march and salute properly.

I was the PMUB (Presbyterian, Methodist and United Board) chaplain. In practice, I got all who were left after the Roman Catholics and Anglicans had claimed theirs. We had our own 'church', a large wooden building. On Sunday mornings the boys were on the parade ground for an hour in their 'best blue' and all weathers, then marched to compulsory worship. It meant a packed service but a hostile atmosphere. There were a few wives of permanent staff at the back but the mostly male attendance was very different from what I call the 'lifeboat' congregations of civilian churches – women and children first. It was a captive audience but I had to work much harder to capture their attention and interest. After the service there was a cocktail party for officers in the Mess, at which the sermon was occasionally discussed.

I was living in the Mess, with a batman to press my uniforms, polish my shoes and bring me a cup of tea each morning. We were waited on at table for meals and had regular 'Mess Night' dinners. A senior chaplain gave me wise advice to slip away from these around 9 p.m. before things got out of hand. I once saw a cartoon on the noticeboard in which two officers, standing at a bar, were contemplating a drunken chaplain, complete with dog collar, lying on the floor. One was saying to the other: 'What I can't stand about the new padre is his "un-holier than thou" attitude.'

I still had 'Dorcas' but I was becoming embarrassed, if not ashamed, to see her standing in the Mess car park alongside superb sports cars and smart saloons. Then I heard of a previous officer owner of an old Austin 7. When he went on leave, his colleagues completely dismantled it and rebuilt it in his bedroom. He had to repeat the exercise to get it out. I quickly sold mine, for £5 more than I had paid for it and bought a 'ragtop', cheese-grater grille, lowlight Morris Minor, which became my pride and joy. Enid and I began our married life with it.

I had reported to the lady officer in charge of married quarters when I arrived, knowing that it took on average two and a half years' service to build up enough points to be eligible for one. Having just got engaged, I was prepared to wait. To my astonishment she offered me one on the spot, explaining that two more than they needed had been built and stood empty. I asked how long they could keep it for me and she asked why I couldn't take it immediately. 'Because I'm not married and will need to get a wife.' She roared with laughter and said she'd hold one for six weeks. Rumour went round the camp that I was looking for a wife, but none applied – the few women on camp were all married already. I phoned Enid and told her that if we could arrange a wedding in six weeks we could have a fully furnished detached house on the same day! She did and we did. But I'll keep most of that story until later.

One regular item in the boy entrants' curriculum was a weekly 'Padre's Hour' when it was my responsibility to 'give them a bit of religion', according to the Wing Commander in charge of them. I had them in batches of about two dozen. My opening gambit was to check denominations, asking them to respond by raising hands. They had all registered when they joined up. 'How many Methodists here? Baptists? Presbyterians? Congregationals? Salvation Army? Etc.!' Hands went up readily. Then, in the same tone of voice, I would say: 'And how many Christians?' Occasionally a hand went up, accompanied by an eager, smiling face. Usually, there was consternation and boys would look at each other to see if any responded. The conversation continued as follows:

'What do you mean by "Christian", Sir?'

'What do you think I mean?'

'Someone who keeps the ten commandments.' (invariably)

'OK. How many Christians here?' (more consternation)

'But nobody can keep all ten, Sir!'

'So how many do you need to keep to be a Christian?'

'Six out of ten, Sir.' (invariably)

'OK. How many Christians here?' (more consternation)

All this led to a lively discussion of what a Christian really is.

Many boys were homesick and regretted signing on. With a married quarter we were able to give many a taste of home, using tins and tins of baked beans. We recall one staring at the table and saying: 'Cor, a tablecloth!' But they weren't supposed to visit officers' homes and this was a black mark against me. Then I persuaded the Air Commodore to try dropping the parade before Sunday morning service, putting the boys on their honour to go to church. At first, this went down well and the atmosphere improved greatly. But it backfired in an unexpected way: many nominal Anglicans started coming to us and their chaplain protested. It was all too much for the authorities and I was posted overseas, to Aden.

So I had to leave my now pregnant wife, promising to find a place out there as soon as possible, so that she could join me. It was at the time of the Suez crisis, so I flew out a long way round via Malta, across the Sahara Desert to Nigeria, then Uganda and finally Aden. In Kano, a fellow officer and I decided to do some sightseeing but a local guide ushered us into a stone hut full of snakes, slammed and locked the door, demanding 'baksheesh' as the price of liberty. While there I experienced a locust swarm, which blotted out the midday sun for an hour and a half, leaving not a trace of vegetation in their wake. I could hear them all munching, while the locals desperately but helplessly tried to save their crops. A bit of the Bible came very much alive.

Aden is a barren place, hot and humid. We had to swallow large salt tablets to replace what was lost in sweat and were supposed to drink thirteen pints of water a day. But the water came from artesian wells through a natural deposit of Epsom salts. It could only be swallowed piping hot or freezing cold, mixed with lemonade powder to make 'jungle juice' or Vimto.

Lukewarm, it acted as an emetic – another bit of the Bible came alive!

I found an apartment in Crater, an Arab town inside an extinct volcano, reached through a cleft in the rim with a bridge over it. It overlooked the town rubbish dump and incinerator. It had no kitchen so I salvaged and installed an old sink and purchased a gas ring. It was all a sharp contrast to our married quarter, but it was our first family home when the baby arrived. We were also free to entertain airmen of all ranks.

There was no church building and only a handful of 'other denominations' meeting together in the Anglican church. The 'vicar' was shocked when he caught me feeding some birds with bread left over from our communion service. I was only following my heavenly Father who feeds them, according to the Sermon on the Mount, but it became increasingly obvious that we needed a place of our own and I managed to obtain a wooden hut, which we decorated and furnished. With copious watering we had a little garden outside, but two sandstorms ended that.

Numbers began to grow. We had an evangelistic outreach called 'Operation Dragnet' and put up posters and bills, with just these two words to arouse interest before telling people personally what it was. But Headquarters got annoyed with all the queries from higher up as to what operation was being planned and we had to remove them. But they had done their job. The best advertising, as always, was one person telling another about us.

My preaching was changing even more. Men want it straight from the shoulder, even if they disagree with you. They also want something they can get their teeth into, a diet of tough meat, though I made an effort to put gravy on it. Something (I would now say Someone, since I know the Holy Spirit better) prompted me to announce a series of talks going right through the Bible 'from Generation to Revolution'. The results were an eye-opener to me and them. We began to grasp the big picture,

God's massive plan of redemption for the whole universe in general and us in particular. It was a milestone in my ministry.

As well as the base in Aden, my parish included stations along the south coast of Arabia and up into the Persian Gulf. I would fly in, take a service and fly on. Commanding officers often ordered staff to attend, until I made it clear I'd rather walk round and invite attendance. One occasion stands out in my memory. My senior chaplain in Cyprus sent me a signal telling me a report had come in about 'unauthorised religious activity' in Bahrain and ordering me to go immediately and close it down. I flew up and found that in the absence of anything official, a corporal had started a Christian fellowship and baptised sixty converts in the swimming pool. I was thrilled, preached the longest sermon in my life (three and a half hours) and flew out. I reported that I could not and would not do anything to discourage such a work of God. After all, I was the 'non-conformist' chaplain! Alas, there was a sad sequel. Many years later I addressed a group of clergy in the north of England on 'Mission' and got all of them interested if not fired up – except for one rather overweight vicar who sat through it with a deadpan expression, his mouth never smiling and his eyes never sparkling. Afterwards, I made a beeline for him, hoping that private conversation might break through where public oratory had failed. He greeted me with: 'We've met before.' Yes, it was the former RAF. corporal, now a professional part of the establishment. I could have wept.

All this, of course, took place in a context of Arab Muslim culture, which surrounded us on all sides. It was my first exposure to a totally different way of life, permeated throughout by a very different religion. An officer had shown me photos of a man caught stealing an orange in the market, having his hand chopped off and the stump cauterised with pitch. His agonised face haunted me for days. On another occasion I was on a second-floor balcony with friends and we saw an excited mob in the street below, dragging along a naked girl in the dust by her hair. When I suggested we should do something I was told not to interfere. She had been caught in adultery and was being taken off to be stoned. Another bit of the Bible came alive.

On Christmas Day I took a group of our new Christians for a picnic, mainly to take them away from the drinking binges in camp. We went to an Arab fishing village and out in a boat with them. A member of the crew told me that the Christian religion was 'mush tamam' (very bad) because Christians celebrated the birthday of their founder by getting drunk (alcohol is forbidden to Muslims but they freely chewed *qat*, leaves with a drug in them). I tried to explain that not everyone born in Britain is a Christian but he could not understand. Everyone in Arabia is automatically a Muslim.

What struck me most about Islam was its fatalism. *Insh'alla* (God wills) was an expression of resignation to God's irresistible power ('muslim' means 'a submitted one'). I was with an Arab fisherman laying out his fish to dry in the sun when one of the extremely rare rain showers came on. We only had one or two a year and loved getting soaked. But this would ruin his fish and I offered to help him gather them, only to be told we must accept God's will.

I made other startling discoveries – for example, that slavery still existed. I thought that William Wilberforce had finished all that. I also found out that in the whole of Saudi Arabia there were only a handful of Arab Christians and most of these were 'secret believers', who knew that open profession was considered treason worthy of death. Being baptised was to sign their own death warrant. The act was seen as the final, irrevocable break with the former life.

This struck me as quite near what the New Testament taught about the rite. I had always had vague doubts about the validity and effectiveness of moistening the foreheads of babies but now questions came to the surface which had to be asked and answered. I found over thirty passages of Scripture dealing with baptism and studied them as if my life depended on it, as later it did. How had I missed it all? I came to three shattering conclusions. First, that it should be by immersion in water. The Greek word 'baptise' meant just that but was only transliterated into English letters. Second, that its subjects should be repenting believers and therefore old enough. Third, and this was decisive, that the New Testament meaning and significance as a bath for the dirty and a burial of the dead could not possibly be applied to babies. I began to read books on the subject and concluded that theological justification for infant baptism was deductive rationalisation.

I had not had any occasion to christen babies while in the RAF but now realised it was going to be a problem when I returned to 'Civvy Street' (civilian life). This happened in an unexpected way. I was now promoted to 'Squadron Leader' but still on a Short Service Commission of three years, with the possibility of a Permanent Commission later. But the abolition of National Service in 1961 meant that far fewer chaplains would be needed, the SSCs being the first to be made redundant. I was not sorry, since most of my most fruitful work was done among the National Servicemen who were serving for two years and whose future was wide open. Permanent staff were a much tougher nut to crack. My wife was pleased for my sake. She had been put off by some of the long-term chaplains we had met, more officers than pastors, and she did not want me to become 'professional'.

As it happened, my return to the UK came sooner than expected, when I became ill and had to be sent home as a 'Casevac' (Casualty Evacuation – the label made me feel like a hero!). My wife and daughter went to her parents' home, where she had our second child. After I came out of hospital I served my remaining few months at Yatesbury, a camp which was completely demolished after I left! During this time I was available to be interviewed for a circuit in the September, when all Methodist ministers move round.

The Chairman of South Wales District was eager to have me

at Tonypandy Central Hall in the Rhondda Valley, where George Thomas, later speaker of the House of Commons and later still Lord Tonypandy, was a member. When I told the Chairman I could no longer conscientiously administer baptism to babies, he offered to provide a deaconess to do all the christenings. When the Methodist hierarchy heard of this, the invitation was cancelled and I was told to appear before a disciplinary committee at the forthcoming annual conference in Bristol. I duly turned up to face half a dozen senior officials, including the well-known Old Testament scholar Professor Norman Snaith, who had written a book in which he said the Baptists were the only denomination with a consistent view on baptism. When asked who had influenced me, I quoted him, among others, and he had the grace to blush. This led to general embarrassment and the interview came to a premature end. I never heard from them again. I guess they didn't quite know what to do about me, perhaps because the name was so widely known, my father having been the Vice-President of the Methodist Conference. And I had an award for being the top probation minister in the country, so my record was clean, except for this.

By that time, all 'stationing' of ministers was completed and approved by Conference, leaving only a few circuits without a full complement. I was 'banished' to one of these at the last minute and our new family home was to be in Eliza Street, Ramsbottom, Lancashire. This was the land of William Blake's 'dark satanic mills', though the cotton industry was already on the way out. It was totally new territory for me and I wondered how I would adapt to it.

In one of my first conversations with a local Methodist I was told that if I wanted to see many people in church I must remember the three 'Ps' – pies, peas and pantomimes. Food and entertainment were the best attractions. Then there were two big annual events in all the churches which drew the crowds – the 'sermons' and the 'walks'. Both dated back to the days when Sunday Schools were just that. The only education for children working in the mills six days a week had to be on a Sunday, when they were taught 'the three Rs' – reading, writing and 'rithmetic. But once a year they got religious instruction and had to listen to a 'sermon'. Skipping that meant expulsion. Habits die hard. Long after State schools took over education during the week and Sunday Schools only taught the Christian religion, crowds still turned up to the Sunday School anniversaries, still called 'The Sermons'. Only they went from one to another each season so that one full service in each church was followed by empty ones. The 'walks' were an annual procession of the Sunday Schools and later all the churches.

The Bury Circuit was a large one, with a team of five ordained ministers and many lay ('local') preachers. There were some large and impressive church buildings, usually ex-Wesleyan Methodist and often erected by wealthy mill-owners and some smaller, simpler ones, usually ex-Primitive Methodist and built by mill-workers. But like the cotton, church life was in decline. One huge Gothic 'cathedral' had a congregation of under twenty. I looked after one large and one small church and a congregation meeting in the community hall of a council estate.

It was frustrating to be preaching in so many different churches, though it required fewer sermons. I longed for the weekly ministry with the same congregation I had had in the RAF. Round the corner from our manse were the remains of a demolished chapel with the basement hall still intact. We renovated it and I began a weeknight Bible School, which soon bore fruit.

There were a few conversions. One couple was shocked into faith when I told them I couldn't christen their baby. And I met with keen young people, who are still active today, in the smaller church, the huge one long since gone. But for the most part, it was routine maintenance of a denominational system. We had to work by a book called *The Constitutional Practice and Discipline of the Methodist Church*, which was then an inch thick, but is now a loose-leaf added to each year and three or four times the size.

As one of my colleagues remarked: 'If revival came by organisation, Methodism would leave all the other denominations standing.' I was not alone in feeling I was serving a structure rather than people.

An invitation from Tom Rees aggravated my frustration. He was planning an evangelistic campaign in the Dominion of Canada (it was called that after the biblical claim that the Lord will 'have dominion from sea to sea'). Tom was going to use the Royal Train to travel from the Atlantic to the Pacific coast, holding rallies in all the major cities en route. He wanted me to be on his team. I applied for six weeks' leave of absence without pay, but was flatly refused.

I was now over thirty years of age and was beginning to have questions about the future. Some would call it the usual 'mid-life crisis'. But it was more than that for me. Was this what the Lord had called me to do? Was I to spend the rest of my working life changing so quickly from one situation to another? Was this the best way to use the gift he had given me?

These and many other questions finally condensed into one crucial issue. Was I in the right denomination? Was this the part of Christ's body he wanted me to be in? I had offered for the Methodist ministry because I was not familiar with any other. Was it now time to look elsewhere? And if so, where should I look?

When I was ordained in Leeds, I had to promise that if ever in dispute with the denomination, I would 'go quietly', that is resign without a fuss or protest, without rocking the boat by agitating others. I now resolved to do just that. When I told my wife it would involve losing my job, pension and our home, and facing an uncertain future, she swiftly replied: 'I want to be married to a man who obeys God.'

Why this door closed and how another opened I will leave for the next chapter.

6

Watery Watershed

Changing horses in midstream can lead to a soaking, which is exactly what happened to me!

I have often been asked why I left the Methodist ministry and why I went into the Baptist ministry, quitting the largest Free Church for a much smaller one. This has led me to examine my reasons and my motives, which are not always the same. The heart can be deceitful and the mind can rationalise. But I feel I must try to explain what proved to be the most significant step I ever took.

The most obvious factor was my changed understanding of baptism, which was contrary to Methodist tradition, in turn derived from Anglican tradition, in which John Wesley had been nurtured and ordained (a Cambridge professor shrewdly observed that he was like a man rowing a boat – he kept his face towards the Established Church but every pull of his oars took him further from it).

In my final circuit, described in the previous chapter, I was a living anomaly. I had stopped christening babies altogether, but no one seemed to be bothered or even to have noticed. We now had three children, all of whom we 'dedicated' to the Lord but none of whom were christened. However, I was not baptising believers either, so was not obeying Christ's mandate to make disciples by baptising and teaching them. Indeed, I was not even baptised myself, though by this time I had discounted what my grandfather had done for me as a baby.

I had taken steps to remedy my personal situation by asking a friend who was pastor of a little church further up in the Pennine hills if he would oblige. Keith agreed and I duly presented myself. I shall never forget it, one of the few occasions when I had a direct 'vision' from the Lord. As I went down into the water, I noticed some green mould on the side of the baptistry. In an instant the pool, congregation and building disappeared from view and I was in the Jordan river and saw Jesus just ahead of me being baptised himself. As I was the next, I was overwhelmed with the joy and privilege of following him. I realised that in baptism he was identifying with us who needed cleaning up and we are identifying with him who didn't, an insight that would cast fresh light on his crucifixion, which he also called a 'baptism'. He was killed, buried and raised for me. Now I had been baptised into his death, buried and raised with him. The issue of baptism was settled so far as I was concerned.

However, underlying this was a far larger problem. I had changed my views on baptism because of what the Bible said. But in letting Scripture be decisive over this, I had to apply the same principle to all other matters of belief and behaviour. I was now a 'Bible man', and others were beginning to label me as a 'conservative', as against a 'liberal', in that I accepted the inspiration and authority of Old and New Testaments as the Word and words of God. Only one other minister in the circuit team held similar convictions. Harry and I experienced increasing isolation.

This came to a head at a quarterly Preachers' Meeting, when ministers and local (lay) preachers came together and reviewed their activities, using a questionnaire that went back to Wesley.

The first query was always: 'Do all our preachers believe and preach our doctrines?' The answer was invariably taken for granted and the Chairman would write 'Yes', without any further discussion. On this occasion I called out 'No' when the question was put. An extraordinary situation had arisen. A leading layman, one of the Circuit Stewards, was following me round the circuit pulpits with a sermon he advertised in the local press: 'New lamps for old – the magic of fundamentalism'. In it he denied that anyone could be 'born again', since human nature can't be changed. Drawing attention to this led to a heated debate, which came to a halt when someone asked: 'What are Wesley's doctrines, anyway?' I said he himself had clearly listed the fundamental truths of salvation, which he insisted must be taught by all Methodist preachers. I was therefore asked to prepare a 'paper' covering these, to be given at the next meeting. I searched Wesley's writings and collected all his references to the 'fundamental' doctrines for which he believed God had raised up Methodism, such as assurance and, above all, holiness (which he defined as 'perfect love').

Delivering this message three months later caused a riot. One after another said that if they were forced to preach such things they would resign. The Superintendent Minister panicked, knowing how difficult it already was to fill the pulpit 'Plan' (Mr 'Supply' already appeared too often, indicating a church would have to find its own preacher). Now he saw a looming impossibility of doing so. He closed the meeting, saying he would meet me privately. When he did so, he begged me not to press the matter any further, lest it lead to serious division and a difficult situation for himself. I agreed to this, but it left me in a difficult situation. I was chafing against an unequal yoke.

By this time I had realised that the tensions in our circuit were not unusual but reflected a wider trend in the whole denomination. I had met others in the same predicament, depressed by the general departure from foundational roots. Their influence was being neutralised by the circuit system.

So it was my view of the Bible, even more than my view on baptism, that was driving me to a parting of the ways. The Methodist drift to liberalism, with its emphasis on a socio-political 'gospel', has gone on apace since then. To be honest, I am constantly grateful to the Lord for prompting me to leave when I did. At the time I was more conscious of being released from a lifetime of frustration and even isolation. I did not realise then I was being released to such a fruitful and fulfilling opportunity of ministry for the rest of my life.

Looking back I can see that the years in Methodism were all a time of training and preparation for the task the Lord had in mind for me, though it could never have developed in that setting. I had had experience of so many churches and situations, far more than the average young minister. I felt I had been favoured, partly because of my name, the family having had such denominational prominence, but primarily because of the truth of the family motto: 'God favours'.

That brings me to another possible motive for my transfer. Since this was psychological, I find it very difficult to gauge how much influence it had. It was certainly present, though I don't think it played a major role. In a word, the name 'Pawson' may have been a help, but it was also a handicap. Since my father had been an impressive Vice-President of the Methodist Conference, I could not but live and minister in his shadow. I was expected to live up to his image and continue the family tradition, stret-ching back to Wesley himself. It was sometimes as difficult for me to be myself as for others to accept me for myself. Dynasties are not always successful. It was only after I left Methodism that I learned that my father and Dr Sangster had a prayer pact that I would one day be President! My father never once mentioned the disappointment he must have felt when I made his dream impossible. That role would be fulfilled by one of my father's 'sons in the gospel', as he called them, one Donald English.

In Baptist circles I was totally unknown. I remember attend-ing my first Baptist Union Annual Assembly as a complete stranger. For a short time I felt very lonely, but this quickly passed. I soon found like-minded friends and, supremely, found myself and my ministry. To be accepted for myself was a welcome relief.

I leave the reader to assess the relative weight of these three factors influencing my decision – my conviction about baptism, my devotion to the Bible and the tradition of my family. Certainly all played a part. The important thing is that I have never once regretted it or questioned its rightness. Had I not made the change, it is highly unlikely that anyone would be reading these memoirs or, for that matter, that I would have written them.

Who was it said that everyone ought to change denominations at least once in a lifetime, then they will know they are acting on conviction rather than tradition? I had become used to people being described as 'good Methodists' and would now hear about 'good Baptists', coming to the conclusion that both phrases described upholders of denominational traditions. By this criterion, I had been a bad Methodist and would turn out to be a bad Baptist!

So why was it the Baptist denomination to which I turned? Quite simply, it was because I could then preach and practise baptism in a scriptural manner. I had considered the Church of Christ, since their teaching on the significance of baptism, as distinct from its practice, was closer to mine than that of many Baptists who seemed to regard baptism as little more than a 'wet witness', an act of obedience, a symbol rather than a sacrament, a human rather than a divine act, a testimony to the unbaptised rather than a means of grace for the baptised. My understanding of the New Testament saw it as a bath to cleanse the dirty and bury the dead, a rite effecting what it symbolised. But the Church of Christ was a tiny shrinking body with little prospect for the future, a cul-de-sac.

Some suggested the Church of England, with its strong and growing evangelical wing. My views on baptism alone would rule that out, to say nothing of the episcopal hierarchy or the political establishment, which blurred the distinction between church and world, neither of which I could see as biblical. I was told that the Prayer Book allowed baptism by immersion, even put this before the baptism of infants. But 're-baptism' as believers of those christened as babies was absolutely forbidden, since it implied denying the validity of the previous rite and the authority of those who had administered it.

My view of the 'church' had also crystallised as I studied the New Testament. Its membership was to be believers only, its boundary marked by baptism. The word 'church' had both a universal and a local application, but it does not have a hierarchical structure linking the two (I believe that came from the Roman Empire). It seems to me that the Baptists had got the balance about right between the independence and interdependence of local churches.

So to the Baptists I turned. So far I have told why I made the change. Now I will tell you how I made the change-over, which is just as much part of my story.

The first step was to send in my notice of resignation to the Methodist authorities. I was informed that I would have to meet the President in person, to explain my reasons. He was due to visit our District (Bolton and Rochdale) and address the ministers, after which he would meet me. That year it was a genial, pipe-smoking expert on social and political affairs, especially Communism, on which he had written. The substance of his talk to us was that Methodism had reached a fork in the road, a crisis of identity, and must either go back into the Church of England or become a true Free Church. Inviting comments from the floor, he was faced with the first question: 'Are you suggesting that we all become Baptists?' He looked straight across at me and grinned! When we met privately, he took time to get his pipe going, then remarked, 'I suppose there is nothing I can say to you?', and I responded with, 'No, Sir, you said it all this morning', and the interview was over, with, 'Well, we're sorry to lose you and wish you well' and a warm handshake. A few days later I received a cheque for £120, my contribution to the pension fund; they kept the employer's part. I was given a date when I could leave.

I went to see the Baptist 'Area Superintendent' in Manchester, who received me in a friendly and welcoming manner. I was not the first Methodist to seek a transfer. He described the main differences between the two denominations, in particular that while the Union could 'accredit' and recommend pastors, they could not appoint them. I would have to find a church that wanted me, which might be a problem since I was unknown and not (yet) a Baptist. I came away wondering how on earth to go about that.

But the Lord had it in hand already and fixed it all up in a most unexpected way. During my time in Aden as a Royal Air Force chaplain, I had bumped into the regional Bible Society representative on a visit from his base in Ethiopia. Lynn Ashley was a Baptist minister and an ex RAF chaplain. When I took him to our flat for a meal, my wife delightedly greeted him as an old friend! As a teenager she had attended Bible Society house parties which he had led. We later visited Lynn in Addis Ababa and he took the dedication of Deborah, our first child, in a fellowship meeting in the former Italian Embassy (from the days when Mussolini's forces invaded the country and it was renamed Abyssinia).

He was now to play a crucial role in my pilgrimage. I'm not sure how he heard about my hope of becoming a Baptist pastor, but he passed the news on to a dear aunt of his who was in membership with a Baptist church in Buckinghamshire, which was without a pastor and looking for one. It was in a village called Chalfont St Peter, and the church was named after its location, adjacent to a large common called 'Gold Hill'. I had never heard of the place, much less been anywhere near.

I was invited to 'preach with a view', spending a weekend meeting leaders and members. Hospitality was provided by the

Church Secretary, in a home which he and his wife had built with their own hands. Frank was an aircraft designer, then working on Britain's biggest helicopter, the Fairey Rotodyne – a practical and spiritual man, after my own heart. On the Saturday evening, before I had seen the church or any other members, I had an absolute assurance that the Lord had chosen this place for me, though that was to be severely tested before it was confirmed.

Within a week of my visit, a members' meeting unanimously decided to invite me to be their pastor. But the invitation was cancelled almost as soon as it was issued. The Baptist Union had intervened and told the church that the Trust Deeds of the building meant that they were limited to 'accredited' pastors and my invitation must be withdrawn. The church was full of apologies that our mutual raised hopes had been dashed. I told Enid that the Lord wanted us there and would get us there. We heard that the church had invited another man to pastor them and he had readily accepted. I still told Enid that we were going there. To remove the initial barrier I applied to the Baptist Union for accreditation. I went all the way to London for an interview with the Ministerial Recognition Committee only to be asked one question, laughable in the light of subsequent events: 'As a Methodist minister you only had to prepare a few sermons a quarter and take them round the circuit; do you think you can produce two sermons a week for one church?' I was longing to do just that, but managed to keep a straight face and said I thought I might be able to! I was duly accepted but too late for Gold Hill. However, the man who had been invited and accepted inexplicably changed his mind and withdrew, leaving the pastorate vacant, for which I was now eligible. I was invited for the second time and accepted. I asked to see their Trust Deeds and discovered there was no such clause limiting them to accredited pastors. All the fuss had either been a mistaken assumption at best, or a deliberate bluff at worst. It was an unfortunate first encounter with Union officialdom.

A whole new era was opening up. Whereas I had been used to serving so many different churches in Methodism, I would serve just two more for the rest of my ministry. The relationship with these could not have been more different than my previous experience. Each deserves a chapter to itself.

7

Chalfont St Peter

It was still a rural village in Buckinghamshire when I arrived, with its parish church near the single line of shops and the Baptist chapel overlooking Gold Hill Common. The cemetery was divided into two parts, consecrated for Anglicans and un-consecrated for everyone else, from Baptists to suicides. There was still a blacksmith. All but one of the Baptist 'board' of deacons had lived there for years. All this was to change during my seven years there, partly due to its neighbour community.

Gerrards Cross, less than a mile away, was a wealthy suburban commuter belt, which had grown up around the railway line to Paddington station in London. It was a dormitory for business tycoons and film stars. The parish church was an architectural hybrid, two wealthy sisters having each financed one half in her own taste.

A number of domestic servants in the 'posh' area had regarded the Baptist chapel in the neighbouring village as their spiritual home, feeling more comfortable with rural artisans. Quite a number were still in membership. But during my time the village was increasingly changed into an extension of the commuter belt and the rural atmosphere changed to a suburban one, which was reflected in the congregation and to which the church had to adapt. The change-over, however, never became a source of tension.

The church building itself belonged to a previous century. A brick box, almost a cube, contained a high gallery and a low pulpit, unrelated to each other. With the increasing population outside and congregation inside, we soon had to build a higher pulpit and steepen the balcony to make maximum use of the space. At the same time we covered the very dark wood of the balcony front and underneath. I spent days sticking up polystyrene tiles. At least the inside began to look as if we were in the twentieth century.

Decades before, the village ironmonger had had a vision of the future in which the church was packed to overflowing and needing far more extensive premises. On this basis, he had persuaded the church to buy four cottages on each side of the chapel and two at the rear, together with all their gardens. We began to see his vision coming true and as four dwellings on one side became vacant we were able to pull them down and build an extension to the church building.

Even before that they had built an architect-designed house for the pastor in some of the disused gardens, the soil of which was very fertile due to generations of privies. We were the first occupants and could at least choose our own furniture and furnishings. By that time we had three children and a Christian German girl who came as an 'au pair' to learn English. So we filled the four-bedroom house, which felt like our first real home.

The 'induction' service seemed more like a wedding complete with reception. Unlike Methodism, where ministers move on so quickly that they are regarded as temporary incumbents, these dear people clearly expected us to stay indefinitely. There was a novel sense of mutual commitment, which augured well for the future, particularly in view of the radical difference between Methodist and Baptist systems of church government.

Each Baptist church is autonomous, conducting its own affairs, believing it is directly responsible to the Head of the Church, the Lord Jesus Christ, and guided by his deputy on earth, the Holy Spirit. There is no hierarchy (I call it 'higher archy'), either outside or inside the local church. Preaching and practising the priesthood of all believers, the major decisions affecting church life are made at regular 'members only' meetings, which are protected from libel laws provided no members of the 'public' are present, a help when matters of discipline arise. For day-to-day running, a board of deacons, chaired by the pastor, manages affairs.

As with all systems, it is open to abuse. At its worst, it is seen as a democracy, in which voting, influenced by lobbying, puts membership in control of ministry, the tail wagging the dog. Many pastors have felt frustrated, even broken, by unco-operative congregations. Churches have split over what amounted to 'political parties' vying for power.

At its best, I believe it to be nearest to the New Testament, a true theocracy (government by God), when leaders and led together seek the mind of Christ, which requires being 'in the Spirit'. Some dismiss this as being idealistic and impractical in the real world of fallen, sinful humanity or at least among believers not yet perfected. But as those already called 'saints' should live up to their calling, so fellowships should aim for the ideal which grace has put within our reach. There will always be some who have a mind of their own rather than the mind of Christ. Whether they can sway decisions will reflect the general quality of membership, in turn reflecting the quality of ministry they have received. Style of leadership is a critical factor in this situation. A leader is someone whom others follow. Not all pastors are good leaders and a poor leader can soon be at loggerheads with members and even deacons, chafing at the very idea of members' meetings.

However, there is a real weakness in the system. The

'diaconate', as the board of deacons is called in this country, deals with all the routine business of the church, practical and spiritual, matters of finance as well as fellowship. Two trends are difficult to avoid: administration dominates the agenda and deacons can be chosen for business ability. Both tend to leave deacons maintaining the status quo and the pastor to take spiritual initiatives on his own, in extreme cases a dictator in a democracy, which can only end in mutual frustration and separation.

I quickly became aware of the hybrid anomaly of the average diaconate and resolved to remove it. Since Baptists justify their separate identity by an appeal to Scripture on baptism, they are open to advocacy on other issues based on biblical arguments. New Testament churches clearly differentiated between their spiritual and practical needs by appointing elders to 'supervise' the former and deacons to 'serve' the latter, though both needed spiritual qualities and both served the body, the difference being purely functional.

I began by teaching the relevant Scriptures, which took some weeks. Then we had free and open discussions in the members' meeting. The change was accepted more readily than I expected. I was asked to choose the first elders but declined. Sheep do not follow a shepherd they do not recognise. It was not an election with rival candidates for the same vacancy, but I asked for at least a four-fifths 'vote of confidence'. Those thus 'selected', not 'elected', were exactly the ones I would have chosen.

It was essential to disband the diaconate as a body. Two 'executives' would soon have overlapping agendas. Henceforth we would have separate deacons for the different spheres of service needed – finance, building, catering, music, etc., each having a team of helpers if necessary and all accountable to the oversight of the elders. The system worked well, primarily because the spiritual leadership was now clearly more corporate than individual. Changes were still brought to the members for their approval and co-operation. But being presented by a united team of trustworthy and increasingly trusted leaders made it far easier to gain a confident consensus. Two familiar objections disappeared: 'We've never done that before so we're not going to do it now' and 'We've tried that before and it didn't work'. I suggested we use the word 'opportunity' instead of 'problem', as in 'I can see a . . .'. A sense of adventure and expectancy began to pervade the members' meetings. 'What will the Lord tell us to do next?' To this day, my wife says she misses these meetings more than anything else, a sentiment which leaves most Baptists utterly amazed!

The most radical change I initiated was presented as an experiment for six months with a promise that we'd go back to the old ways if the members wanted to then. In the event, no one even asked for discussion.

It was to reverse the order of service on Sunday morning, taking the Word before the worship. This was the order of service Jesus knew and is still practised in every synagogue today. It was the order in the early Church, as we know from the book of Acts where the apostles' teaching preceded the prayers and is confirmed in a full account in an early Christian document called the 'Didache' (teaching). It is both logical and theological to listen to the Lord before talking to him, an appropriate dialogue. Who would rush into the presence of a royal monarch and open the conversation with self-chosen topics? How much more should we let the King of kings have the first word.

Few are ready to worship when they arrive in church. It takes about twenty minutes before they are thinking more about the Lord than themselves or each other, which is when true worship begins. But if they have listened to Scripture read and explained in a real and relevant way, they are ready to respond, in spirit and in truth, instead of being dismissed with one final hymn. The tone of worship was much more varied, sometimes solemn, sometimes exuberant, depending on what the Lord had been saying. Of course, it makes more demands on preacher and worship leader to be sensitive to the Spirit's leading. In those days I was both but made room for contributions from the congregation, prepared and spontaneous.

The children benefited as well as the adults. Arriving at church, they went straight to their own sections of what we called our 'All-age Bible School'. Instead of going out of worship, they came back into it later, by which time the parents were really worshipping and the atmosphere produced a much higher standard of behaviour than before. I had a concern for the increasing number of teachers required, so met them every Thursday evening, when I gave them next Sunday's adult Bible study before they prepared their own materials in sectional groups. Teachers need to be taught, and it gave me a chance to 'rehearse' my material before giving it to the adults. I have spent time on this because too many think of me only as a preacher and interpret growing congregations as a preacher's fan club. But I was first and foremost a pastor, seeking to build up a strong local church that could be salt and light in the immediate vicinity. Some mature Christians who chose to come a distance to attend our services were surprised and even offended by my reluctance to back their application for membership. My principle was that the further you go to church, the more you may receive, but the less you can give, only seeing other members on Sunday.

Another major development during my time was the opening of 'Rock House'. We had a concern for some of our elderly members and others no longer able to care for themselves. Just over the road were two very large Victorian semi-detached homes with extensive gardens. Our dentist occupied one but had decided to move so we approached the other and found that they, too, would consider an offer. The elders and a few members prayed and each was 'given' exactly the same figure: £27,000 (this in the sixties). This offer was accepted. I spent a few days in bed with flu, planning the bed-sitting rooms. After extensive operations, it was opened by Lady Petter, the widow of the oil engine magnate, now in her nineties and a fine

Christian, who had nursed Florence Nightingale in her final illness, singing hymns to her as she was dying. Since then flatlets have been added for those who can still care for themselves with some supervision and a nursing home cum hospice with eight beds, providing complete care in three phases.

There are many other tales to be told of our seven and a half years there, during which we became very fond of the people and the place. Our three children began their education there in a village school with some exceptional staff. One teacher remained a dear family friend and decades later the headmistress turned up to one of my meetings in Nottinghamshire. And I should mention another member of the household, our marmalade-coloured Border Collie called Trixie, who once bounded up the aisle in church, exactly on cue as I was reading the words: 'Beware of the dogs', from Paul's letter to the Philippians. No, I had not arranged this as a visual aid, though I was capable of such a gimmick. I once put a huge red poster on the outside noticeboard, reading 'Danger – God at work!' Every passenger on passing buses saw it and made varying comments. But a local decorator chose that time to fulfil a contract to paint the external woodwork of the church building. He refused to climb a ladder, in full view of drinkers at a pub on the opposite corner, until the poster was removed. There is a streak of mischief in my make-up, which can interfere with the dignity of my calling!

I thought we were settled there for many years, but it was not to be. When the Lord made it crystal clear that he wanted me elsewhere, as I shall explain, I was heartbroken at the thought of leaving. I went into nearby woods and wept like a baby. Tears have filled my eyes as I recall and write this.

I asked the Lord to 'seal' my departure by providing a successor quickly. One of the elders had taken a holiday in Scotland, staying on the east coast in his parents' home. Visiting an elderly saint, he had asked whether this godly man knew of any minister in Scotland who would be suitable. After listening carefully to an account of the past, present and potential future of our fellowship, he replied: 'There's only one man in Scotland I believe could do it: Jim Graham of Dunfermline.' Returning home, the elder urged me to telephone him and see if he was open to consider a call. I was reluctant, considering this church business rather than mine, but he prevailed. On a Monday night I found myself phoning a complete stranger and plunged in with: 'I'm a Baptist pastor in England. I don't know you and you don't know me, but would you be willing to take over from me down here?' There was a long pause and then, without any further comment or questions, he simply said, 'Yes', explaining that a few days previously the Lord had told him to expect such a call. I later met him and we became friends. He came to visit the church. A few days after I left he accepted a unanimous invitation to follow me, surely one of the smoothest change-overs ever. I could not have wished for a better successor. He suffered a little from my shadow but quickly made a name for himself which he carries today. He was to stay in the village eight times as long as I did, but like me is 'retired' with a wider ministry than ever. Some time after he had taken over, the little old lady who had given my name to the church years before, wrote to say that 'things have been even better since you left'. I'm sure she was quite unconscious of the ways her remark could be taken!

Before moving on with my story, I want to deal with three strands in my later life and ministry which began during my time in Buckinghamshire, each of which requires a chapter of its own.

Two of these were completely fresh developments. Both were related to events outside the church in the 1960s. First, I became one of the early participants in what later became known as the 'charismatic renewal'. Second, I became aware of God's present and future purposes for Israel, the people and the place.

The third was a development of what I had been doing for many years. It was the maturing of my preaching, in style and content, in preparation and delivery. The thrice-weekly opportunity to use my gift, which I classify as 'teaching' since it was more used for the edification of the saints than the evangelism of the sinners, had taken me some way towards fulfilling the proverb 'Practice makes perfect', though I am still learning.

Since this last would become that for which I am best known, I'll talk about that first.

8

Sermons Galore

I guess I'll be remembered as a preacher more than anything else. Indeed, when a stranger asks me what I do for a living I usually say I'm a preacher, which leads to an awkward hiatus in the conversation, while the enquirer recalls church connections of distant relatives or distant memories.

I have certainly devoted more time, energy and attention to preaching than anything else. In a real sense it has been my life. Looking back, I can see how it has developed, in content, preparation and delivery.*

My first attempt was a dismal failure. The congregation numbered three, my mother and two sisters. Father was away and for some reason we couldn't attend church that Sunday, so we improvised at home. I was 'volunteered' to be the preacher and my pulpit was an armchair facing backwards. I chose the parable of the Labourers in the Vineyard as my subject. First I

---

* Publisher's footnote: David shares further insights about his long pilgrimage as a preacher in the forthcoming collection of lectures entitled *Preach the Word!* (Sovereign World, to be published in 2006), gathered from the 2003/4 conference for preachers held at Westminster Chapel in London.

read it from the Bible. Then I retold it in my own words. Then I went through it a third time to find what lessons I could from the narrative. At this point, one of my sisters interrupted, in an exasperated tone, with 'Isn't that vineyard full yet?' The atmosphere of worship collapsed into unseemly mirth and my sermon came to an untimely end. Her remark became a family saying, a secret code for a boring preacher.

I cannot recall any repetition of this domestic experiment, yet it was prophetic in a way. That parable later became one of my favourite and oft-repeated messages on the mercy of God, with more visible fruits than any other. It was also significant in that I 'expounded' a passage rather than a text, which later became my invariable custom.

My first sermon in church was a shock for me and a surprise for the congregation. My friend Jack, the converted bookmaker, was due to preach one Sunday evening in Spennymoor Methodist Church in County Durham. After tea at his house, I went with him on the bus. When I asked him what he was going to speak about, he told me I was to do the preaching while he would conduct the service. Shaking with nerves, I gave my testimony, quoted all the texts I could remember and sum-marised my entire theology – all in seven minutes flat, an achievement I've never been able to repeat (today I average 60–100 minutes).

I have already described my progress through the Methodist system for preachers. I am grateful for the experience thus gained and marvel at the patience of the congregations. Had they not been so accustomed to passivity, they might have stoned me. But there were two limiting factors in the experience gained.

One was the widespread practice of preaching on a text (one verse) or a topic (many verses). In practice, many texts were taken out of context and used as hooks on which the preacher could hang his own thoughts, giving them a semblance of biblical authority. In my early days I adopted this practice and was guilty of using (abusing?) Scripture to support what I wanted to say.

The other was lack of continuity. Each sermon had to be entirely self-contained, as it was hawked round a 'circuit' of churches. Even as a full-time minister, Sunday services gave no chance of a sequence of messages, much less an expository series.

All this began to change when I was a Royal Air Force chaplain, in sole charge of Forces fellowships. But the development came to fruition when I became a Baptist pastor, preaching twice a week to the same people. It was therefore while I was at Chalfont St Peter that my preaching was moulded and matured. Since a congregation plays a silent but significant role in shaping a preacher, I owe a great debt of gratitude to the people there, especially for their honest comments afterwards.

It was here that I found my calling – to be a Bible teacher. I resolved to preach whole books of the Bible, at roughly a chapter at a time. If that meant a series of more than a dozen I would give breaks for a mental change. I began each book with an overview and background, to whet the appetite. When I finished one book, I asked the Lord to show me which was the next needed for the church. Invariably, the answer came from the pews. Two or three would say: 'When are we going to study Deuteronomy?' for example.

I also resolved to teach the whole Bible, as well as whole books. I planned to do this over a decade. Only a knowledge of the whole Bible can lead to a whole knowledge, and love, of God. Too many make their own image of God, a mental idolatry, by a highly selective use of Scripture, concentrating on those attributes that appeal to them (his love and blessing, for example), while ignoring those that don't (his hatred and cursing). A sentimental view of God can be very different from a truly scriptural one. Even our understanding of Jesus can be faulty if we derive it entirely from the Gospels and ignore his self-portrait and letters in the book of Revelation. My ambition has been to preach the truth, the whole truth and nothing but the truth.

My hearers got quite the wrong impression that I knew the whole Bible inside out and my sermons were simply the overflow of vast familiarity with Scripture. The truth is very different. I simply knew one chapter better than they did. I have always maintained that teachers need two qualifications – to keep at least one step ahead of pupils and to be teachable themselves, the latter enabling the former. Wanting to learn must come before wanting to teach.

Preaching is like cooking, taking far longer to prepare than to be consumed. Both bring the satisfaction of feeding hungry appetites. Both require a digestible and balanced diet and will be more eagerly accepted if made appetising.

All this takes time. I gave it top priority, finding I needed up to an hour in the study for every five minutes in the pulpit. There is no short cut in my experience. Effective preaching is as much perspiration as inspiration. Come with me into the study and watch me as I prepare.

After prayer for illumination by the Holy Spirit, I begin with my Bible and a stack of plain paper – and nothing else. I want to get as much by myself as I can before consulting anyone else. I read through the passage to be expounded again and again and again and again, jotting down a jumble of thoughts that come to me, filling many pages. Then I seek to come to grips with the passage by analysing it, giving it a structured outline, using 'A.1.a.i.' for the main headings and sub-sections. This helps me more than anything to see the flow and direction of the narrative or argument. I am often tempted to alliterate the headings (giving them rhyming syllables or identical word-beginnings or endings). It is said to be the province of fools, poets and Plymouth Brethren. I have never been one of these last, hope I am not one of the first and would like to think I have a poetic streak in me. They can be forced and somewhat artificial, as in the classic example about the Prodigal Son:

A HIS MADNESS
   1. He cavilled
   2. He travelled
   3. He revelled

B HIS SADNESS
   1. He went to the dogs
   2. He lost his togs
   3. He ate with the hogs

C HIS GLADNESS
   1. He got the seal
   2. He ate the veal
   3. He danced the reel

But in my case, when it worked well and fitted the passage, it served three functions. First, it gave me a sense of real satisfaction, that I had 'mastered' the passage properly. Second, it helped me to memorise the outline and be less dependent on notes in the pulpit. Third, I gave the outline to the congregation, on a blackboard, screen or service sheet and they seemed to find it helpful to follow (and estimate how much longer I'd be going on!).

Only after getting my outline and fitting my jumbled thoughts into it, did I consult other books, mainly comment-aries, to check on whether I was on the right track. I have never collected books of other preachers' sermons so avoid the temptation of pinching their material, using their outlines or even their illustrations. Usually commentaries confirm my find-ings, often giving fresh insights that I can add in, but occasionally seem to have missed what I have found. This drives me to re-examine my case very carefully but if I convince myself I keep it in, bringing the delight of fresh insight to me and my hearers, who often confirm such from their own private study. Quite often I would write out my own translation or, rather, paraphrase of the passage, which is a quick way to find out if it has really been understood. Summarising its major theme or thrust in a single sentence is another way of doing this.

With controversial passages, where commentators differ widely on interpretation, I have made it a practice to tell the congregation the various views, while leaving them in no doubt about my own and giving them reasons for my choice.

The final step is to add interest, information and instruction. I regard this as adding gravy to the meat to make it palatable. A gripping introductory remark or story should quickly lead in to the main topic. (Who said: 'If you don't strike oil in two minutes, stop boring'? It has been attributed to George Jessell, Mark Twain and Oscar Wilde!) A practical conclusion tells people what you hope they will do about it. Good illustrations will both interest and illuminate, especially if taken from real life or contemporary events.

To be boring is surely the unforgivable sin for a preacher of 'good news'. I have discovered that the secret of capturing and keeping attention is pace. I do not mean speed of speech but rapid movement of thought. Someone once analysed a few of my sermons and found each had an average of over seventy distinct ideas. I am not concerned that all should be remembered. One will become a living word from the Lord to this person and another to that. With many thoughts this is likely to happen to more people. While not ruling out the oratorical value of repetition, belabouring a single point is the quickest way to lose attention. When the mind is less active the body becomes more active. Fidgeting is a warning sign! I reckon I have failed if I can't keep a twelve-year-old boy listening and I am thrilled with a remark like 'That was great!' from one such.

Summing up my preparation, my two single objectives are to make Scripture real and relevant. Real, by going back into the past and making it 'live' for the congregation, which means focusing on the human side of the divine revelation, the situations, tragic and comic, into which God spoke and in which he acted. My aim is to touch the emotions so that people feel as well as think, sharing the joy and sorrow, the anger and frustration, the depression and optimism of God's people.

Relevant, by coming back into the present with insight and encouragement from the past, relating Scripture to life as lived today, returning the focus to the divine side of revelation. Again, the aim is to touch the emotions as well as inform the mind, since without both, the will is unlikely to be stirred into action. Too much evangelical preaching has been cerebral, information for the mind, Sunday School lessons for adults. I want my hearers to share the heart as well as the mind of God and so be the more eager to do his will. The Bible is full of his feelings, far removed from Greek notions of an impassive deity, unmoved by anything we do or say.

Of course, I am not likely to stir up anyone else's feelings if I have not first excited my own. Both in the study and the pulpit God's Word has moved me to laughter and tears (more often the latter but that has never embarrassed me, even when my words are choked). And of course, emotion is of little value in itself, unless it leads to action. I remember a lady thanking me for my sermon, which she said she found 'really moving'. Without thinking, I blurted out: 'Where to?' She was offended and strutted away. Later she told me she couldn't get my question out of her mind, confessed to the Lord an honest answer ('nowhere') and then made a real response to his Word.

So now I have a message which I hope will be real and relevant, touching the hearts, minds and wills of those who hear it. All that remains is to deliver it effectively. I have often quoted the black American preacher who said: 'I thinks myself clear; I prays myself hot; and then I just lets go.'

I have always taken very full notes into the pulpit, so full that someone else could use them. But I have never written out a sermon, never had a full manuscript, so never 'read' one. Even with full notes I try to 'photograph' them in my memory so that I need not refer to them very often. My main reason for wanting to be as free from them as possible, even though they are all there, is not to give a false impression of knowing so much and having it all at my fingertips, but for a far simpler reason: to keep my eyes on the congregation. Eye contact is a vital element in effective communication. If the speaker spends time looking down, his hearers are encouraged to look away. I make a point of trying to look directly into the eyes of every member of the congregation some time during my discourse. Surprisingly, this has often left an individual with the impression the whole message was directed to or at them personally. Incidentally, it is easier to 'hide' from a preacher in the front rows of seats than at the back, since it is harder to focus on nearer than distant faces. The same applies to the audience: it is harder for them to focus attention for long on a face that is more than two metres away from a background.

I have learned more about preaching itself from watching the congregation than any other source. In fact, I feel it is a dialogue, even if it sounds like a monologue. I am very dependent on the congregation and constantly respond to their response. Eager expressions are a great encouragement. There is an element of truth in the saying that 'a congregation gets the preacher it deserves'. Even when making an audio or video recording I usually have a visible audience.

I use expressions on my face and gestures with my hands but do not move the rest of my body. It can be quite hazardous these days, with so many electric wires around one's feet. But moving around can be very distracting, drawing more attention to the messenger than the message. I shall never forget a judge's observation that a barrister who is sure of his ground when summing up a defendant's guilt or innocence keeps his feet still, while one who is unsure tends to walk backwards and forwards. Our body language strengthens or weakens our case. So I remain on one spot equally comfortable with a lapel radio or a stand microphone.

Language is crucial. Few are aware that there are two sorts of

English. On the one hand, Anglo-Saxon vocabulary tends to have shorter, concrete, picturesque, blunt, even crude words, but it touches the heart and is understood by the man in the street. On the other hand, Latin English has longer, multi-syllable, abstract, refined words, intended for the mind and used by scholars, philosophers and theologians. Too many preachers betray their university education or reading. Winston Churchill used a vocabulary of 25,000 Latin words to write his books but only 5,000 Anglo-Saxon words in his radio broadcasts, which upheld the British people's morale during their hour of greatest peril. He promised nothing but 'blood, tears, toil and sweat' rather than 'sacrifice, sorrow, labour and perspiration'. In paying tribute to the gallant pilots who won the Battle of Britain he did not talk about the 'gratitude of the majority for the minority' but simply said: 'Never in the field of conflict was so much owed by so many to so few.' One of the reasons for the popularity of the Authorised (King James) Version of the Bible was that it owed so much to William Tyndale's translation, using words with Anglo-Saxon roots ('a city set on a hill cannot be hid'). By contrast the New English Bible, intended for the 'common' people, uses phrases like 'oracular utterance'! Theologians use such Latinised words as justification, sanctification and glorification. I love the pidgin English equivalent for the first of those three words: 'God 'e say 'im alright.' My heart responds to that, not just my mind. Early in my ministry I resolved to use simple Saxon English as much as possible, not only for the sake of that twelve-year-old boy, but for all adults, whatever their education. Little did I realise that this would later facilitate (sorry, I should have said 'help') a worldwide tape ministry, understood by all who had learned Primary Standards English. Even the New Testament was written in common (koine) not classical Greek, so I am following in the footsteps of the apostles.

Probably the most common comment on my preaching is: 'Well, you certainly gave us something to think about!' It is said in a tone of mild reproach, implying: 'I didn't expect to have to think in the meeting.' I usually reply by pointing out that we are called to love God with all our minds as well as our other attributes and that the greatest unexplored territory in the universe is between our ears. I've never lost my northern bluntness!

I'm more thrilled when a remark containing genuine repentance reveals that the Holy Spirit has been busy while I was preaching. As when I spoke to members of both Houses of Parliament in Canberra, Australia, and a cabinet minister told me afterwards he was going home to re-write his income tax returns. I am only too aware that the finest oratory cannot convict people of sin, righteousness and judgement. Only the Holy Spirit can do that but he chooses to do it through preaching. So I am confident that preaching is not old-fashioned, obsolete or past its sell-by date, but equally convinced that without the Holy Spirit it can achieve nothing of eternal value.

So I intend to go on preaching as long as I am able and as long as the Lord uses it. I once addressed a large gathering of doctors and told them their calling would be obsolete one day. One of them shouted: 'And so will yours!' Like other gifts of speech, prophecy and tongues for example, preaching will 'cease' and we shall know the Lord as well as he knows us. I look forward to that day. Even though it has been the craft of a lifetime, I'm sure he will find something else for me to do, even more exciting and satisfying. And my tongue will still be used, if only in praise.

9

When the Wind Blows

By concentrating on Bible teaching, I found myself labelled as an 'evangelical', which opened up wider opportunities for ministry outside my adopted denomination.

I began to be invited to address conferences and conventions which were inter-denominational (perhaps 'non-denominational' would be more appropriate for some). My name was suggested for the well-known Keswick Convention. I spoke at evangelical colleges. The Anglican London College of Divinity was one, only a few miles away. At one stage many students suddenly began attending our morning services, when I was working through the book of Isaiah. It transpired that it was the set book that year, on which they would be examined! All Nations Missionary College was then at Taplow, near Maidenhead, and I became a regular part-time teacher. I revelled in teaching those who would become future teachers. But the students became so adept at reproducing my material that the staff coined the word 'impawsonation'! Nearly fifty years later I returned as visiting lecturer, invited by one of my former students, now the Vice-Principal of the College, in Ware, Hertfordshire.

A flourishing 'career' was beckoning for this evangelical Baptist. Then I had to go and spoil it all – I became a 'charismatic', which closed doors even more quickly than they were opening, including Keswick, where earlier teaching on the Spirit might have been more sympathetic but later views were rather different. One of its most prominent speakers asked me if I had lost my critical faculties. Actually, I would become as critical as any of the more bizarre aspects of the 'Renewal', as it came to be called.

It was in the early 1960s that I began to hear hints and rumours of new happenings in traditional churches, which were being attributed to the Holy Spirit. My first direct encounter was at a conference for pastors at Herne Bay Court, run by the Evangelical Alliance. When I arrived an older brother told me: 'I've just seen the rooming list and you've been put in with someone who *speaks in tongues*.' He spoke in such hushed horror that he might have been warning me about crocodiles in the bath. I went to the bedroom that night in a state of apprehension, fearing that I'd be kept awake all night by strange sounds, Winnie the Pooh locked up with Tigger! Instead I found a relaxed, humble and approachable brother with whom I felt immediately at ease. To tell the truth, I felt more at home with him than with the one who had warned me about him. He did not talk about his new experience, much less try to convince me I needed it. A friendship began which has lasted to this day. Mike Pusey was the Baptist pastor in Basingstoke (now my address) and he is currently on the staff of Guildford Baptist Church (where I used to be pastor). I was impressed by what he was rather than anything he said or did and later visited him in his home to find out more.

Michael Harper, one of John Stott's colleagues at All Soul's Langham Place, next to the BBC in London, had been caught up in this new 'movement', as had other members of the staff, though John disassociated himself from it. Michael would do more than anyone to promote what was happening through his

'Fountain Trust'. In the early days he organised a house party in a small conference centre in Stoke Poges (where Gray wrote his 'Elegy Written in a Country Churchyard'). This was just down the road from me and I asked if I could gatecrash the select group event. Among others present was Harry Greenwood, from Chard in Somerset. He was the first person I ever heard pray and praise in another 'tongue'. It is a horrid word, implying uncontrolled babbling; the Greek *glossai* should always be translated 'languages'. What I was hearing was a clear, confident speech with an impression of distinct grammar and syntax. I singled Harry out for private conversation and he prayed for me, but nothing happened.

So what was my spiritual state at that time? I was a full-time Christian minister, serving the Lord as faithfully as I knew how, preaching his Word and seeing fruit. Was this not proof that I had the Holy Spirit? What more did I need? I did quite a bit of self-examination at the time but in hindsight can now see the answers to these questions more clearly.

I was typical of many Christians, who are fully Trinitarian in profession and principle, believing that there are three persons in the 'Godhead', Father, Son and Spirit, as contained in the creeds, hymns and benedictions of Christian worship. But in practice, and even in preaching, I and they are actually Binitarian, focusing our faith on two persons, Father and Son. We had come to know the Son and through him the Father, so had a conscious relationship with both, which enabled us to talk to others about both. But we did not talk about the Spirit in the same way. We rationalised this by saying that his function was to glorify the Son, not himself. But the same is said of the Son, that he would glorify the Father, not himself – yet we did not hesitate to talk about Jesus. The truth was that we didn't 'know' the Spirit personally, so could not talk about him with the same intimacy or confidence.

Once a year, the ecclesiastical calendar had forced me to speak about the Holy Spirit, on Pentecost Sunday. I had managed to do so by swatting up commentaries and other books. But I was passing on information rather than experience, preaching a doctrine rather than a dynamic, proving he was a person rather than a power. Whit Sunday was celebrating the 'birthday of the Church' two thousand years ago, an historical event of yesterday, not a continuing experience for today. I was relieved when this Sunday was over and I could get back to 'the gospel'!

Now I realised my neglect and omission and resolved to put things right – in the pulpit rather than in private. I announced that I would preach a series of twenty sermons on the Holy Spirit, covering everything the Bible said about him, from the first page to the last. I was doing this as much for my sake as anyone else's and was reminded of the lady who said to her vicar: 'Please don't preach your doubts, I've enough of my own.' But I also recalled the Moravian Peter Bohler's advice to the Rev. John Wesley, before his conversion: 'Preach faith until you have it.'

As I prepared the series I was surprised to find how much the Bible said about the Spirit. We can miss so much in Scripture when we are not looking for something, particularly in the Old Testament. I discovered that the Spirit was responsible for the achievements of the prophets, priests and kings, even the skills of the craftsmen who constructed the tabernacle, the physical strength of Samson, the wisdom of Solomon and many other exploits which I had unconsciously attributed to unique human abilities. But these were all historical events and could be retold without disturbing implications.

When I got to the New Testament I began to feel disturbed and even fearful. I had planned to reach Acts chapter 2 on Pentecost Sunday. How appropriate! But what was I going to say? I was still somewhere between Easter and Pentecost myself, with no personal experience of what happened to the first disciples. I was in a panic and even considered how I could postpone the rest of the series and save face, without anyone guessing why I'd done so. But I could not think of a way of getting off the hook. I was already into the Gospel of John and all that Jesus said about sending 'another standby' to take his place. I couldn't stop now.

Life with the Lord can be full of surprises. He intervened in a totally unexpected way which not only released me from my dilemma but also changed the course of my ministry.

I must digress at this point and tell you about James, a highly intelligent patent agent, who was the self-appointed leader of the opposition at our church meetings. I suppose every fellowship has to have one to keep the rest of us on our toes. His contributions greatly irritated, even frustrated me, but my wife would tell me not to get upset, because 'the rest are all with you'. Once a year, in the spring, I had relief from his presence. He was vulnerable to severe hay fever and had to take to his bed with congested lungs, which could last for weeks. I am ashamed to admit I welcomed his affliction and took advantage of it.

That year it occurred right in the middle of my 'crisis' over the sermon series on the Holy Spirit. Reluctantly, I felt I must make a pastoral visit to his sickbed. All the way there I kept hearing a voice in my head, repeating the phrase: 'James 5, James 5.' Well, that was his name, but what did '5' mean? Then I remembered that in chapter 5 of the epistle of James, sick believers are to call for the elders and an anointing with oil, which would bring healing. I had never done that, certainly did not want to do it in this case, so decided not to mention it. But his first words to me were: 'What do you think about James 5?' He explained that he was due to fly to Switzerland four days later for important business. Would I anoint and heal him? I said I'd pray about it (a useful cop-out) and spent the next day or two asking the Lord to give me a convincing reason (excuse?) for not doing so, but the heavens were silent.

The day before he was due to fly, his wife rang to ask when I was coming. I promised to bring one or two leaders that evening and purchased a bottle of olive oil in anticipation. But

I was full of doubts and questions. What was I getting into? How could I be used to heal anyone? The apostles may have had such 'power', but I didn't. Above all, if it didn't work, James would be more of a thorn in my flesh than ever before, with contempt for my ministry. I went into the chapel, knelt in the pulpit and tried to pray, sharing my mental turmoil with the Lord. I could not pray successfully for his healing, confessing that I was glad he was sick. I didn't know what else to say, so stopped talking. Quite suddenly, I began to intercede for James with all my heart and soul, pouring out words from the depths of my spirit. Only they weren't in English! It sounded more like Chinese. I recall pausing, looking at my watch and finding, to my astonishment, that I'd been going for an hour without stopping, a novel experience in my devotions. I wondered if I could do that again, opened my mouth and did, in a totally different language. It was more like Russian this time.

I was not excited emotionally but mentally felt profound relief. So this was it, what the disciples experienced on the first Pentecost. I would be able to preach about Acts 2. More immediately I found myself eager to visit James and anoint him with oil. Now I was confident it would work.

We went that evening and found him lying flat with a grey face, gasping for breath. We worked through James 5 as if it was a car service manual, so we began with confession. I told him I'd never liked him and he said that had been mutual. I emptied the bottle of olive oil over his head. We then prayed. Guess what happened – absolutely nothing! We checked James 5 but we'd done everything by the book. I was desperately disappointed. Devastated would be a better word. I got up from my knees and ran to the bedroom door, just to escape. Something (Someone) stopped me just long enough to ask whether James still had his airline ticket for the next morning and when he said, 'Of course', I blurted out that I'd drive him to Heathrow airport – and fled.

I didn't dare to contact him next day but he rang me, asking me to pick him up. I couldn't believe he was better and able to travel, so asked if he'd got his doctor's approval. He had and had also had his hair cut, the barber insisting on a shampoo first (he said he'd never seen such greasy hair!). Apparently in the middle of the night, he felt his lungs were being crushed, as if by two giant hands, and coughed up a bowl full of liquid.

There were three wonderful long-term results. First, he never had this condition again, though he had suffered it every year since childhood. Second, he and his wife were both filled with the Spirit (his father was a keen Pentecostal and had longed for this to happen). Third, he became my best friend and closest confidant. I am therefore baffled when a Christian tells me he thinks tongues is of the devil. Indeed, I think that comes perilously near the unforgivable sin.

The next Sunday I was still in John 16 and the 'Comforter' and preached from my prepared notes as usual, or so I thought. Afterwards, a young carpenter asked me: 'What happened to you this week?' When I enquired why he asked, he replied: 'Because this week you know what you're talking about.' I then shared my experience with him. A year or two later he was accepted for the Baptist ministry himself and began with a better knowledge of the Spirit than I had had.

So what had been my spiritual state and status before all this? And had either now changed? I now talked about this new experience as both 'receiving' and being 'baptised in Holy Spirit', which are one and the same thing in the New Testament. As for describing my former ministry I found that what had happened to me was remarkably similar to what had happened to the first apostles. On the night before he died, Jesus had told them that the 'Comforter', the new 'Paraclete' (Stand-by), was a complete stranger to the world and would necessarily remain so, but was not a total unknown to them. He had been *with* them (they had healed the sick and cast out demons by his power, without realising where their ability came from) but would soon be *in* them. When they had thus received him for themselves as

Jesus himself had done after his baptism in water, they would be able to do what he had done, in even 'greater' measure. And so they did, after their Pentecost.

And so did I begin to do, after my 'Pentecost'. Praying and praising in unlearned languages was just a beginning, for me as well. My 'main' gift was still 'teaching' God's Word, though others detected new notes were sounding – greater clarity, confidence, conviction and challenge. To this day a discernible change comes over me quite quickly when I speak in public. But other gifts, supernatural abilities I never had before, began to surprise me and others. I had to learn how to recognise the promptings of the Spirit in my spirit and respond by doing what he wanted me to do and saying what he wanted me to say. He uses words even more than actions to get results. Some are so simple and straightforward that they hardly seem to be sent from heaven, until the results prove them divine.

After a meeting in London, a delightful young couple came up to me and faced me with:

'Mr Pawson, you've got to help us or we're going to get divorced!'

'Are you both Christians?'

'Oh, yes.'

'How long have you been married?'

'Three months.'

'Why are you thinking of divorce?'

'We can't stand each other.'

'How did you meet?'

Then it all came out. She had volunteered to be a prison visitor and had been allocated to a men's prison. She had led a young convict to the Lord, discipled him well and over his remaining term fallen in love. Neither she nor he had close relatives or friends, so on his release they had married and moved into her flat together. They quickly discovered how different their social backgrounds had been. He never used cutlery, eating with his fingers, and at night left all his clothes in a heap on the floor, ready to pull them up and on in the morning. She liked everything tidily put away in drawers, flowers and lace curtains. They had never seen each other outside a prison cell. They had made a terrible mistake. I felt that months of patient counselling would be needed. Silently I asked the Lord for help and four totally unexpected words came to mind: 'Week on, week off.' I spoke them out and added: 'I think that means you are to take turns; one week you *both* do everything *his* way, but the next week you *both* do everything *her* way.' The girl said: 'That's so weird it's got to be of the Lord . . . is that all?' I said: 'The Lord told me no more.' Off they went and I've never seen them again. But six months later I got a delightful letter, bubbling with joy and telling me how wonderful marriage was, how happy they were and how grateful for 'my' advice! But they didn't tell me if they were still doing 'week on/week off'. I thought that would make an excellent title and technique for a handbook on marriage guidance, but the Lord told me it was a 'word of wisdom' for that couple alone. I felt a kinship with Solomon when he told the arguing women to cut the baby in half. I was impressed with how economical in time and effective in result an inspired word can be.

A word of knowledge is equally potent. After a meeting in Sheffield, a woman asked me how she could be a better witness to her neighbour. I replied, 'You don't need to take those pills', which surprised me as much as her. The conversation went on:

'How did you know I take pills?'

'I didn't but the Lord did. Did the doctor prescribe them?'

'No.'

'The Lord wants you to have his peace. Does that mean the pills are tranquillisers?'

'Yes.'

'Then receive his peace and flush the pills down the toilet.'

Her face lit up with joy and she rushed away in excitement. I complained to the Lord that he hadn't let me answer her initial question about witnessing to her neighbour, but he replied,

'Who do you think will be the first person she'll talk to about tonight?' and I chuckled. What a sense of humour he must have.

Words of knowledge led to healing. I was guest speaker at a convention in a large marquee. When I got up to address the crowd, the Spirit led me into healing before I spoke and gave me a list of six most unusual ailments, including cancer of the tongue. But the most striking was a middle finger of a left hand. As soon as I said this, a man leapt to his feet and held up a hand with a black middle finger. He had cut it off in an accident at work, had it sewn back on again, only for it to become gangrenous – and was having it permanently amputated the next day. But that was never needed. Next morning it was as healthy as the others.

One Sunday I found myself preaching in the church attended by Princess Anne. She wasn't there that morning but there was a full congregation, many looking as if they had arrived on horseback. It was a very 'high' Anglo-Catholic setting and before I ascended the pulpit I had to stand on the chancel steps to be 'fumigated' by two small robed boys with swinging incense burners. I was given fifteen minutes to speak on the lesson for the day, the unforgivable sin! I took nineteen minutes and managed to include freemasonry! The vicar was very excited and demanded my notes so he could preach the sermon again himself. He asked me to administer the cup at communion, but with many large 'Gainsborough' style hats and bowed heads I was bumping ladies' noses and chins. By the end of the service I wondered what the Lord could do, if anything, but I was in for a humbling surprise when we gathered for a coffee at the rear. A well-dressed gentleman told me he had just come to faith and quite literally danced for joy. Then a little old lady with a terribly bent back, almost at right angles to her legs and supporting herself with a stick, told me she had served the Lord faithfully as a missionary overseas for many decades but was finding her crippled old age hard to bear. Would I pray for her? Before the amazed onlookers who knew her well, her back straightened up in an instant and she walked upright without her stick. My wife and I drove away rejoicing in what turned out to be one of the best Sunday morning services we've ever attended. Some time later I was visiting a friend's house and found myself sitting on a sofa with a boy of nine, whose hands were covered in warts, much to his embarrassment at school. With my arm round him I asked Jesus to take them away. A day or two later they were all gone, leaving pink flesh. Whether these things happen to young or old, in private or in public, I confess I still find it a battle to believe the prayer will be answered and am filled with grateful wonder when it is. But I have learned to seek the Lord's mind before praying for the sick. Sympathy is no substitute for obedient faith.

Gifts of healing and miracles are quite distinct. I define 'miracle' as a natural event with a supernatural cause. I exclude 'happenings' in the psycho-somatic sphere and in the spiritual realm. The word seems to be limited to occurrences in the physical world outside human beings. Jesus stilling the storm or multiplying bread and fish are examples. In my experience I have, on rare occasions, affected the weather pattern in the name of Jesus.

In the north of Northumberland are the Otterburn moors, where a farmer and friends arranged an open-air rally in a field. They had had a vision of me preaching and even the date on which it would happen. They telephoned, confident that I would be available on that Saturday, which I was. But when I arrived they gave me a complete set of waterproof clothing (the right size), since the forecast predicted a heavy belt of rain crossing the county that very afternoon. I dared to tell them they had wasted their money, since I wouldn't need any protection from the rain. But as we began the meeting the sky went darker and darker. The people were sitting on hay bales and I was on a four-wheel trailer as a platform. Just before I was due to speak the first drops of rain began to fall and umbrellas sprouted among the audience. I'm afraid I became quite angry with the Lord and rebuked him for arranging the meeting but not the weather. I even told him to split the black rain cloud in two, above our heads. To my astonishment (o ye of little faith!) he did just that. The rain poured down on fields either side of us but we were in a shaft of sunlight, which even burnt my lower lip. Reports in the Alnwick newspaper and *Farmers' Weekly* both used the word 'miracle' of this extraordinary occurrence but the *Methodist Recorder* simply talked about the 'meeting'!

Perhaps the most common gift of the Spirit is prophecy. In popular parlance this is limited to predictions about the future. But it can be just as much about the present, giving insight, rebuke and encouragement to God's people, forth-telling as well as foretelling. Nevertheless, predictive prophecy is a real and relevant component of messages from God. It is not given to satisfy curiosity about the future, much less to impress others with secret knowledge. Its purpose is solely to prepare people for what lies ahead and to give them confidence in the God who knows and shapes coming events. I have found myself making such announcements from time to time.

In the next chapter I will tell you how I came to tell Margaret Thatcher she would become Prime Minister of the United Kingdom and her response. Lest you think I believe God favours right-wing politics, I hasten to add that in Australia I urged congregations to pray for a relatively unknown Trade Union official called Bob Hawke, whom God had chosen to be their future Prime Minister. I was told not to mention 'that boozing womaniser' in church, but I told them that they'd have to pray for him when he was in office, so if they interceded for him beforehand he could turn out better than they feared. And he did.

I suppose the 'prophecy' for which I am best known is that Islam will become the dominant faith in Britain. The story of how I came to this conviction (or rather how it came to me) and its implications for the Church is told in my book *The Challenge of Islam to Christians*. No timing accompanied the intuition, so I may not live to see its fulfilment – or failure. In my flesh I hope I was wrong, but in my spirit I fear I was right. Since I first went public with it, many reported trends and events seem to be confirmation, not least the declining influence of institutional Christianity and the increasing attention given by public authorities to the growing Muslim minority.

In this chapter I have tried to give a taste of the new dimensions to my ministry that came with a more conscious relationship with the third person of the Trinity, the Holy Spirit.

What excited me most was not what was happening to me but what began to happen to others as well. People with few natural gifts could all have supernatural gifts. It would take another book to tell stories of members who had formerly played little part in church life, now finding they could edify the whole body in ways beyond their wildest dreams. I began to think of ministry as something everybody could exercise. I lost all interest in ordination as a transition from amateur to professional status. I had already dropped clerical dress and now stopped using the title 'Reverend'. Fellow ministers accused me of trying to abolish the clergy. I retorted that I was trying to abolish the laity. In theological terms my 'pneumatology' (theology of the Holy Spirit) had turned my 'ecclesiology' (theology of the Church) upside down. Receiving the Spirit had redefined the church for me. I began to receive ministry from those I had ministered to. I realised I needed them as much as they needed me, a sobering, yet liberating discovery.

10

Let My People Stay

In 1961, when I went to Israel for the first time, it was to see the place, not the people. My growing love for the Bible had bred a curiosity to see the land where most of its events had taken place. I booked for a commercial tour (advertised as a 'pilgrimage') and found myself with a surprisingly jolly party of Presbyterian ministers from Northern Ireland. In those days the land was deeply divided by a 'no-man's-land' of minefields and we had to carry our bags through the Mandelbaum Gate, the only crossing point between the Jewish and Arab zones. But we managed to visit most major sites of biblical importance. I came home with dozens of colour slides, some useful souvenirs, many new insights into the history and geography of Scripture and, quite unexpectedly, a strong feeling that I must and would return. As the plane flew away, tears filled my eyes. I felt I was leaving home, not going home!

The cheapest way to return was to lead a group, which I did a few years later. I quickly raised the number required for free places. This time we had a stark introduction to the politics of the place. The 'old city' of Jerusalem was still in Arab hands and under the control of Jordan. Colonel Nasser had risen to power in Egypt and there were ominous rumblings throughout the Middle East.

We were on the Temple Mount when stones began to fly, followed by bullets as a full-scale riot erupted. Our Arab guide fled and left me to shepherd our group out of the Damascus Gate and back to our hotel, where we learned that King Hussein had been on the radio to impose a three-day curfew on the whole city, warning that anyone who ventured out on to the streets was liable to be shot. His Arab Legion, trained by the British Glubb Pasha, would ensure its observance.

By an amazing coincidence, his senior officers took over part of our hotel as temporary headquarters. Hours later they were in the bar while we were singing in the lounge, the two rooms joined by an open archway. We were led by Eric Wood, a former opera singer whose sister and her husband led the London Emmanuel Choir. The army officers were fascinated by his fine tenor voice and asked him to entertain them. He told them he only sang Christian songs now, but they were already so bored they would accept any diversion. So he sang the gospel to them for an hour or so. The result was that we were given written permission to explore Jerusalem. The streets were totally deserted. It was a weird experience. We seemed to be taken back through the centuries and would not have been surprised if the apostles themselves had come round a corner. We had the whole city to ourselves for three days before life returned to normal.

One of these was Easter Sunday and we debated whether to worship in the hotel or go out looking for some local believers. We decided on the latter and set off through the empty streets, not knowing where to look, but asking the Lord to guide us. After a short time we heard a shout above us. An Arab was leaning over the parapet of a flat roof, beckoning us to join him, pointing to an open staircase at the side of his house. To our astonishment he led us into a meeting room with chairs and hymn-books laid out ready for a service. Nammour told us he was the pastor. Knowing his congregation could not come and desperate to preach his prepared sermon on the resurrected Christ, he had prayed for two hours, asking the Lord to provide a congregation. Finally, the Lord said his prayer was heard and told him to look down into the street to see the answer. And there we were!

After the service was over, I asked him to share his testimony, sensing it would be a remarkable story. It was even more amazing than I had anticipated. He had been a college lecturer and political agitator, stirring up his students to create civil unrest in the Hashemite Kingdom of Jordan, on behalf of Nasser with the hope of power and prominence when Egypt took over. He had two other ambitions: to marry a beautiful girl and start a family, both of which he achieved. But their first child was a 'blue baby' and quickly died. He was literally heart-broken and taken to hospital after a severe cardiac arrest. There, Jesus had appeared at the foot of his bed and said: 'Three days.' He told his visiting wife he would either die or recover in that time. He recovered and led many of his former students to Christian faith and formed them into a church. We listened spellbound, recalling the empty Garden Tomb a few hundred yards away. Alas, shortly after this he was kidnapped by Syrian Ba'athists and has never been seen again. I believe he joined 'the noble army of martyrs' and look forward to seeing him again in glory.

As my interest in Israel grew, so did that of our church. I resisted the temptation to start every sermon with, 'When I was in . . .', but inevitably my description of biblical locations became more real. The director of our Bible School told me he could pick out the teachers I had already taken with me by the way they retold Bible stories. Gone was the tone of a fairy tale: 'Now, children, I'm going to tell you a story about . . .' And in its place was the matter-of-fact tone with which last Saturday's football match was discussed. They had seen the real places and realised these things had really happened.

I had no difficulty, therefore, in gathering a full group for a further visit, little realising that this would affect me quite profoundly for the rest of my life, by shifting my attention from the place to the people of Israel. I had booked everything for June 1967. Then the famous 'Six-Day War' broke out. I sat glued to the television screen throughout the astounding conflict. I admit freely that my interest at first was purely selfish. Would it be over in time for us to hold our planned tour or would we have to cancel everything? But as I watched I became aware of a unique event of historical significance. Against overwhelming odds, the Israelis were winning. I began to see them in a new light and even to wonder if their God was on their side.

I tore myself away to fit in some pastoral visits. Among others I went to see Joe, a distant relative through my wife. He was now quite old, a life-long diabetic who had controlled the handicap with a careful diet and worked in the nearby 'Colony' for sufferers of epilepsy. We discussed the Middle East battle and he assured me that Israel was bound to succeed and survive. The Bible said so! He gave me a book about biblical prophecies, entitled *The Rebirth of the State of Israel – is it of God or Man?* by Arthur W. Kac (Marshall, Morgan and Scott, 1958). To say I was flabbergasted when I read it would be an understatement. How had I missed such a vital element in God's purposes? It was as if a blazing light had been switched on. So the God of Israel and the Father of Jesus were one and the same person! And Jesus himself was, still is and always will be a Jew! My Bible is a Jewish book, all forty authors except one being of the same race! The Jews are still his chosen people and he has future plans for them!

It was all a mental revolution for me, a Damascus Road experience for this Gentile who now realised he was by faith a true son of Abraham. On the very next Sunday, I preached about the God of Israel and the Israel of God. It was like putting a light bulb into a socket and finding it was already switched on. Recordings of that talk went far and wide, into synagogues as well as churches. I just knew that life would never be quite the same again.

We did manage to go, during the last 'cleaning up' phase. I was in a jeep with an army major on the Golan Heights, viewing the Russian guns overlooking the Israeli kibbutzim down the steep slopes below. I could not believe such a fortified position could ever have been taken and asked him how it was possible. He spoke not a word in answer but simply pointed to the blue sky above.

We were staying in a hotel in West Jerusalem and one day set off in a coach to go down to Jericho, the Dead Sea and Masada. We bumped over a dusty track through the former no-man's-land, from which the mines had been cleared. When we returned in the evening, we crossed an asphalt road with concrete pavements and lighted street lamps. By the time United Nations' inspectors arrived there was no trace of the city ever having been divided. Jerusalem was back in Jewish hands after nineteen centuries, an unprecedented event in the whole of human history. The 'Wailing Wall', now renamed the 'Western Wall' (the former name now transferred to the tax office!), was wet with tears of joy.

I was there again in 1973, watching the Independence Day military parade passing right through the conquered Arab zone of the city and was struck by the arrogance on the faces of the triumphant national leaders, Ben Gurion, Moshe Dayan and Golda Meir among them. I turned to one of our elders and said: 'God will surely humble them.' Months later they were taken by complete surprise on the holy day of Yom Kippur (Day of Atonement) when everything is shut down and everyone is at home. It would be a costly conflict as well as a humbling one. The myth of invincibility was shattered.

My growing links with the place and people of Israel stimulated new depths and dimensions in my ministry. I found myself looking at other people with new insight, since the God of Israel is also the God of all nations, including Britain. Was it just a coincidence that we lost our worldwide empire within a few years of washing our hands of the mandate to look after

Palestine? Or that six of our Prime Ministers disappeared from the political scene after reneging on Israel, from Neville Chamberlain, through Winston Churchill, to James Callaghan. Or that our two longest serving premiers, Harold Wilson (see his major book *The Chariots of Israel*) and Margaret Thatcher, were both openly 'Friends of Israel'?

Mention of our first lady PM reminds me of my 1979 visit. By now I had two groups from Guildford keen to go and arranged two consecutive tours, between which I would spend a week with friends in Jerusalem. When the first party left the airport, my wife reminded me of the forthcoming general election and asked if I had remembered to register for a postal vote. I hadn't but told her I could still use prayer to influence the outcome. It was Independence Day and crowds filled the streets of Tel Aviv that night and I danced with them, jealous of their 'family' patriotism. I returned to my hotel in the early hours. Believing the Lord has the casting vote in every election, giving us either in justice the leader we deserve or in mercy the leader we need, I asked him whom he would vote for and the name 'Margaret Thatcher' came straight into my mind. I then asked him if he had any word for her and two things followed the name – that she should return to the faith of her father (a Grantham grocer who was also a Methodist 'Local' preacher) and soon seek a relationship with Menachin Begin, then Prime Minister of Israel.

I seized a piece of hotel notepaper and wrote all this down in a letter to her, beginning: 'I want to be the first in the country to congratulate you; God is granting you this high office and responsibility.' Then my natural reticence (cowardice?) took over and I feared to send it. I decided to go out for a walk to think it over and seek guidance from the Lord. Walking down the main 'Dizengorf' street in Tel Aviv, I came to a bookshop window. Central to the display was a framed text from Isaiah: 'For Zion's sake I will not keep silent; for Jerusalem's sake I will not hold my peace.' That settled it!

The next morning my friends from Jerusalem, the musical couple Merv and Merla Watson, came to drive me to their home and I asked to be taken to the Post Office first. I insisted on sending it by Express, which meant many stamps and cost many shekels. Merv, intrigued by the name and address on the envelope, asked what was inside and I explained I had told her she would win the coming election. He laughed and said if she lost the election he would throw me out of their house – 'We don't entertain false prophets in our home!' In the event, she didn't lose and I stayed on with them.

The second group of our church members then joined me and after showing them as much as possible (our Israeli guide called us 'the group that runs where Jesus walked') we went to the airport for the flight home. In those days our tickets were collected on arrival and returned at departure. They were duly distributed to the group, all for a flight on British Airways, but I, the leader responsible for seeing them home safely, was given a ticket for a flight on the national airline El-Al (no, it doesn't stand for: 'every landing always late'). I protested, but was told security would not exchange it or allow me to, at which a church member said she believed the Lord was responsible. So I climbed aboard an Israeli 747 – with a slight man called Menachin Begin, who was going to London with the hope of meeting our new premier, Margaret Thatcher. I was able to tell him about my letter to her and later learned that at her first meeting with press reporters outside 10 Downing Street, she had quoted from my letter, adding a prayer of St Francis.

I have since been to Israel many times and my passport is full of their stamped image. This could have been difficult when I flew to a Muslim country known to refuse admittance to anyone who had such entries in their record. Handing my passport to the Immigration Officer, I asked the Lord to blind his eyes. He turned over every page, while staring into the distance over my shoulder, then handed it back to me.

Perhaps my most memorable visit was by myself. For two

months I travelled the length of the land, from Beersheba to Dan, staying in both Arab and Israeli houses, where friends and neighbours would gather in the evening to hear me speak. The most moving encounters were with Arab Christians who believed that God was keeping his promises to his chosen people by bringing them back to their own land. When I pointed out that this had brought material loss to them, they simply replied: 'Ah, but it also means the return of our Lord Jesus Christ is getting nearer.' One asked: 'Why has Israel given Jericho away, the first city God gave them?' Another told me that back in 1948 he had taken all his money out of an Arab bank and put it in an Israeli bank. His neighbours said he was crazy, but he said he was simply putting his money where his faith was. He kept all his and they lost all theirs. It has to be said that most with this outlook belonged to 'Brethren' style fellowships, well versed in Scripture. Anglican Palestinians are usually extremely hostile towards Israel and Israelis. So even the Palestinian believers are deeply divided among themselves. But it is touching to know that Israeli believers risk their lives to bring aid to their Palestinian brethren. That brings another event to my memory.

Some years ago, leaders of Christian fellowships in Israel, Arab and Jewish, met in Tiberias for a conference, but were soon at loggerheads over major issues. Things looked like coming to a standstill until someone suggested calling in a person from right outside the situation, whom all knew and trusted, to chair the gathering before it broke up altogether. My name was suggested and accepted, so they telephoned to ask me to fly out immediately. I was free but a flight by scheduled service at short notice would cost over £800, which I didn't have and didn't feel I could expect them to meet. Some of the younger ones there went to prayer, believed the Lord told them he could get me there if they pooled their spare cash, which they did, raising the equivalent of £120 in shekels. Meanwhile, I went to Luton airport and asked if they had a charter flight leaving for Israel. There was one but all seats were taken. When I persuaded them that my travel was very urgent, they finally offered me a rear-facing upright cabin-crew folding seat – for £120!

After I boarded I realised I was the only Gentile on the plane and found myself facing three rabbis. After a Kosher meal, I opened the conversation by asking whether they kept the Torah, the laws of Moses. They protested at being asked. Of course they did. When I quoted some that I knew they couldn't (because they no longer had a temple, priesthood or altar for sacrifices) or didn't (because the chief rabbi had substituted a more convenient contemporary alternative), they became quite agitated and demanded to know whether I was 'orthodox' or 'liberal'. When I said I was neither, they fell silent and studied me with shrewd eyes. Finally, one burst out with: 'I know – you're a Christian and you think Jesus set you free from all Moses' law.' I told him he could not have put it better and how good it was to be so free, since neither I nor they could ever keep them all all the time, which was what their forefathers had promised at Sinai. All too quickly the time passed in discussion and we landed at Lod (now Ben Gurion) airport.

I had long had a desire to climb Mount Sinai, though I recalled a Scottish cleric who, when informed of one of his church members' intention to do so and shout the Ten Commandments from the top, rebuked him with: 'You'd do far better to bide at home and keep them!' I set off from Jerusalem in a bus for Eilat and found myself sitting next to a female army officer, who told me her family had discovered they were descended from King Solomon, after archaeologists had uncovered an ancestral tomb. When I told her that made me very envious of her and how I wished I could have been a descendant of the king whose name I bore she burst into tears and cried out: 'Why do we Jews have to be such special people? I just want to be like everybody else!' But that was something she could never be and I found myself running through Paul's list of answers to the question: 'What advantage has the Jew?'

I arrived in Eilat with nowhere to stay for the night. There were no resort hotels then and no street lamps. But I had been told there was a Messianic Jewish couple in town who might be able to help. I had nothing but a name, no address. I stood in the pitch dark and asked the Lord to show me where they lived. I felt he was directing me to a block of flats at the top of a hill, so I trudged up and found their name against the bell push of the top apartment. I climbed many flights of stairs, knocked on their door and was greeted with: 'Come in – we've been expecting you all day!' When I asked if someone had told them I was coming, the answer was: 'The Lord told us in our morning prayer time to prepare for an important visitor.' So I had a comfortable bed for the night. Next morning I found it was their bed and they had slept on the kitchen floor. Arabs don't have a monopoly on generous hospitality.

Next day I boarded a bus for Sinai and again I was the only Gentile. There were a number of spare tyres on the roof rack and we would need them all. The rough stony tracks cut through them at regular intervals, over the same routes where the Israelites' shoes and sandals never wore out over forty years. We finally reached St Catherine's monastery late at night in pitch darkness, to find everything closed and the few monks in bed. We knocked at the gate until one got up to open up the bunkhouses where tourists can get a few hours' sleep before ascending the mountain at sunrise. The monk was in a bad temper, grumbling that he had not been warned about our arrival and pointing to doors he had unlocked, through which we could see three-tiered bunks. He was shouting at us: 'Men this way; women that way!' The group became very agitated and one or two bordered on hysteria. I moved among them trying to calm things.

I woke very early next morning and being a bit of a nosey parker went for an exploratory walk. Opening the door of a nearby stone building, I found it full of skulls, knee-deep on the floor – the mortal remains of many monks. I told no one and rejoined the others for the climb. Reaching the summit I came across a Jewish girl reading the Ten Commandments aloud in Hebrew. I asked for her name and she replied: 'Miriam.' I said: 'My! You've been here for a very long time.' She laughed.

After descending, we boarded the bus for the return journey. I was sitting alone on a double seat. Another passenger soon joined me and asked me: 'What is the secret of your peace?' I was surprised by the question, since I have never been a very placid person. Then I realised he was referring to the previous night when I had tried to calm the agitated group. I said I did not understand why everybody had been so upset by the monk's impatience with us. For answer he pulled up his left sleeve and showed me a tattooed number on his forearm. He told me that all the others on the bus were survivors of German extermination camps and when the men and women were shouted at by the monk in the darkness and separated into bunkhouses, they were all reliving their arrivals at the camps and final glimpses of loved ones they would never see again. I wept for them and was thankful they had not seen the charnel house full of skulls next door, which could have tipped some of them over the edge.

Years later I would stand in the poison gas chamber at Auschwitz, where thousands of naked Jews were massacred before their hair was cut off to stuff cushions, gold fillings pulled out with pincers, tattooed skin peeled and dried for lampshades, body fat made into soap and their ashes sold off as fertiliser – some within an hour and a half of their arrival. A Polish Jew showed me round the remains of the Warsaw ghetto, then took me to Treblinka where we had to walk over a layer of ash and clinker, the remains of so many cremated Jews. At the stone memorial was a group of Israeli children mourning their grandparents. I joined in their lamentations unabashedly.

I have had a unique rapport with artists and sculptors in Israel. It's as if their imagination has brought them next door to faith.

I found 'Jackson' in a tiny studio. I have rarely met anyone so crippled in body. He had fought in Israel's many wars but stepped on a land mine. His broken body was held together by straps, slings and splints. With the aid of a huge magnifying glass he was fashioning, in silver, tiny human figures about an inch high, combining them in scenes from the Old Testament, mounting them on pieces of rock taken from the very places where the event happened. Dozens of these exquisite works stood on shelves behind him, tempting me to break the tenth commandment. He opened the conversation with:

'Why have you come to Israel?'

'Because I love the Bible, amongst other reasons.'

'How well do you know it?'

'Well, I've studied it for some years.'

'Let me test you – how old was Isaac when Abraham was told by God to sacrifice him?'

'Twelve?'

'No, he was in his early thirties!'

I have since found out that the very next incident recorded in Genesis was the death of Sarah when Isaac was thirty-seven. Jackson told me then that Isaac could easily have overcome his elderly father but voluntarily submitted to be killed. It all made for much more insight into the incident as a 'type' of Jesus' crucifixion on the very same Mt Moriah. He then showed me a miniature sculpture of it, complete with an adult Isaac (as in all Jewish portrayals), an Abraham with uplifted knife and an angel with outstretched hands forbidding him to proceed. It is sitting in front of me as I write this. He gave it into my custody but said it will always be his.

Then there was the artist Motke Blum, whose studio was on the other side of the street, near the Jaffa Gate. He had painted a magnificent impressionist picture of Jerusalem, so subtle that you couldn't be sure whether you were looking at the old earthly city or the new heavenly one (there was no temple, anyway). I fell in love with it and asked how much he wanted for it. After looking me up and down, he frankly told me I probably couldn't afford it (actually, I had a friend with me who probably could). He had been offered £13,000 but had refused because it was 'my best picture'. The conversation then proceeded as follows, starting with:

'When the Messiah comes, he will love your picture, because he loves this city.'

'If the Messiah comes [his tone was jocular], I'll give it to him for free.'

'Do you mean that?'

'Did I mean what?'

'What you just said.'

'What did I say?'

'That you'd give it to the Messiah for nothing, when he comes.'

'But who knows if he'll ever come?'

'I do!'

'How?'

'Because God has promised to send him, in your Scriptures, and he never breaks a promise.'

He looked thoughtful and said no more. The next day two ladies from our group lightened upon the same studio and asked the painting's price, only to be told it wasn't for sale but was being kept for the Messiah. They excitedly reported this to me, unaware that I knew anything about it. A few years later I went back to see the picture but it had gone. Knowing how hard it is for artists in Israel to make a living and thinking he must have sold it to make ends meet, I turned to leave the shop quickly, not wanting to embarrass him. But he spotted me and called me back. I told him I'd called to see the picture again but he pointed to the ceiling and said it was somewhere in the loft. I thought he was being evasive and pressed him to show it to me. Finally, he got a ladder, climbed up through a trap-door and brought it down, to my surprise and humiliation. I asked him why he was hiding his best picture up there, only to be told he was receiving so many big offers for it, he was being constantly tempted too much to sell it. So he was keeping it where only God knew about it and it would be kept safe for the Messiah. He later painted a beautiful picture of the coming of the Messiah in glory to the Mount of Olives and sent me a print copy.

But it was not these experiences which introduced a new note into my preaching. My motivation was scriptural rather than sentimental. It was the clear prophecies about Israel's future in both Old and New Testaments that convinced me that our destiny is tied up with theirs. I could no longer accept the pervasive 'replacement' theology that the Church is God's 'new Israel', displacing the 'old'. In my New Testament, 'Israel' occurs over seventy times, always referring to the Jewish people, with only one possible exception (then only by changing 'and' into 'even'). Gentile believers are not a new tree planted by God, but are wild olive shoots grafted into a Jewish native olive tree among their remaining faithful branches. Paul wrote his whole letter to the Romans to warn Gentile believers not to boast about replacing some Jewish branches since they too will be cut out if they do not continue in God's kindness.

My interest in the people of Israel has separated me from mainstream thinking and my support for the place has furthered my isolation. Their right to their promised land is widely questioned by churches whose sympathy is more inclined to the Palestinian cause. However, I want to make clear that while the people and the place belong to each other, I believe that their ownership of the land is unconditional, but their occupation is conditional, depending on their just and righteous dealings with each other and aliens living among them.

So I do not support Israel right or wrong. Indeed, on one occasion I addressed hundreds of Jews and Christians outside the Yad Vashem (the Holocaust museum on Mount Herzl). I pointed out that the one and a half million children who perished in that bloodbath were now matched by the same number of babies aborted in Israel since 1948. Shortly after-wards, I found myself in the President's residence, presenting my faith. Sadly, he ended the interview by admitting he was an agnostic!

Although I became known as the 'Israel man', this only accounts for a tiny fraction of my teaching: 15 out of 1200 tapes (1.25 per cent). I am troubled when extreme Christian Zionists only listen to these and don't balance them with all my other teaching. Indeed, I have come unstuck with some of them because I don't believe that Gentile believers should start behaving like Jews, that Jews can be 'saved' without knowing Jesus or that Jewish sufferings are over yet. Above all, I do not accept the eccentric interpretation of Scripture known as 'Dispensationalism', propounded by Nelson Darby and promulgated in Brethren and Pentecostal circles. This has had a great influence on Christian Zionism, with what I call its 'reverse replacement' theology. This is the belief that the Church will be 'raptured' to heaven well before Christ and its mission taken over by Israel, the physical separation continuing into eternity with Gentiles in the new heaven and Jews on the new earth. I believe that there will be one flock under one shepherd in a new Jerusalem (inscribed with twenty-four Jewish names) which has come down from heaven to earth.

So I have been shot at from both sides on this issue (as on many others!), which makes me wonder if I might just be getting the balance right. But 'no-man's-land' can feel lonely and vulnerable and it can be painful when both extremes assume you belong to the other. If only they would check out what I have said and am still saying. Despite rumours to the contrary, I have not changed my basic understanding of Israel since 1967. My latest talk, given at a meeting in East London organised by a Messianic Fellowship, was entitled 'The God who keeps his promise – to curse and bless his people'. If Israel's survival is a great miracle, her suffering is a great mystery, until his righteousness is taken into account. Then one understands why he has preserved his chosen people yet not protected them from the worst that nature and human nature can do to them, both coming to a climax in the 1940s, with the Holocaust and the foundation of their own State, yet the ambiguity continues to this day and will do so until they fulfil the purpose of their election.

I have often wished I had Jewish blood in my veins. A few who know me well are convinced I must have. Two of my grandchildren have, our son-in-law being descended from the chief rabbi of Manchester. But I rejoice in being a true son of Abraham, by sharing his faith in God's promises until they are all fulfilled in the city we both look forward to inhabiting, whose 'architect and builder is God'.

11

Guildford and Millmead

I did not want to go to Guildford. For one thing, it was a Cathedral town. A new diocese had been carved out of the commuter belt in Surrey and a new cathedral built. In keeping with a long tradition local materials were used (red bricks had been baked from nearby clay, the North Downs chalk being far too soft). Standing on a prominent hill, it dominated the town. And cathedrals tend to cast an Anglican shadow over the ecclesiastical scene, partly because they represent the established, i.e. official, Christianity, politically and socially. I had visited the site to watch building progress and had also located the Baptist church. Typically, it was a nineteenth-century Gothic-style box in grey brick, squeezed into a back street behind the shops. Though the population of Guildford was then over 60,000, the building was smaller than the one I ministered in at Chalfont St Peter and had no attached hall, only a tiny vestry and an upstairs room.

Apparently the Guildford Baptists had sent spies to check me out. They must have reported back favourably, for I had a letter asking if I would consider an invitation. I simply wrote back to say I was not interested, being happily settled where I was, thank you! I had already told the Lord that if he ever moved me I had two requests – a building fit for the twentieth century and access to university students, whom I regarded as a key group for the future Church. Since I did not think Guildford could provide either, I turned down a second enquiry as well. They had looked elsewhere but found themselves coming back to my name.

Some time later I was in bed with influenza. After my wife had risen and gone downstairs I was chatting with the Lord. To my astonishment a word appeared on the wallpaper opposite, as clear as any graffiti. It simply read 'Guildford' and then faded away. My wife came up with the breakfast on a tray and the morning mail next to the toast. The top letter bore a Guildford postmark and before opening it, I told her: 'We're moving to Guildford!' This third time they pressed me to meet them to discuss it face to face. I drove over and got two surprises, after telling them I had decided to go.

The first was they would soon have to leave their building, which had been requisitioned by the council for redevelopment (it became a small car park). They would have to find a new site, and plan and erect new premises. They asked if I was willing to face the extra demands this would involve. Was I willing?! The second was that they felt they should plan for larger numbers, to accommodate the students from the new university then being built next to the cathedral. So I got both my wishes, but only after I had consented to go. The Lord has unique ways of testing our obedience.

Shortly after we arrived we found the streets under water, after unusually heavy cloudbursts of rain, causing jokes about the new Baptist minister hitting town! We moved into the best house we've ever lived in, two miles from the centre and ideal for teenage children needing their own space and distance from church affairs. But on Sunday nights it was packed with young people, peaking at ninety, who called it 'The Pawsonage'. As regards the adults, I arranged a monthly series of social evenings (fun, games and supper) for fifty members at a time until we had all 'let our hair down' together, which created a 'family' feeling quickly.

I was determined to repeat the two radical changes I had made at Gold Hill. I had already realised that major differences are more easily made in the first months of a new pastorate, when it is expected that a new broom will sweep clean, than later when modifications can be seen as a reflection on others and taken personally.

The new Sunday morning programme was accepted readily, since it was already halfway there. My predecessor had only stayed long enough to introduce an American-style All-Age Sunday School, before leaving for the States to head up the Southern Baptist Sunday School headquarters in Nashville, Tennessee. But the adult section was sparsely attended, most still coming to the later morning service. I was expected to prepare for teaching in both. It was a simple step to integrate them and there was never any desire or demand to go back. All ages went to their respective age groups on arrival and after an hour came together for half an hour of worship.

While this change had been quite easy, the other was much harder – introducing an eldership to replace the diaconate. The problem was that I insisted that elders had to be male (among the biblical qualifications is 'husband to one wife'). Leadership of any family in church or home is a masculine responsibility in Scripture, as I understand it. But there was already a woman on the small board of deacons (half a dozen), as was her husband. He was treasurer and she led the women's meeting. Though they did not dominate, their joint approval or disapproval could be decisive. And it became painfully clear that I could not accept them both as elders. When, under increasing pressure from them, I tactlessly said I believed the church had been mistaken in its former thinking, they took offence, resigned their membership and took up pastoral responsibility for a village church a few miles away. But we got our elders, now free to concentrate on spiritual oversight, while the deacons took up their separate tasks with efficiency and enthusiasm.

Of course the early years were dominated by what became widely known as the 'Millmead Centre'. I was heavily involved in a number of ways. The first was in the drawing up of plans. An architect had been chosen. He had been involved in church restoration (cathedrals like St Paul's in London and Chichester) as well as designing new parish churches. But he did not yet have a personal faith and still saw a church as a 'house of God', rather than a home for God's people, more concerned with form (soaring roofs) than function (lounges). We became good friends, sending many plans back and forward to each other, eventually arriving at a blend of his ideas and mine, which pleased everyone. The most radical innovation was to put the 'sanctuary' (worship area cum preaching auditorium) at the back, out of sight, with the social facilities (lounge, games hall, food services) at the front. So the dynamics emphasised meeting rather than meetings, informal ministry as much as formal, horizontal relationship with each other as well as vertical with the Lord.

Particular care was taken with the auditorium, which had to be multi-purpose, as suitable for musical and dramatic presentations as for worship. A sloping site enabled us to tier the seating. The optimum 'shape' of a crowd of over 200 is a quarter circle, which fits easily into a square space with the pulpit, table and baptismal pool in one corner. The whole building is only 90 by 110 feet, but includes an incredible variety of facilities, from shower rooms to a caretaker's flat. I was even dreaming about it. One morning my wife told me I had been talking in my sleep, a rare event for me, and said: 'We must have an invalid toilet.' Sure enough that had been overlooked. It is the most workable set of church premises I know and we had a steady stream of visitors, eager to incorporate its features into their own schemes.

The second was in the raising of money. The lowest estimate from a contractor was for £175,000, a considerable sum back then. The problem with church buildings is that one generation has to find the capital so that succeeding ones can use it rent-free! I got cold feet at this stage, fearing it could be a financial millstone round our necks for years and even considered whether it would be better to rent existing buildings from others than invest so much in our own. However, one members' meeting settled the matter for all of us. Two people brought 'words' from the Lord which lifted our faith. A driving instructor said he believed the Lord was promising to supply all the funds by the time the new building was opened. Another lady added that he would prove this by giving us £25,000 from an unexpected source to start the fund. Just a week or two later I showed her a cheque for this amount, from a wealthy Christian who had never been to our church and didn't belong to our denomination. But we had to find the rest and did so in a variety of ways.

Emulating the children of Israel providing for the tabernacle, I asked every member to give something precious to them and valuable to others. A local auctioneer was so impressed he offered his services and saleroom for the event. I also asked each member to raise at least £50, asking the Lord to give it to them, if they could think of no other way to raise it. One nearly blind pensioner was very cross with me for suggesting it. But she went home, sat by her fireside, closed her eyes and prayed. Opening her eyes, she saw glints of sunlight reflected in some unused brass implements and ornaments in the fireplace. Gathering them up, she made for the nearest second-hand 'junk' shop. Most only raised a pound or two, but one was an antique plant pot. She came home with £48 and was the first to bring the fifty. With delight she told me she had never thought she could have a ministry of giving but was now determined to continue exercising it. She was to bring five more lots, totalling £300. Sadly, she died before the building was completed, so was never in it. But maybe she saw it from above.

We felt it a matter of honour to pay the builder's monthly bill immediately. So we approached our 'NatWest' bank manager for a 'bridging' loan, to tide us over lean times. But it was a time of financial stringency and loans had been suspended. However, next day he bumped into his top boss in a London car park and was given approval, offering us £35,000. Eighteen months later he telephoned me to ask when we were going to use it. Embarrassed, I had to tell him we wouldn't be needing it, the Lord supplying every month exactly what we needed. I had to apologise for troubling him. He was not a Christian but later gave a 'testimony' in our church, based on our accounts, noting that they were emptied every 31 December and the contents given away, so that we faced the next year with corporate faith that the carefully worked-out budget would be met. The last contribution to the building fund came in just in time to open free of debt.

The third was in the erecting of the building itself. I virtually acted as clerk of works on behalf of the church, visiting the site daily and insisting on everything being just right. I had to point out that a grated floor drain had been put right in the middle of the lounge. The auditorium floor with its critically angled tiers had to be re-laid three times. But I loved doing it and was fascinated to see our plans taking shape. I have kept in contact with the architect, Robert Potter, now in his nineties and still active. He has since worked on All Souls, Langham Place, squeezing a superb meeting area between the floor and the Underground rail tunnels. He and his wife now have a real faith in the Lord as a result of witnessing the 'miracles' at Millmead, not least obtaining a 'plum' site on the riverbank in the centre of town for the princely sum of £100. And I have kept on designing churches, almost as a hobby. Perhaps my best example is the Coton Green Christian Centre, last building on the right as you leave Tamworth on the A513 for Burton on Trent. There is another at Hedge End, near Junction 7 on the M27 on the way to Portsmouth, but this still awaits the main auditorium. Buildings do not make the church, much less extend the Kingdom, but they can be either a help or a hindrance.

The church was, is and always will be people. After the Centre was opened, it was used every day of the week, from a club for the handicapped to trade union meetings. We wanted to share it with the town. And we put on a variety of activities to build bridges with the community. Our drama group presented some superb plays which drew full houses on a Saturday evening and often supplied the first link to Sunday services. In one of them, my daughter played the title role in *The Diary of Anne Frank*, to whom she bore a striking resemblance. We sent a photo to Anne Frank's surviving father, Otto, living in Switzerland and read his moving reply at each performance. A musical, *Children of the King*, had to be repeated so many times that attendances totalled 10,000. We held a three-day Arts and Crafts Festival, with musical concerts each evening, all done by members. Many visitors were surprised that Christians could do such interesting things. I encouraged some men to become a Barbershop quartet and even now, decades later, the ministry of 'The Millionheirs' is still in great demand. I am a great believer in pre-evangelism, establishing relationships before seeking to convert people. One of my father's favourite sayings was: 'Don't try to board a human soul without pulling alongside first.'

We had very few specifically 'evangelistic' events and I very rarely made 'altar calls' in the services even after baptisms, which is customary in Baptist churches. We found that making friends and bringing them under the sound of God's Word of truth, made real and relevant in a systematic way, enabled the Holy Spirit to do his convicting and converting work. Rarely a Sunday passed without someone repenting and believing. We needed to hold multiple baptisms every first Sunday evening of each month. These began with the baptisms and ended around the table of the Lord's Supper, to emphasise the corporate aspect of being baptised into the body. While the candidates were drying and dressing we had the preaching and prayers, before they returned. There were always two of us in the pool, so the emphasis was not on the baptiser and I invited members to share this. One gardener found it such a deep spiritual experience to share in baptising others, that I was left ashamed that for me it had almost become routine and realised that I had been robbing others of the privilege.

As in most churches, the pastor was expected to 'do' the weddings and funerals but later I began to delegate these as well. Actually, I had an agreement with local funeral directors that I would only take burials and cremations of practising Christians (Jesus did say: 'Let the dead bury the dead'). I never found funerals an evangelistic opportunity, finding it difficult to get the balance between saying too little, giving false comfort, and too much, giving offence. With Christian funerals, I sought to make them joyful occasions, praising the Lord rather than eulogising the deceased, celebrating their present state and future prospects rather than nostalgic memories.

Our congregation grew and we had to extend our capacity with closed circuit television to the games hall. Many preferred to sit on the floor in the auditorium. For the evening service it was necessary to come up to forty minutes early to be sure of a seat. Many were visitors, either to 'charge up their batteries', as they put it, or out of curiosity, like the Queen of Sheba, to see what they had heard. But we kept membership local to discourage those who passed good churches to come to us. At one stage we had an influx of people from the main parish church. I went straight to the Rector and told him that I did not approve of sheep stealing or even sheep straying from other flocks. He thanked me for telling him but said he had sent them to learn what they could and come back with a new experience and enthusiasm. I told Michael he was a bigger man than I since I had never once considered whether he could offer anything to our people. I didn't add that that was because he was Liberal/ Catholic in his churchmanship! When his people returned they took some of ours with them, to start home groups for prayer and Bible study. The pastor of the Strict Baptist Church accused me of taking a couple of his members from him. I pointed out that four of ours were now coming to him (they didn't like a crowded congregation!), so that we were more than quits.

The Lord was calling us to help other churches in town. We began sending a fifth of our evening congregation to other fellowships, with their permission, sometimes overwhelming their smaller evening congregations. Our visits were very welcome, often followed by a provided supper. Our reputation as a cuckoo in the nest, displacing other fledglings as we grew, began to fade. We took pains to avoid such offence. Our church notepaper was headed 'The Millmead Centre of the Baptist Church – part of the body of Christ in Guildford'. We did not need to define what we thought the other parts were but wanted to avoid the arrogance of 'The Guildford Christian Fellowship', implying it was the only true one.

Then came the day when someone brought a word to the monthly members' meeting that the Lord wanted us to share our financial resources with other churches in town. By that time our offerings had increased from £6,000 to £100,000 per annum, of which we gave away about a third to overseas missions and other worthy causes, but never to other local churches, whatever their need. So we opened a new account with our bank manager (Julius Caesar!) and soon there were hundreds of pounds sitting in it. The problem was how to disburse it without seeming to be patronising. Then a tornado tore off the flat roof of a comparatively recent Roman Catholic church – but not the charismatic one with whom we already had some links. We did not want to use our savings for this, but the Lord did. When I presented the priest with a large cheque, he could hardly believe it and declared it must be a world first, Baptists financing Catholics! He then said: 'You're a Bible church, aren't you?' After admitting that his congregation and he himself were not familiar with Scripture, he asked if some of our members would come to teach him and them the Bible. We gladly obliged with a carefully chosen team, led by an elder.

The reason why he called us a 'Bible' church was that we had recently completed a public reading of Scripture non-stop, twenty-four hours a day. It took over eighty hours from Sunday evening to Thursday morning. Each reader signed up for fifteen minutes, promising to listen to the preceding and following readers. We used the 'Living' translation, its colloquial-style paraphrase easier to read and listen to. This exercise drew an aggregate audience of 2000 and we sold half a ton of Bibles. Some dropped in for an hour in the evening and were still there next morning. Cries of 'just one more book, then I must go' were common. And lives were touched and changed. Two examples spring to mind:

One woman put her name down for a time just before an appointment with her solicitor to institute divorce proceedings against her husband. She found herself reading Malachi ('I hate divorce, says the Lord'). She never did see her lawyer and is still married. The Mayor of Guildford, called Alderman Sparrow, a nominal Roman Catholic, asked if he could take part and represent the Council in this unique event. Would we mind if he wore his gold chain of office? Not at all if he wore something else as well! We found him a slot at 3.30 p.m. on Tuesday. He said he'd bring his wife but turned up without her, explaining that she had been up since dawn, cooking, cleaning and preparing for unexpected visitors. He then found himself reading Proverbs 31, all about the ideal wife working hard in the home and came to: 'Her husband is well known for he sits in the council chamber with the other civic leaders!' He was so excited he wanted to take a Bible home to read it to his wife.

I have been singling out some of the highlights, but in between there was all the normal pastoral work to be done. On Monday evenings I held a 'clinic' when anyone could book a half-hour with me. I wanted to be accessible to any in need. On Friday evenings I held 'classes' to prepare enquirers for baptism and church membership. For the rest of the week I gave priority to preparing my two Sunday messages.

I mention these routine activities because many assumed, quite wrongly, that Millmead was little more than a preaching centre and the congregation little more than a preacher's fan club. Far from it, my primary aim throughout was to build up a local family of God, making a significant impact on the whole community. One young mother with journalistic skills asked me what she could do to serve the church while tied to the home. I set her a target of getting a news item about us in the local newspaper every week, not the usual notice of past or future events but stories of real human interest. She succeeded magnificently and got the town talking about us.

But growth brings its own problems. Anonymity was one, reflected in pew conversations – 'Are you just visiting?' answered by: 'No, I've been a member for two years.' The average person can only cope with about 200 names and faces and we were getting on for a thousand men, women and young people. The biggest problem was providing for the developments of gifts, with nothing between small house groups and the large celebrations, the latter needing quite mature leadership and ministry. The answer was to develop a middle layer, defined geographically. So between over forty house groups and celebrations at the centre we developed five 'areas', each with two elders. These had their own gatherings, especially on Sunday evenings, either in another part of our premises or in a borrowed building in their own region. Later ecclesiologists called this triple-tier system: cell, congregation and celebration, ideal numbers being respectively 20, 200 and 2,000,000 (the largest ever on a Korean airport runway). Most 'church' life was experienced in the areas (membership, baby dedications, pastoral care, etc.) where numbers were sufficiently small for anyone to know everyone else and where 'amateur' preachers and singers could be encouraged to develop their gifts in a supportive atmosphere until they were ready for bigger things. However, with three levels of fellowship we had to be careful not to overload members' diaries, so we had to work out a delicate balance between them. For example, house groups were reduced from weekly to fortnightly.

The system worked well and, above all, developed far more ministry than one large congregation could ever have produced. But this in turn demanded more full-time staff particularly at the training level. Before mentioning this development, I must pay tribute to two colleagues who gave me such support when I carried most of the responsibility myself.

Ruth Henshall came to us from the Evangelical Alliance to be my PA (personal assistant). Even before the new centre was completed she manned a church office in a caravan on site. She provided a vital link between us and the people, getting on well with everyone and handling administration with efficiency and enthusiasm. That Millmead was such a happy place to visit or serve was largely due to her. Don Martin was a big man, in every way. He had been with Rentokil, dealing with dry rot, and answered our advertisement for a caretaker, to live in and look after the new centre. It is a thankless job, keeping a building clean and tidy whilst it is used by so many different individuals and organisations. He was an amazing worker with his hands and we hatched up many ideas for improving the premises. He is the only church warden I know who, when a tramp came to his door begging, would give him a bath, wash his clothes and give him a cooked meal, all with his sweet wife's co-operation. He was a brilliant carpenter, so we sent him to Nazareth to fit out a new wing in the Arab hospital there. He had never flown, much less to another country. It was a highlight in his life. Ruth, Don and I worked at the Centre in happy harmony.

We had a gifted team of elders to share the oversight of the growing fellowship, but these all held down full-time jobs and came under increasing pressure, as did I, and the need to augment the full-time staff was obvious. There was no shortage of applicants. But it was at this stage that my own weaknesses became apparent. I am not much good at either selection or delegation. In short, I am not a good team member, let alone a team leader. I made some serious mistakes and people were hurt, which I deeply regret. On top of all this, I had a breakdown lasting a few months, which I will describe in a later chapter, leaving the work in the hands of two colleagues, our youth pastor and our lady worker. They kept things going until I was able to return.

Even then I wondered whether I was part of the church's future or not. I could see very clearly what the next phase of the fellowship could and should be, but doubted whether I could lead them into it. I preached my way through the book of Jeremiah, twice having to interrupt the series because I became too emotionally identified with him (he is still my favourite biblical character). When I had finished what was to be my last-ever systematic exposition, I had a number of surprising comments from the congregation. I was told I was preaching 'over their heads'. I thought they meant I was too intellectual, too abstract, too obscure, but they explained they meant none of those. They had an increasing sense that I was no longer speaking pastorally to them, but prophetically to the wider Church and the nation as a whole. One or two said: 'We're going to have to let you go.' It was an omen of the final phase of my ministry though I did not realise it then.

One of my last practical contributions was to plan an extension to the premises, a second storey with a much-needed extra meeting room and a suite of offices for the staff. I selfishly included a penthouse room for myself, with a magnificent view over the river and town. While it was being built I stood in the room and imagined how congenial a workplace it would be.

I was never to occupy it. Before relating the surprising call which prevented me doing so, I must mention other aspects of ministry that developed while I was in Guildford. In one way, my time there was the 'peak of my career' and I shall always be grateful to the people in the church who gave me such loyal support. Neither they nor I guessed that the Millmead Centre would become such a sounding board for the Word of God, sending its truth far and wide.

12

Miscellaneous Ministry

I am not an evangelist. Knowing one's gifting and staying within it makes for satisfying ministry. Just occasionally I have been asked to give a 'gospel' talk at an evangelistic event but it has usually proved a mistake, both for myself and others, even though the Lord has honoured it with results. I cannot speak of the cross without the resurrection, ascension and return to follow or the incarnation that came before. Above all, I cannot speak about Jesus until I have made sure that people understand what God is like. So I cannot preach what some call 'the simple gospel', especially in a brief talk, and am comforted that the apostles couldn't either.

Nevertheless, I revel in teaching the truth to unbelievers and seize every opportunity to do so. It is too easy for pastors to live in a sheltered world of 'preaching to the converted' from a pulpit 'six feet above contradiction'. It is both challenging and stimulating to be confronted with alternative opinions and face scepticism about our own. Scripture exhorts us to give a reason for the hope within us. To have to do this publicly can shake or strengthen our own convictions.

Perhaps because it is known that I enjoy such challenges, I have often been asked to take part in public debates, three of which readily spring to mind.

One was in Guildford University, before students and staff in one of the larger lecture theatres, to debate the relative merits of Humanism and Christianity. My opponent was the well-known Professor of Education, himself an atheist Jew. He spoke first and concluded his quite brilliant address with the memorable statement: 'So then, I believe that mankind can and must solve all its own problems – and if he can't, God help us!' This remark was greeted with howls of glee and erupting applause, which produced bewilderment on his face. Clearly, he had not realised what he'd just said. I began with: 'I'm a preacher and I take as my text the last three words of the previous speaker: "God help us".' Technically, we won the debate but in reality he had lost it by that careless throwaway remark.

Another was in the Inns of Court before over a hundred lawyers. The issue was whether Jesus was a liar, a lunatic or the Lord. Roger Forster and I stood for the latter, opposed by a Professor of Psychology, convinced Jesus was schizophrenic and deceiving himself, and the President of the British Humanist Association, claiming he knew what he was doing in deceiving others. We concentrated on the crucial question of his resurrection and the combination of eye-witness testimony and circumstantial evidence which would convince any jury and had convinced a higher proportion of lawyers than any other profession. The voting was 5 per cent lunatic, 10 per cent liar and 85 per cent Lord.

The most memorable was in Birmingham University, one of the official student debates. At very short notice I was asked to propose the motion 'That Jesus is the only way to God' and warned that it would be opposed by John Hick, the notorious Professor of Theology, author of the infamous book *The Myth of God Incarnate*. He turned up for the preceding dinner in evening dress and a dog collar, while his seconder wore a large wooden cross hanging from her neck, whereas my seconder and I had normal suits with collar and tie. In appearance, you'd have thought they were the ones supporting the motion. As we approached the debating chamber, which was crammed to capacity, the Student President expressed surprise that a religious topic should create such interest. The debate was fierce and heated. A confessed communist shouted abuse at me and I nearly gave him as good as I was getting but paused to ask the Lord how he felt about him. To my astonishment my eyes filled with tears and I wept for him in his anger. As proposer of the motion I was given the last word and I had a page of notes made during the debate, all points to score. But the Lord forbade me to make any and gave me a vision instead, telling me simply to describe it.

I saw a crowd in a market-place, watching a puppet-theatre surrounded by a large curtain. They were discussing how the puppets were able to do such antics. A scientist in a white coat explained that if you went up close you would see that they were being pulled by strings. When asked who or what was pulling the stings, he contemptuously replied: 'No one and nothing; the strings pull themselves.' Most of the crowd found this unacceptable and discussed who could be behind the curtain pulling the strings. An Indian suggested there could be millions of people behind the curtain, while an Arab insisted there could only be one. A man wearing a clerical collar said that everybody's idea was right for them and no one could be sure who or what lay behind the curtain. The crowd seemed satisfied with this answer, which brought all arguments to a peaceful conclusion.

The puppet play was over and the crowd drifted away, leaving a beggar who had hoped to get a coin or two for a first meal that day. Just then a small boy came out from behind the curtain. The beggar asked him if he did the puppets. The boy said no, but his dad did, adding: 'I'll introduce you to him if you like.' The beggar did like and asked the father if he could spare any of the day's takings for a starving man, only to get the surprising reply: 'I'll do better than that. My boy will take you home while I pack the theatre up. A square meal and a warm bed are waiting for you.'

Later that night, all the characters were lying in their beds thinking about the puppets. The scientist said to himself: 'I'm sure there's no one pulling those strings.' The Hindu and Muslim were both sure their numbers were correct. The clergyman felt he had been a peacemaker in agreeing with all of them. But the beggar patted his stomach and thought that was the best meal he'd had in years, leaned back on the soft pillow, pulled up the covers and was soon fast asleep.

I could hardly believe I was seeing all this, much less saying it. Was I going crazy? What would all these intellectuals make of it? They listened in total silence. I thought it was 'stony' but it turned out to be 'rapt'. I slowly realised it had made Professor Hick's religious relativism look ridiculous. The President put the motion to the vote and four out of five supported the motion (that only the Son could introduce anyone to the invisible Father). The President announced the motion defeated! To protesting cries of 'Carried! Carried!', he apologised for his 'slip of the tongue', excusing himself by explaining that he had never expected it to be carried. Afterwards, John Hick stormed out without a word, while I had quite a queue of people wanting to talk. The first was a medical student who told me he had come into the hall an agnostic, but was leaving it 'believing in the Lord'. I was counselling long after most had left. A few days later I got a letter from the Christian Union saying they had 'heard' about my 'victory' and would I come and speak at one of their meetings? They hadn't even bothered to come and support me. I'm afraid I didn't reply.

Among my 'outside' engagements have been marches of witness, climaxing in a public gathering, indoors or outdoors.

One such was in Ilford, on the Saturday before Easter Sunday. On Good Friday morning my wife and I were driving along the

Mile End Road when traffic came to a complete standstill while the huge new mosque disgorged its congregation through the front entrance. There were hundreds of men in their prime, unembarrassed and unashamed to be seen in public as religious. The next day the march of Christians was good, lots of rejoicing women and children, young men and older men – but a noticeable lack of men in between. The contrast with the Muslim crowd, who were not even trying to 'witness' to their faith, was striking. I said to my wife at the time: 'If you were a gambler, would you put your money on Islam or Christianity as the future religion of this country?' Without hesitation she replied: 'Islam.' I remembered that when God numbered Israel, he counted all the men over twenty who could fight for him and that a synagogue had to have a minimum of ten men (is that why they called Jesus 'Rabbi', as he began to build his Church by discipling twelve working men?). I have found such thinking a useful guide to measure the 'strength' of Christian groups and events.

Another march I took part in was very nearly a complete disaster. It was born in the vision of a bus driver in Hull. This used to be a royal town: Kingston (King's Town) upon Hull. But in 1641 the gates had been shut against King Charles II by 'Plotters' led by the MP Sir John Hotham, beheaded a few years later. The bus driver's idea was to march round the city walls, declaring the gates open to the King of Kings, Jesus, culminating in a meeting in the main parish church, at which he asked me to be the speaker. I was glad to go, especially since all the denominations had welcomed the venture and promised to take part.

Then a week before, Eddie rang to tell me it had to be cancelled. A false rumour had quickly spread that it was an attempt to revive the anti-Catholic sentiments of the seventeenth century, so the Catholics had withdrawn, followed by the Anglicans, the Methodists and all the rest. The parish church cancelled the booking. I told Eddie this was simply an attempt on the part of Satan, the father of lies, to neutralise the testimony, which had already attracted widespread interest. I felt real anger towards the devil and was determined to counter his interference. I told Eddie I was still coming, that we'd march even if there were only two of us and asked him to find another venue for the final meeting. On the day itself, which was a bank holiday, the two of us walked to the rallying point, appropriately at the statue of William Wilberforce. The streets were deserted, except for police at many corners and police vans strategically placed to remove any arrested. Because of the rumours they were expecting riots! Eventually about two dozen others joined us. We spread them out in a long, thin line but it was a vain attempt to be impressive. There were far more police than us along the route, smiling contemptuously at our pathetic column and resentful about their extra and unnecessary duty. We duly upheld the name of Jesus at each 'gate' and made our way to the civic hall, our alternative venue for the finale. Waiting for us was a packed crowd, many ashamed that they had believed the rumour. Clergy from different denominations were there, most disguised as laymen with collar and tie. I called them to sit with me on the platform while I spoke on the real objectives and the need of Hull for the gospel. As a result I was given a whole hour on local radio to address the population. So it didn't turn out too badly after all. However, there was a sad sequel. Eddie's young wife died quite unexpectedly, sitting by the fire. There was a spectacular funeral, with many clergy attending and many churches represented in the large congregation, perhaps seeking to atone for their withdrawal from the march.

I was invited to preach at the annual service for the legal profession in the Temple off the Strand in London, a building notorious for confusing echoes. It was no comfort to be told a special amplification system was to be installed a week after my visit. Lord Denning was to read the lesson. The high pulpit closely resembled the dock in a court and when I mounted it and faced judges, barristers and solicitors I felt I was on trial. I began by saying I had been told the agnostics in the building were quite shocking. This went off like a lead balloon. No one even smiled, let alone laughed. Even without wigs and gowns, they looked a grim lot. So I launched into the sermon, based on a phrase from Romans 8: 'What the law could not do, God did . . .' My theme was that the law can punish and deter, but cannot make bad people into good, wicked into righteous, sinners into saints. Only God and the gospel can do that and it's happening every day. Afterwards we gathered in 'Chambers' for a cocktail party. A solicitor took me aside and explained why my initial humour had not been appreciated. The agnostics (acoustics) remark was Lord Denning's favourite and oft-repeated joke, especially in that building! I was suitably abashed, resolving never to use it again (though I have).

I have sat through many court cases to support both the innocent and the guilty, from a case for fraud in the Old Bailey to a case of murder in Lewes Crown Court. In the latter case, a pharmacist and a nurse were accused of killing his wife by neglect after she had a serious fall. I was convinced the nurse was innocent. The case was highly publicised, especially when he was sentenced to prison and she was acquitted. The press besieged our house for days, without guessing she was hidden upstairs in a bedroom. Finally, they consented to leave if I would give an interview about my involvement. It's the only time I've ever filled the front page of the *Daily Mirror*.

I have been to prison myself, but only to visit and speak to inmates. In one top security jail there has been a remarkable work of God. A whole wing has been transformed, with every prisoner a believer. Security is hardly necessary now. Most are 'lifers', in for serious crimes like murder and drug dealing. I found them hungry for Bible teaching and had no difficulty holding their attention. On one occasion I spoke for so long a warder rushed in, stopped me in mid-sentence and told me the gates were being locked for the night in a few minutes and I must leave immediately unless I wished to spend the night 'inside'. I didn't! I shall never forget the expression on their faces when I told them that if they remained faithful to the Lord and hungry for his righteousness, they might find themselves one day administering justice to others when he returns to reign. I have seen vicious criminals not only reformed but transformed by grace, among them Chris Lambrianou, sent down with the Kray brothers' gang for being an accomplice to murder. He and I met on a radio broadcast and became friends within minutes.

Another unlikely group I have been involved with are the gypsies. I refer to the genuine Romany folk, not the travellers who have chosen their lifestyle. There has been a remarkable move of the Spirit among them, coming here from France and Spain. In proportion to their numbers they have a higher percentage of believers than any other ethnic group. A friend and I were visiting a campsite near Leicester. Every caravan was adorned with Jesus stickers. A barn had been emptied of old horse-drawn vans and turned into a chapel, filled with an assortment of salvaged chairs. We were sitting in a caravan, with children and dogs dashing in and out, when our host looked at me and said: 'You're gorgeous.' I didn't know quite how to take that – until I discovered that *gaujes* was really their word for a non-gypsy, as 'Gentile' is to a Jew. I was also shaken when they prayed, addressing the Lord with a word that sounded remarkably like 'Devil'. But the reality of their repentance and faith is both impressive and humbling. They renounce so many things, from lying, stealing and cheating to telling fortunes. They may not be well educated but they have a shrewd wisdom which sees right through hypocrisy. One of them telephones me regularly to check up on his biblical interpretation, but I have rarely needed to correct him! The Holy Spirit is his mentor, giving him remarkable insight and accuracy.

Even unbelievers seem happy to arrange and attend Christmas carol services and I have been invited to speak at a wide range of these. Typical was a gathering of hundreds of businessmen and office workers from premises near St Paul's Cathedral, but in another church nearby. But I am rarely asked twice, since sponsors find my Christmas messages are not to their taste. On the one hand, I strip away the sentimental myths and associations to reveal the stark truth of what really happened. On the other, I always go on to Jesus' second coming to planet earth, its more severe purpose and the need to be more ready to meet 'the Man' than the world was, and is, to greet the baby. I have no ambition to be a popular preacher. I tell my audiences what I believe they need to hear rather than what they want to hear or, rather, what I believe God wants them to hear. This leads to many of what I call my 'double visits' – first and last rolled into one! My wife often greets me on returning with: 'Well, was that another double?'

I enjoy speaking in schools and colleges, where young minds are still open to new concepts. One grammar school was buzzing with interest in Islam, after visits from a mullah. The head of the religious department was a declared atheist, but another member of staff urged me to come and counter the situation. I was given fifteen minutes to address the teachers and 800 boys. I plunged straight in with the statement that 'all the religions in the world could be wrong, but only one can be right', focusing on the irreconcilable differences between the major faiths over such basic issues as:

Is God personal? (he or it)

How many persons does 'God' cover? (1, 3, or millions)

I pointed out that Allah cannot be called 'Father' because he never had a Son and that he cannot be 'love' because he is only one person all on his own. When I finished there was a rowdy ovation, surprising the headmaster. The atheist religious teacher let me loose on his classes for the rest of the morning and said if he ever became a Christian, it would be one of my sort. Interest in Islam died away, apparently. I am as surprised as anyone by such results and am careful to give credit where it is due. Without the Lord I wouldn't have anything at all to say, much less say it with the clarity and confidence that makes an impact.

Some evangelicals are surprised that I speak in Roman Catholic settings, both here and overseas. I defend myself by saying I will teach the Bible wherever anyone will listen and would do so in the Vatican, if invited. Catholics are showing a new, and for them a novel, interest in Scripture and some are more eager to learn than many Protestants. But I pull no punches with them either. I was addressing a gathering of priests and clergy in a continental Catholic seminary and chose as my subject 'What the Bible really says about Mary'. I said I was happy to call her 'Blessed', because she prophesied 'all generations' would, but I could not call her the 'Blessed Virgin' because she had at least four boys and two girls after Jesus. I pointed out that during his three years' ministry Jesus increasingly removed himself from her, calling her 'Woman' at his first miracle, saying, 'Who is my mother?' when told she was in the crowd and giving her to John as he died. The last we hear of her was when she spoke in tongues at Pentecost, but she had been a charismatic ever since she allowed the Holy Spirit to impregnate her, willing to face the cost. I concluded by confessing that because Catholics had added so much non-biblical teaching about Mary (her immaculate conception, perpetual virginity, bodily assumption, etc.) and practised prayer to her (to the detriment of the present humanity of Jesus our only mediator and high priest), we Protestants were frightened to talk about her. They had said too much and we were saying too little. Someone followed me with a prophetic vision of flowers growing in a dark case, which was interpreted as a sign of hope in the dark history of Catholic/Protestant hostility. A priest wept on my shoulder and said he really understood now why Protestants seem scared of mentioning Mary. But a cardinal, who had sat three feet in front of me throughout with a stony face, told me he would 'pray that our Lady will appear to you in a vision'. To date she hasn't.

When speaking to Catholics I have used some funny stories early on in my address to see if they can see themselves as others see them and even laugh at themselves, which can be very reassuring. A friend of mine was preaching in Australia and invited all who wanted to be filled with the Spirit to come and kneel at the front. Down the aisle waddled a little nun in a black and white habit, for all the world like a penguin. She knelt down and prayed in a loud voice: 'Lord Jesus, fill me to overflowing with your Holy Spirit and if you don't I'll tell your mother of you.' What happened next implied that he didn't want his mother involved! I told this in a meeting on the Isle of Wight and two nuns fell right off their seats in hysterical laughter.

Then there was a hymn-singing programme on television from a charismatic Catholic church in West London, during which the anchorman interviewed members of the congregation, including an elderly woman. The conversation went like this:

'How long have you been in this church?'

'Since I was a little girl.'

'My! You must have seen some big changes in that time.'

'I have! If Jesus himself knew about all the changes our new priest has made, he'd turn in his grave.'

The interviewer never even smiled! There is a sad element of truth in her remark. Catholic church buildings themselves can impress simple souls with a dead Son and a living mother.

While encouraging Catholics to laugh at themselves, I have had to laugh at myself as well. At a Catholic meeting in Italy, two nuns in brown habits, one quite small and the other quite large, asked me to pray for them. When asked exactly what they wanted me to ask for them, the surprising response was: 'To fall on the floor.' Apparently their sisters had been 'slain in the Spirit' (a horrid phrase, only applicable to Ananias and Sapphira) and they felt they were missing out on a vital experience. I declined their request as nicely as I could and turned away to others wanting to talk with me. The next thing I knew there was a loud thump and there they both were, lying on the floor, the big one on top of the little one, both with beatific smiles and closed eyes. Was the Lord saying: 'If you won't do what they want, I will'? A Pentecostal missionary who saw the whole thing has never stopped teasing me about it – and I chuckle every time he does. A sense of humour is basically a sense of proportion and we can all look ridiculous.

All these and many other opportunities of ministry outside our church kept me fresh inside it. I was stimulated and enriched by the new challenges they presented. The one thing I can say with confidence is that serving the Lord is never boring. I never tried to open any of these doors but the Lord did and pushed me through them. But he didn't have to push very hard!

13

Invisible Congregation

Great oaks from tiny acorns grow. There were times at the beginning of my ministry (in Shetland) when I preached to just one person. Now at seventy-five I have a larger congregation than ever, numbering many thousands. But most of them are invisible to me. It's all due to the modern marvels of technology.

It began when I was still at Chalfont St Peter. Chris was a member of the congregation but not of the church. He had been exposed to some rather peculiar 'Berean' teaching which limited baptism and communion to Jewish believers. But he enjoyed our fellowship and (most of) my teaching. He was the first in the church to acquire a recorder using large reels of tape. I heard my voice for the first time and was as surprised as others have been. Anxious to use his new acquisition for the Lord, he asked me if he could record my sermons and take them round to members who were housebound by age or sickness. I thought that was a great idea and readily agreed. Little did either of us realise what we had begun. It was the seed of a worldwide ministry, reaching all seven continents. Yes, even Antarctica, where tapes would be used by scientists at the South Pole.

Reels could be passed on and listened to many times over. And they were, soon after they became available. The speed with which they spread was astonishing. But the real breakthrough came with the invention of the audio cassette. These could be easily mailed and, above all, were standardised for every country. Would that all later developments were the same, particularly for video recording.

I have thanked the Lord many times for my voice. Apparently it was well suited to this medium. As the saying goes: 'By your consonants people will hear what you say, but by your vowels they will know where you come from.' My short 'a's give away my northern origin. It seems that my speech is easy to listen to, partly because my preaching style is conversational, rather than pompous or strident.

A silversmith in Canterbury wrote to tell me what a blessing my tapes had been to his family. His wife was suffering from a difficult pregnancy and severe insomnia. She didn't like reading books so found the night hours long and empty. So he got some of my messages for her to listen to. Within ten minutes of starting on the first she was sleeping like a baby and woke up the next morning fully refreshed. The same thing happened on every subsequent occasion, so the whole family benefited from her renewed vitality. I so enjoyed his letter of appreciation that I had to call and meet him next time I was in their district.

In this way, many got to know my voice and even quite a lot about me, through personal references in the messages. But my appearance was a matter of speculation. From my clear, confident and even commanding speech (their words not mine), many assumed I was tall, dark and handsome, which led to some disillusion when they met me. An Australian woman turned up one day. She had listened to me for fifteen years and was 'curious to see the face behind the voice'. I asked her for her response to enlightenment and she said, 'I think I prefer the tapes', a classic case of 'speaking the truth in love'!

When I moved to Guildford, with the reels made so far, the

service was to expand far and wide. Ralph was a retired civil servant, son of a Strict Baptist pastor. His Calvinist upbringing had left him with a dour voice, appearance and manner. He volunteered to look after the tape ministry. His voice went round the world with mine, instructing listeners when to turn over the tape. It gave him a new lease of life and his four-storey Victorian town house was soon jammed with equipment and stock. He gathered around him a team of retired helpers, giving hours of their time. I remember him telling me, with a rare smile on his face, that he'd always wanted to be a missionary and was now in touch with 120 countries. He was to die in harness, on his way to the bank to put money into the tape account. It was as he would have wished.

John and Betty lived up in Hartlepool. But when he retired, she insisted that they moved near Guildford, so she could be part of our church, having listened to tapes. He acquiesced, unaware that he would not only be soundly converted but take a leading role in tape production and distribution. He once told me that he was convinced God brought me to Guildford to give me an ideal platform and sounding board from which to proclaim his Word far and wide. It certainly proved to be that. The majority of the 1200 messages now available were recorded there.

I can honestly say that I was never conscious of this huge, invisible congregation while I was speaking. Had I been I might have been much more careful about what I said, particularly in asides or comments on contemporary events and personalities. When I am speaking, my attention is focused exclusively on the people in front of me. This has given a freshness and spontaneity to the recordings which has helped listeners to feel they have been present, part of the congregation.

When I left Guildford, I was faced with a difficult dilemma. To leave the whole business where it was would be both unfair and discourteous to my successor, constantly tempting the church to make odious comparisons or indulge in nostalgia. But where could I take it all? I certainly couldn't handle it myself.

I had heard of a tape library, founded by Arthur Wallis' brother Peter, under the name 'Anchor', now directed by Jim Harris. I contacted Jim and tentatively asked whether it was within the bounds of possibility to add mine to their catalogue. To my utter astonishment he said he had been waiting for me to come and ask him! Many months before, the Lord had told him he was to be my agent, but he did not feel he should mention that until I took the initiative.

This has led to a quarter of a century's close co-operation, with weekly telephone contact. Jim has become one of my closest friends and most objective critics. He regards it as a matter of conscience and testimony to fulfil all orders by return of post. Our judgements about free distribution to those who cannot afford to pay are in remarkable harmony. Anchor is a charitable company with its own trust, but Jim, backed by his wife Linden and devoted staff, has been a God-send, quite literally, without whom my ministry could never have been what it is. When cassettes gave way to CDs and videos to DVDs and messages could be put on the Internet for downloading, he took it all in his stride, investing large amounts of time and money to keep up with accelerating technology. If giving a drink of water to a prophet gets a prophet's reward, as Jesus claimed, I can only rejoice over what will come to him for his self-effacing service to this servant of God.

Since Jim took over this arduous task, the Lord has raised up distributors in other countries. One of the first was Peter Bettson, a second-hand car dealer in Brisbane, Australia, who auctioned a vehicle every fifty seconds on Tuesdays and Thursdays, becoming a millionaire in the process. My tapes had been a profound influence in his life and he gained a reputation for his honesty in what was widely assumed to be a 'crook's' business. With the simple faith of a late convert, he developed a ministry of healing, not just of people, but diseases affecting poultry and even vineyards and orchards. (I've tasted the delicious fruit, more luscious than that grown before the disease struck.) From his office premises he distributed thousands upon thousands of my tapes, often freely, flooding his own country with my teaching and getting it into others (from Burma to South Africa). Now, after years of exciting ministry he has handed it on to John, a Baptist pastor and missionary (especially to the Pacific Island of Vanuatu, where he has been used in a miraculous way). With his wife Jean's sacrificial help he got my recordings on to over a hundred local radio stations.

In New Zealand there was Bob and now John, great-nephew of one of my boyhood preacher heroes, Dr Norman Dunning of Cliff College. In America there is another Bob, an acoustics expert formerly involved in investigating the notorious tapes which brought down President Nixon and the videotape of President Kennedy's assassination (how many shots were there?). His skills are now used in 'Good Seed Ministries'. In Africa there has been a succession of distributors, right now three Afrikaners, Johann and two young cousins, both called DeWet. Rudi is in Switzerland, Valerie in Canada. All of these felt a call from the Lord and made the first approach to us.

The hand of the Lord has also been seen in financial ways, not least in touching millionaires with the tapes and thus giving them an interest in spreading the truth. I have already mentioned Peter in Australia. Then there was Nelson, in the Philippines. He had made a fortune through a monopoly of supplying spare parts for the hundreds of 'jeepnies', a cross between a taxi and a bus, highly decorated vehicles originally built around ex-US army vehicles. In Malaysia there is Francis, who has built up a family business into an international corporation, concentrating on the supply of utilities and a chain of hotels, including Pangkor Laut, a former leper colony island, now considered the top luxury resort in the world. When he took over his first company in the UK (Wessex Water), he celebrated by holding a concert in the Royal Crescent, Bath, at which the three tenors, Pavarotti, Domingo and Carreras, made their last appearance together. Free tickets were given to 35,000 people. Francis began with a 25-minute testimony to his faith, during which he embarrassed me by introducing me to the crowd as 'my spiritual father and the spiritual grandfather of my children'. He and his family watch one of my videos every Sunday afternoon. The Personnel Director of the Company, Chung Sieu Leng, is also the distributor of my teaching material in that Muslim country, where I am probably better known than in my own.

Where all the tapes and videos have gone and what results they have had, only the Lord knows. Perhaps I'll find out when I get to heaven. Meanwhile, a steady stream of correspondence has given some clues. The letters can be easily classified. At the bottom of the pile are a few from religious cranks, like the garage mechanic from Stoke-on-Trent who bought a tape thinking I was a pop singer. Disappointed that there was no musical content, he nevertheless listened to all I had to say and wrote to tell me I was talking about himself throughout. Yes, he was the Saviour sent by God to redeem the world but still unrecognised by anyone else. Fourteen pages of excellent handwriting and good grammar failed to convince me either. But I recalled that it must have been equally difficult for first-century Jews to believe the claims of the carpenter from Nazareth.

Next come those who feel they are called to give me the benefit of being put right, sometimes over petty details but often over major doctrines, particularly from members of sects and cults. At one stage, the latter were using carefully edited tapes of mine to support their teaching, which led us to print the word 'Copyright' on the label, not that we would ever take legal action. Some of the corrections were valid and I was grateful for the help. Quite a few of my 'mistakes' are due to looking at my notes as little as possible, since eye contact with an audience is so important. Others were due to having picked up wrong information from books, articles or newspaper cuttings.

Then there were those full of questions about biblical

'problems', often of the 'Where did Cain get his wife from?' variety (to which there are three possible answers but please don't write and ask me for them or I might ask you why you are so interested in other people's partners!). I only answered those queries directly relevant to the enquirer's salvation or lifestyle. I do not feel called to spend time satisfying intellectual curiosity. Life is too short.

But many wrote seeking a solution to personal problems, sometimes claiming that the Lord had guided them to me (a subtle pressure implying it was my duty to reply). These letters tended to be rather long, including pages of biographical background. Even with all that information, I still found it difficult to counsel people I did not know, having heard only their version of events. Contacting their pastors often revealed a rather different story. In case of dispute, I occasionally quoted Jesus' response: 'Who made me a judge [i.e. adjudicator] over you?' I did send many handwritten letters where I felt I could and should offer help and advice, but I always urged the recipients to check it out with the Lord and responsible Christians before acting on it.

However, the bulk of correspondence brought appreciation and encouragement. Some of them were kind enough to include 'no reply needed', but I nevertheless thanked them, sending one of my booklets for their bedtime reading. Many had come to faith and even more were sustained and deepened in the faith. For some it was 'a lifeline', the only solid teaching they were getting. Isolated missionaries overseas were in this category. To have 'kept them going' was a humbling privilege.

The letters that touched me most deeply came from those who were spiritually sensitive enough to realise that my uncompromising stand for the truth as I perceived it inevitably became a lonely and even costly ministry. They offered support rather than sympathy, assuring me of prayers that I would never allow fear of men to overcome my fear of the Lord. Such reassurance often came at just the right time, when I was feeling like a voice crying in the wilderness. So while I have kept others going, others have kept me going.

So much of my ministry has been breeding and feeding 'tapeworms', as I naughtily call them, as distinct from 'bookworms'! Indeed, I am more widely known for my tapes than for anything else I have ever done. They have opened up other opportunities for me, both here and overseas. I know they have encouraged other preachers. When we had to increase the price of cassettes because of rising costs, particularly mailing, there were howls of protest from vicars asking where we thought they would get their sermons from now! Actually, I would have thought that one of my messages, usually lasting for fifty minutes would have supplied typical Anglican homilies for weeks. I was sitting at the back of a Bradford fellowship one Sunday, doing my favourite imitation of the wallpaper, listening to a sermon on Jeremiah. The preacher was good, breaking up the passage as I would have done. Suddenly I realised it was as I had done and I had the interesting experience of listening to one of my own sermons in a different voice. He did at one point admit he had been listening to a tape, but did not mention whose it was. When the service was nearly over I discreetly slipped out, lest he was embarrassed to discover my presence.

Tapes have gone to unusual places in unusual ways. They have taken God's Word into countries where missionaries cannot go, sometimes in diplomatic bags through British Embassies. One man parked his car on an open space in Amsterdam only to discover next morning that thieves had broken into it. All they had taken was a complete set of my tapes on Paul's letter to the Romans. I hope they listened to them and repented. Others have found their way into Buckingham Palace. If tapes could talk, their adventures would make a fascinating story.

They have also reached and touched many interesting people of whom I will mention three. One day, while I was away on ministry, my wife answered the doorbell to find a man with an Australian accent on the doorstep. Disappointed that I was not at home, he explained that he was returning to Tasmania next day but would she please thank me for my tapes, which had given him 'a deeper understanding and biblical knowledge' following a 'recent commitment to Christ and his service'. It was Douglas Gresham, the stepson of C.S. Lewis, prolific author of books like *Mere Christianity* and *The Lion, the Witch and the Wardrobe* (now the blockbuster movie *Narnia*, of which Douglas Gresham is co-producer). As a boy he had been brought from America to England by his divorced mother Joy, whom C.S. Lewis had married to enable her to stay here, then fallen in love with and quickly lost her to cancer, leaving the boy in a strange country with a grieving stepfather. Like many others, I owe a great deal to C.S. Lewis's writing, particularly his *Mere Christianity*. And felt I had repaid part of my debt by helping his adopted boy to find his Christian convictions.

Then there was the time when I found myself in a trans-atlantic television studio with Billy Graham's daughter. To my astonishment she was a regular listener to my tapes. Once again I felt I was repaying part of a debt to a father's inspiration.

But I was most moved by hearing, after her death, something about that amazing Dutch lady, Corrie ten Boom, who, with her family, had paid such a high cost for providing a 'hiding place' for Jews during the Nazi occupation. Though she survived the war to travel the world with her story and message of forgive-ness, she eventually succumbed to a severe stroke and was comatose for the final part of her earthly pilgrimage. During that sad time, she only showed any sign of response, by feeble bodily movements, to two sounds. One was violin music, played by her nephew Peter van Woorden (who as a boy had dressed in girls' clothes to escape German attention when cycling around occupied Haarlem). The other my voice, expounding the Bible she loved. I never knew how her nursing companion came across my tapes. I simply thanked the Lord that I could minister to her in her final trial. I have found with others that the spirit can be reached when the body and mind are out of communication.

These days I am adding fewer new messages to my repertoire, no longer having to produce two new ones every week. And those recordings I do make are no longer systematic exposition, as I shall explain. In an itinerant ministry, I am never in the same place more than a day or two, so have reverted to a topical rather than an exegetical approach. But some of these are among the most significant messages I have ever given. The Lord hasn't finished with me yet.

But I'm getting nearer to the end of my ministry. And Scripture tells us to number our days and get a heart of wisdom, which means using remaining time strategically. So I have begun to think about the future of my ministry and, in particular, the body of teaching material recorded over the last fifty years. Part of me wants it all to disappear from the scene when I do. But two factors have persuaded me otherwise.

On the one hand, demand for it is still rising and looks as if it will continue to do so after I've gone. On the other hand, the need for it is great. There are many evangelists reaping a huge harvest around the world, but the need for solid and balanced biblical teaching to stabilise and mature the converts is immense. We have begun to translate tapes, videos and books into other languages, primarily Spanish and Chinese, the two most widely used after English, but also French, Dutch, German and Italian. But all this is only a drop in the bucket and will require co-ordination and investment of time and money.

It seems the time has come to establish a charitable trust to look after all my teaching material both before and after my decease. We have already taken legal steps to establish what will be known as the 'David Pawson Teaching Trust', or 'DPTT' for short. This will not be supporting me personally; the Lord already does that in his own faithful way. I will not even be a trustee. But the Trust will be able to receive donations and legacies and employ a much needed international co-ordinator to oversee the preservation and protection of existing material in digital form, the present worldwide distribution network and the opening up of new 'markets' in more countries and languages. Already there have been urgent pleas for help in China, where there are millions of new Christians and Mandarin is now a compulsory second language in all schools (otherwise it would have meant over two hundred very different dialects).

So the 'invisible congregation' is likely to go on growing, perhaps exponentially. More people will get to know about me but I will get to know less. I have always wanted to have as much personal contact with my hearers as possible. Indeed, at Guildford I used to stand at the door and shake hands with everyone attending, not just after the service, which is common, but also before, as they arrived. I cannot do this with tape listeners or video watchers in this world but fully intend to do so in the next, which should take up quite a bit of time in eternity. Only then will I discover the size of the congregation and what the recorded Word has meant to them. How I look forward to meeting them all!

14

Travels with a Jumbo

I suppose it was inevitable. The tapes of my teaching were by now travelling round the world, so I was becoming quite well known in other countries. I began to receive invitations for ministry trips overseas. I did not consider them until the work at the new Millmead Centre was well established but there came a time when the leaders felt they could spare me and share me for such visits. They thought that this could not only broaden my experience but would also help to give the church a world outlook. I had already put a veneered map of the world above the pulpit, without realising the congregation would use it to pinpoint and pray for my travels. The world is now much smaller. Jumbo jets have shrunk the globe. Distant countries were only a day away. Journeys which had taken early missionaries months could be done in hours.

I had never thought I would one day have an international ministry. It is a merciful Lord who hides the future from us until we are ready to face it. As I write these words I can feel again the nervous apprehension in the pit of my stomach, which I experienced almost every time I set off. I was beset with anxiety about being a disappointment to those who seemed to expect far more from me in person than they could get from my teaching on tape. I feared they would discover how very ordinary I really am out of the pulpit. I guess by now readers have realised I'm also quite insecure and lacking in self-confidence – except when I'm speaking. I took comfort from the American definition of 'expert': an ordinary person far from home.

My first venture could not have been further from home. I flew to New Zealand by the western route, via Los Angeles and Honolulu. We left Hawaii late on Thursday evening. I was in the middle seat of three, squeezed between two enormous South Sea Island ladies, both wearing large bands of scented flowers. Sleep escaped me but I comforted myself that I had all of Friday to rest up in Auckland before my first preaching engagement on Saturday afternoon. To my horror the pilot announced that we had just crossed the date-line into Saturday morning! I was whisked straight from the airport to the back door of the large Baptist Church in Queen Street, Auckland, and found myself in the pulpit and in jetlag. To this day neither I nor the congregation have any recollection of anything I said, except for one extraordinary thing. I had a vision in the middle of it, which many still recall.

I need to explain that not long before the new ocean liner *Queen Elizabeth II* had broken down off Bermuda, due to a ruptured oil supply to her engines. While she drifted helplessly, the passengers were taken off in little boats. In the vision I saw all this happening again, but with one extraordinary difference. The ship's bridge had been replaced by the portico of a Greek temple. In fact, what I was 'seeing' was the front elevation of the church I was speaking in, though I did not know this at the time, having entered from the rear. I soon found out that the church was in decline, with members leaving in twos and threes, mainly transferring to a lively Pentecostal fellowship meeting in the Town Hall. The pastor had invited me to come, in the hope of stopping the rot and even inaugurating a revival in the church. But I am not a 'revivalist' and after two weeks had made no discernible impact on the sad situation. I phoned my wife to tell her that I feared I had made a terrible mistake and was of a mind to stay at home in the future. She shed tears of disappointment with me. It could have been the end of my travels.

But after a few days' rest in the beautiful Bay of Islands, the rest of the planned tour, including a mission to students in Christchurch University, was as encouraging as Auckland had been discouraging. It led to a number of return visits, the most memorable being a Christmas youth camp of over a thousand, including some Maori street gangs. Each morning they gathered in a woolshed, sitting on bales of straw, and I taught them about the Kingdom of God. On the Tuesday morning, just before I got up to speak, the Lord whispered to me: 'You've told them about my power and authority but you haven't shown them.' I asked him how I should begin to do this and one word clearly came to mind: 'Dandruff'! So I got up and announced that Jesus was Lord over all things, including dandruff. My wife's face was a picture and I know it well enough to read her thoughts. This time it said: 'He's finally flipped; I've been expecting it for years and now it's happened.' She glanced at the nearest exit, clearly wondering how quickly she could leave. Then the Lord said 'Warts' to me. I suddenly realised he was graciously dealing with what can seem very big problems to teenagers. But sitting next to Enid was an older Salvation Army man, both of whose hands were covered in them. A few minutes previously a surgeon, sitting on his other side, had made an appointment with him to remove them in his hospital, using a local anaesthetic. Two days later they'd all dropped off, of their own accord. The next ailment, which began to stretch my faith, was a useless hand. It belonged to a girl who, though naturally right-handed, had never been able to use that hand, which led to stress and strain. An hour later she wrote to her parents, writing with that hand. Things reached a climax with a delightful sixteen-year-old boy on crutches. His left arm was useless after a car crash when he was two. He had recently been using a motorised chain saw, while kneeling on a large log – and taken his knee right off. His leg had been saved by joining the lower to the upper bone, giving a much shorter leg. To our amazement the Lord enabled him to run round the sports field and dance on the platform, without crutches. Two days later he told us all that the Lord had also dealt with a persistent bed-wetting habit requiring sleeping on a rubber sheet, even in camp.

By Friday all conditions were healed, except the dandruff. Without mentioning this specifically, I asked any who had been healed but not told anyone yet to come and see me afterwards, especially if it was from a condition I had named. A girl with shining brunette hair came and said: 'Was it the dandruff? I used to have a permanent snowstorm on my shoulders, and tried many shampoos and medications without any benefit – and now it's all gone!' She was followed by a young man with ginger hair and beard, muttering repeatedly: 'I don't believe it.' When I asked him what he didn't believe, he said it was 'the bit about the dandruff'. I invited him to come and inspect the girl's hair, but he protested: 'No, me! I've really suffered from that but it seemed better this morning, so I went to the medical tent and the nurse couldn't find any trace. But I can't believe it.' I told him not to try to but go home and enjoy it.

That morning I told them all that they had now heard and seen the Kingdom but needed to enter it. If they came back to the woolshed that afternoon I would tell them how to. I have more than once made such a delayed appeal, which quickly sorts out emotional response from a conviction of the Spirit. The latter passes the test of time. But that afternoon was a perfect summer's day and they all headed for a Pacific beach two miles away and were soon swimming, watched by a team of burly lifeguards. But one of these was desperate to come back to the woolshed for my extra session. He asked the others to cover his stretch, only to find out that they all wanted to come as well. They got together in a group and, hardly knowing how to pray, asked God to get them to the meeting. They opened their eyes again and saw shark fins out in the bay. They yelled, 'Sharks!', and the swimmers were out of the water in minutes – and into my meeting as a body. So now I know how to get people to attend meetings!

I could easily fill a whole book with my adventures overseas, but will select one or two from different continents to illustrate how the Lord has led and used my willingness to travel, though I do not enjoy living out of a suitcase and the novelty of sitting in a Jumbo jet wears off in about ten minutes. I enjoy meeting new people and seeing new places, but getting there and back is not such fun.

Sometimes the tedium has been relieved in an unexpected way. I only know one British Airways pilot, out of the three thousand they employ. When I boarded a 747 bound for Hong Kong, I had a strong intuition that he was our captain. Sure enough he was and I spent the entire flight in the cockpit, a good part of it in the co-pilot's seat while he took a nap. The plane flew itself the whole way, avoiding storms, mountains and cities without manual aid. The pilot only took control when we were in line with the colony's runway – and he needn't have even then, but enjoyed handling the giant aircraft. The time on that flight had simply 'flown' by.

Turning to Australasia for a moment, I recall my introduction to an aboriginal audience in the heart of Australia. My tape distributor had arranged a full programme all over that vast country but left the last few days, actually Whit Sunday and Monday, for me to speak to native people in the bush. But he had no contacts himself, so asked the Lord to make the arrangements. On the Saturday evening I had a final meeting in Alice Springs, with still no hint of any possible use of the next few days. Afterwards a woman approached me and asked if there was any possibility of my sparing a day or two to visit an aboriginal settlement where she and her husband, both keen Christians, were government officers. The next morning she drove me for five hours in a Land Rover to the hills of the Murray Ranges. I asked how she would let the people know I was coming and she said word would quickly spread in the village, where there was a church, pioneered by a missionary later living in Basingstoke. But as we drew near our destination, we saw a large cloud of dust in the distance and diverted to investigate. It was a horse race meeting with hundreds of aboriginal people from the whole area. A track was marked out and races were announced from an amplifier on the back of a truck. We found a Christian in the crowd. When the races ended at sunset he took the microphone and told everybody they must stay on to hear a special speaker from a long way away. They all stayed, built fires and sat around them with their children and their dogs. In the darkness I could see the whites of their eyes but little more. I had an interpreter but soon discovered they had no word for 'forgiveness', punishment being the consistent response to wrong-doing. I knew nothing of their culture so sent a telegram prayer for the help of the Spirit. Since it was Pentecost Sunday (which unusually coincided with that event in the Jewish calendar), I told them why, to the two 'tribes' of Israel and the Church, this day was very special. On it centuries ago, the Jews received the laws of God and were quickly punished for breaking them, three thousand being put to death. Centuries later, the Christians received the Spirit of God, writing God's laws in their hearts, enabling them to keep them and removing fear of punishment. Three thousand lives were saved.

I spoke for about fifty minutes but got no response from the audience, who sat immobile with blank faces. I felt an utter failure and apologised to the couple who'd invited me to come for my inability to communicate. Their response was a complete surprise. 'Didn't you realise? They were spellbound. We've never known them sit still that long for any speaker. Even the dogs never moved. And they are asking who told you all about them. Their elders want to spend tomorrow morning talking with you.' I was mystified, until it was explained that government policy was to give them back all their old culture, including its laws and punishments, which they did not want, knowing their own weaknesses. Now they realised there might be another way of controlling behaviour – from the inside by the divine Spirit. I spent a memorable time the next day, sitting in the dust with their leaders, expanding on the text that the law came through Moses, but grace and truth came through Jesus.

On another occasion, I was in a huge indoor stadium in Melbourne, speaking to many thousands through a radio microphone. But it was faulty and kept cutting out. I asked for a replacement and was given a new Japanese model, 'the very latest and the only one in the country as yet'. It worked perfectly, but none of us realised it was tuned to the wavelength of the Victoria State Police. All their patrol cars were forced to listen to this English preacher! They sent out detection vans to track down the illegal broadcast. Towards the end of my talk I noticed a posse of police invading the hall. I assumed an escaped criminal was hiding in the audience, oblivious of the fact that it was me they would arrest and question. But they were very good about it all, asking the stewards how much longer I'd be speaking. On learning it would be less than ten minutes, they dryly commented: 'Well, we've heard the rest; we might as well hear the lot.' So when I'm given a radio mike, I often begin with a greeting to the local police, congratulating them on a fine service.

Asia could well be the most significant continent of the twenty-first century and it has been my privilege to serve in many of its countries. In China my input has moved from smuggling Bibles to dubbing my videos into Mandarin. My first visit to India was to speak for Bakt Singh (the 'Watchman Nee of India') in Hyderabad, for one of his large conventions. People sat cross-legged on a concrete floor for hours, leaning forward with foreheads on the ground for prayer. I was in agony until they took pity on me and provided a small stool. I had to speak without any notes, which were seen as a failure to rely on the

Holy Spirit. In Tamil Nadu in the south, the state with the greatest proportion of Christians, ever since the work of the apostle Thomas who is buried there, I gave lectures to 600 pastors, evangelists and church workers, astonished to discover they were given a written examination at the end of the week on what I had said. I had some of my books with me, which were used as prizes. The temperature was in the forties, rats ate my soap, and I failed to eat soup with my fingers. But their enthusiasm and devotion was humbling.

In Singapore I was most excited by the state of the Anglican churches, the result of a succession of evangelical, charismatic bishops. I told them this was the only diocese in the world where I would feel free to be an Anglican, a remark which filtered back home to haunt me! Of course, one factor is that Anglicans overseas are a 'Free' Church, like all others, without the superiority and security of being part of the Establishment. On one occasion I was passing through Singapore airport, with a few hours to spare. A pastor somehow heard about this and arranged to whisk me off to his house where a roomful of his people had hastily assembled. It was hot and humid so he took my jacket and threw it on a bed, inadvertently tipping out my passport and ticket! I did not discover the loss until after he'd dropped me back again at the airport and left. I had no idea of his surname, address or telephone number or even what part of the city I'd been in. Surrounded by milling crowds of all nationalities I did not know whom to turn to, except the Lord. Within a few minutes, a young Chinese couple asked me if I was David Pawson, having seen my videos. I shared my predicament and gave them a physical description of the pastor. They didn't recognise it but thought they knew someone who might. The result of a number of phone calls brought the pastor and my papers just before my flight was called.

The demand for my teaching in Malaysia, both recorded and personal, has probably been greater than in any other Asian country. On one visit, a thousand videos were sold in one week.

In East Malaysia (Borneo) I discovered that my voice can be heard in jungle 'long houses'. There is much evangelism but a shortage of biblical teaching here as in many other parts of the world. I am so thankful that recordings can go where I cannot.

Jackie Pullinger took me into the notorious 'walled city' in Hong Kong, a filthy, ten-storey pile of sin, vice and crime, a tiny territory subject to no legal authority. I watched her praying in tongues for drug addicts and felt totally helpless and humbled. The Dean of Hong Kong cathedral was at the same time writing a booklet to warn his fellow Freemasons about me, after I had addressed a convention of Full Gospel Businessmen.

Moving on to the vast continent of Africa, I will begin with the South, to which I have paid a number of eventful visits. The first was in 1982, when apartheid still held sway. Exception was taken to my simple statement that 'a God of righteousness is as concerned about injustice as about immorality'. For various reasons my meetings in Durban and Cape Town were cancelled, one of which was that I was a 'charismatic'. I dared to make a number of prophetic predictions, which came only too true not many years later, leading to a warm welcome back. I have now spoken in Durban and Cape Town. One of my precious memories is of a flight out with SAA (South African Airlines). I noticed one of the stewards was wearing a 'fish' badge in his lapel. I told him I was comforted that the aircrew included a Christian. He told me there were four on board and they had begun the flight with prayer. I asked him how many SAA aircrew were believers and he said: 'Sixty so far.' Only after we landed did I find out he was personally responsible for this. He would ask the Lord to give him the next name to pray for and then fast until that person came to faith. Wow! I had already noticed that one of the music channels on the headphones was entirely gospel music and he admitted responsibility for this. Alas, towards the end of the flight he received an urgent message that his eight-year-old daughter was desperately ill and he must go home as soon as possible. That same evening I was preaching in a large, modern Dutch Reformed church at Kempton Park, next door to the Johannesburg airport, and before I spoke I led the congregation in a prayer of faith for the little girl. This was at 8 p.m. Days later I learned that she got up from her bed, perfectly well, at that precise hour. Jesus doesn't change, does he?

In Zimbabwe, a pastor volunteered to show me round Harare, asking me what I'd like to see. I mentioned two unique sights, neither of which he'd ever heard of. So I took him round (I make a point of reading up about a place before I go, mainly for relevant illustrations). One was a large cross, made of cigar boxes, now in a cathedral side-chapel. The early tobacco growers had no church building so they gathered round this home-made cross for worship. The other was David Livingstone's last diary, written in pencil, and held in the city vaults, which we managed to get into. We later visited the magnificent Victoria Falls, which Livingstone discovered and named. I was taken up river in a motor launch to a place called Monkey Island. As I got out of the boat a man walked up to me and said: 'David Pawson, I presume.' It's a small world! My meeting in Harare had been arranged in the main civic hall but at the last minute President Mugabe wanted it for a rally of his own, so everything else had to be cancelled and we met in the Italian Ballroom.

My trip to Kenya and the Congo led to a serious breakdown, which I'll keep for a later chapter. In Upper Congo I preached to hundreds of Africans in a huge concrete shell of a church. I was struck by the unusual music of an orchestra made up of about forty ladies in colourful costumes, each holding a Coke bottle hanging on a string, with carefully graded amounts of water, tapped with a key or other piece of metal. The sound produced was beautiful and I'm sure the Lord loved it as much as I did. Later I spent time with my sister-in-law and her husband who were doing valiant work among Angolan refugees in Lower Congo.

For years I was reluctant to cross the Atlantic, convinced that America had more than enough ministries and preferring to go where I felt I was needed. But I have been persuaded that my type of biblical teaching is needed over there, where topical relevance or apocalyptic sensationalism can dominate. So Florida, Texas, Kansas, Virginia (Pat Robertson's '700 Club' television channel) and Carolina have figured on my itinerary. However, I felt more at home in Canada (perhaps because it is more British?). I have appeared on *100, Huntley Street*, the national Christian television programme, a number of times. On the first, the director asked me what I would like to talk about and I immediately said: 'The Kingdom of God, Jesus' favourite topic and mine.' He looked disappointed and reminded me we had to keep viewers interested and switched on. But he had given me the choice and I insisted, speaking for about twenty minutes. There were phones in the studio and a team ready to deal with calls from viewers. One caller asked for me personally and the following conversation took place:

'Hello, is that Mr Pawson?'

'Yes.'

'I'm a hooker [prostitute] on Yonge Street [red light area], and I've been watching your programme. Can I ask you something?'

'Of course, go ahead.'

'How can I get into that Kingdom you've been talking about?'

'Why do you want to?'

'It's time I got my life straightened out.'

I almost shouted 'Hallelujah'. I remember thinking I must be preaching the right gospel at last, the one Jesus preached, which got a response from just this kind of person.

In Vancouver I was invited to help with a summer course at Regent College on 'Spiritual Gifts', substituting for David Watson who had recently died of cancer. One attending Anglican clergyman was quite sceptical, particularly of the gift of healing and challenged me to a demonstration in front of the students. So we laid hands on a girl with a twisted spine and with a shriek of joy she straightened up. We told her to go straight over the road to the University Hospital and return with medical proof of her healing, which she did. That certainly gained more attention to our lectures.

As I have travelled the continents, I have revelled in the variety of God's family, which cuts across all human divisions into black and white, rich and poor, East and West. Christians are accused of living narrow lives but our social contacts are broader than any unbeliever's. This was brought home to me forcibly in South America.

One day I was in Brasilia, the inland capital of Brazil, the guest of an ambassador in a luxurious modern ranch-style mansion that seemed to be largely made of glass. After a superb dinner we gathered round a grand piano in a huge split-level lounge through which a stream flowed – to sing hymns of praise to the Lord. Later, I was shown to one of the guest suites down the garden, each with its bedroom, bathroom and sitting-room and all joined by a glass corridor. The next day I was flown in a small plane into the Amazon jungle and entered a long house crammed with people, children, dogs and pigs. It was full of smoke from an open fire, on which stood a boiling cauldron being stirred with a stalk of sugar cane. As far as I could see, formal dress was little more than a G-string. Their faces full of the joy of the Lord, they extended hospitality in every way they could, bringing me a common brick to sit on and asking if I'd like a drink of tea. In that heat I eagerly said I would. Someone found a glass tumbler, which looked as if it had never been washed and was caked with food remains, dipped it in the cauldron and bore it to me. I took one look and asked the Lord to take away any sensation of the utensil and enable me to enjoy the contents. The prayer was answered and I really relished the refreshing drink. As I left I marvelled that our faith opens doors to the top and bottom of society. While the spirit protests against the wide disparities in circumstances, so obvious in South America, I rejoice that the Lord is no respecter of persons, has no favourites and looks on the inside of people not the outside.

I could hardly have experienced a greater contrast within forty-eight hours, yet felt equally relaxed singing the songs of Zion in both companies. And the only inequalities in heaven will be those of rewards for our time on earth.

Finally, let me bring you back to my home continent of Europe. I have ministered in so many countries here that I can only show you a few brief snapshots.

France – where I tried to use my schoolboy French and shocked an audience by repeatedly using a slang phrase for emptying one's bowels. Germany where I told 120 men I'd come again the following year if they each brought ten more men and next time there were exactly 1200. Italy – where the only handwritten manuscript of my book on hell was in mislaid luggage at Bologna airport and was mysteriously (miraculously) handed to me two days later in Rimini, a hundred miles away. Belgium – which was not my Waterloo. Holland where I spoke at the Opwekking (Revival) Pentecost camps on a polder (reclaimed land) in the Zuider Zee, with 30,000 to 40,000 campers. Spain – where I addressed flourishing indigenous Pentecostal fellowships. Portugal – where meetings were attended by expatriates from all over the world, settled in the Algarve. Norway – which was covered in sheet-ice after rain, snow and frost. Sweden – where the Lutherans banned tapes of my talks. Denmark – where church youth leaders were sleeping together.

I was able to get through the Iron Curtain before it came down. The first trip was to what was then Czechoslovakia. We took money to help build a church in Jablonec, laying the foundation stone in twelve feet of snow. Secret police attended the service and years later I learned that the pastor went to prison for six months for refusing to sign a list of statements I was accused of making. He knew they were lies, but even though I was safely out of reach, would not bear false witness and paid the price without ever telling me. I was translated by Milos, who had trained pre-war Wimbledon tennis champions and whose son nearly created an international crisis when his ice-hockey team trounced the Russians in Moscow.

Let me finish with a story from Romania, in the days when they were still behind the Iron Curtain and under the tyranny of an evil dictator and his wife. My wife and I went by train through Hungary. I had a large suitcase, full of Christian literature, too big to put up on the rack in the compartment, so it was standing just outside in the corridor, where I could keep an eye on it. When we reached the border a forbidding woman in grey uniform subjected us to an exhaustive search for contraband goods, even pulling out the seat cushions to inspect underneath. Finally, she pointed at my case and shouted: 'Whose is that?' I said it was mine and whispered to the Lord that it was time for a little miracle. On cue, a drunken soldier grabbed a fire extinguisher, set it going and filled the carriage with dense foam and fumes. We were all ordered off the train and down onto the tracks, where we waited for the carriage to clear. By the time we clambered back on the inspector had disappeared. My case was covered with white powder but all its contents were intact and unspoiled. Thank you, Lord, for intervening in the nick of time.

And thank you, reader, for wading through these rambling reminiscences. As I have re-lived them, I have been reminded again of the Good Shepherd's two sheepdogs, Goodness and Mercy, which have dogged my footsteps wherever I have gone.

15

The Wandering Gentile

It was becoming increasingly clear that it is difficult, if not impossible, to be pastoring a church and travelling the world at the same time. It was simply not fair on the members to be here today and gone tomorrow. I was beginning to realise it would have to be one or the other. But which was it to be?

It was the third major fork in the road I had faced. The first was whether to be a farmer or a preacher. The second was whether to be a Methodist or a Baptist. Now this was whether to be an itinerant or a resident. (I nearly wrote 'to itinerate or vegetate'!) I needed just as clear guidance for this as I had had for the other two. A change would have far-reaching implications.

I have already mentioned in an earlier chapter that the work in Guildford was developing beyond my capacity at the end of the seventies. I could see very clearly where the church needed to be taken or needed to go in the next decade, but I could not see as clearly my role in its future.

I resorted to my usual practice for seeking guidance from the Lord. I resolved to continue what I was doing unless and until the Lord clearly told me otherwise. I've seen too many Christians wandering in the wilderness because they came out of a situation before they knew the one they were being called into. Then I promised the Lord I would be obedient, provided he fulfilled his responsibility and gave me clear orders. I don't believe we have to try and read his mind or guess his plans.

I had booked in for a pastors' conference in Ashburnham Place in Sussex. Over a hundred attended. It gave me a chance to get away from all duties and wait on the Lord. Alex Buchanan was one of the speakers, a man with a genuine prophetic gift, fostered by brushes with his mortality which have removed all fear of man and replaced it with a healthy fear of God. After one of his talks, he announced that he had 'four words from the Lord for four men here'. He didn't know who they were but they would. That got our undivided attention. The first three proverbially went in one ear and out of the other. But the fourth electrified my mind and entered my heart. I can recite it to this day. This is how it went:

My son, you have ministered to the extent of your gift in the place where I certainly put you. You are no longer bound to stay in that place. I set you free and I set the land before you. But one thing I require of you, that you surrender all that remains to be done in that place into my hands, for it is my church and my congregation. And I want you to go out and so serve me that one day you will be able to look me in the face and say: 'Lord, we did it.'

I asked him afterwards if he knew who that word was for and he said he didn't when he began it but did by the time he finished it. It was me.

It was all I needed. I had clearly taken the fellowship in Guildford as far as I could and needed to make room for someone else. And there was more than a hint that I would be engaging in a wider, even nationwide, ministry, rather than another pastorate. However, I have never acted on a single 'prophecy' until it is confirmed by others. Fortunately, this had been recorded and I was able to take it home to be weighed and judged by my fellow elders. They took time to reach a conclusion but unanimously agreed it was from the Lord. They were reluctant to implement it so I finally gave them a date when I would relinquish my responsibilities.

The church was very generous towards us, allowing us to stay in the manse until they needed it for my successor and subsidising our income until I was well established in my new vocation. I think they realised what a leap into the unknown it all was and wished to share the step of faith with us. However, doors opened very quickly and within two years I had spoken in over two hundred places in the United Kingdom.

At first I accepted most invitations, not yet having a clear idea of what I should be doing. I soon grew disillusioned with being a 'special visiting speaker', filling programmes for those using known names to draw people to their events. I realised that if I was to use my time and energy strategically I must begin to analyse the effectiveness of brief visits and focus attention on the most profitable events. I don't mean numbers attending but long-term effects. I developed a habit of asking a key person in each place to write to me six months after my visit, with a frank and honest report of what results, if any, were still discernible. I was basing this on the belief that anything the Lord does is lasting, while human efforts by themselves are soon forgotten. I did not return to places unless there was clear evidence that the Lord had used me there. I was not into oratorical entertainment!

I quickly found I could do more good where churches were willing to come together for my visit and gave priority to such united events. I was already speaking in many denominations, from Pentecostal to Roman Catholic, from traditional to radical, old to new. I was more and more inter-denominational in my thinking and speaking. When occasionally asked about my denominational affiliation, I said I was a 'Methobaptican', having been ordained a Methodist, accredited a Baptist and had two Anglican bishops lay hands on me for my itinerant ministry (at their request). I saw myself as serving the whole body of Christ, or at least any part of it willing to use my services. Nor were my opportunities limited to the evangelical stream within each denomination. The ministry had widened ecclesiastically as well as geographically.

I soon realised that I would have little or no impact on churches as such unless I could influence their leaders. So I seized every chance I got to conduct seminars for clergy and ministers, pastors and elders. I have to say that they were tougher audiences than their members but correspondingly more rewarding, and with such an audience it was an advantage to have pastored churches which had become well known. I had faced and tackled their problems myself, if not always successfully. I could at least offer sympathy, if not solutions.

One totally unexpected development was that I began to concentrate on meetings for men only. I couldn't help noticing that in most congregations women outnumbered men, in some cases by as much as five to one. Coupled with this was an alarming trend of an increasingly feminist Church, with disturbing consequences in doctrine and discipline. I resolved to redress the imbalance and began to hold one to three days of conference under a title taken from the book of Revelation: 'Men for God'. This was one of the best things I have ever done, as well as one of the most popular. Men of all ages, occupations and temperaments attended, as many who worked with their hands as their heads. It was surprisingly easy to fire them up with enthusiasm, but few churches were willing to take up my suggested monthly programme for discipling their men, which was the only method Jesus used for building his Church. One pastor who did take it up told me two years later that he now faced two totally new 'problems' – more men than women and too many leaders! Part of him was thrilled but another part was at a loss to deal with this unfamiliar situation. You'd think all clergy would welcome such a change. Not so. Some are afraid of women, even their wives. Some are not men's men and quite effeminate. Some don't want strong men in the pews, competing for control. Some simply don't want any extra responsibilities. But if I had my time over again, I'd make this my top priority, as Jesus did. I had many letters of thanks, mostly from wives, for their new husbands.

So my very different ministry was taking a quite distinct shape. And it became financially self-supporting, supplemented by some royalties. But I had to work out some financial principles for myself, no longer receiving a regular 'salary'. The first was that I would never send out begging letters in any shape or form, though I would not refuse any gifts. Nor would I ever ask for a 'fee'. I was sometimes asked what I expected and simply said: 'Nothing.' And I refused to accept any remuneration until all other costs of my visit had been met (hire of premises, publicity, etc.). I invariably stayed in homes rather than hotels, enjoying such hospitality, especially where there were children. We receive no regular support from any church and only a few individuals give us gifts from time to time. But all our needs have been provided for and I value the freedom of speech financial independence allows. One of the subtle temptations of an itinerant ministry is to tell people what they want to hear, rather than what they need to hear, especially on an initial visit, and thus build up a 'circuit' of opportunities and support. I cannot take any credit for resisting this seduction, not having any ambitions in that direction.

An itinerant ministry needs a base, however. In any case, we would have to find a home of our own as soon as the Guildford manse was needed. Where should we look? Ideally, it would be where we could make a contribution as well as receive support in a relationship of mutual benefit, being sent out and welcomed back. To remain in Guildford among people whom we had come to know and love, and who knew me so well, might have seemed an obvious choice. Two factors persuaded us otherwise.

First, I did not think it would be fair to my successor, whoever that might be. Even if I could be disciplined enough not to interfere with his leadership (many, including my wife, doubted this), my presence alone could embarrass or even intimidate him. In any case, I have always believed that pastors, like headmasters (apart from the fictional 'Mr Chips'), should leave a clear field for successors, who are bound to have their own ways of doing things. So when I leave a sphere of service I stay right away unless or until my return is requested or needed.

Second, there was a crisis in the church at Guildford which made it more compelling to move away. I had a colleague on the staff who had originally come to assist me, with special responsibility for the youth work. He took an increasing share of the load and acted as my deputy when I was elsewhere. When I was out of action for a few months he manfully took over and kept things going. When the elders accepted that my work was done and that I should be released for wider ministry, they seemed reluctant to initiate a search for my successor while I continued, so eventually I gave them a date for my resignation. Again my associate stepped into the breach. It soon became clear that he felt he could and should step into my shoes on a permanent footing. To be fair, he genuinely believed he was the right man for the job. But the church did not yet share this conviction and was not ready to make such a major decision. Indeed, someone else was already being considered (a former Liverpool 'Teddy Boy', now a Baptist pastor in Canada, seeking a return to his native land, and he was later invited). The upshot of all this was that my associate left the church, taking many younger members with him and even one of the elders, setting up a new church. It was all done so secretly and suddenly that it came as a complete surprise, in fact a great shock, to many of us. I was ministering in South Africa at the time and the first I knew of it was when someone showed me a printed headline: 'CLIFF RICHARD'S CHURCH SPLITS'. I was sorry to see his name dragged into it! The article went on to say it was another example of division over charismatic principles and practice. That really hurt. I know I was too charismatic for some and not enough for others but we had kept the bond of peace in mutual love and respect. If that had been said it was an excuse, not the reason.

By the time I returned, it was a fait accompli, too late to be reversed. There was widespread pain. Families were divided, friendships sundered. I felt as if my baby had been cut in half. Millmead would never be the same again. A generation had gone missing, many of whom I had baptised. And for me personally, any potential base for my itinerant ministry had disintegrated. Our potential supporters were now in two camps. We wanted to keep in touch with both and felt this would only be possible if we were not identified with either.

There was a secondary factor supporting a move, but it hardly influenced the decision. We could not afford to buy a house in Guildford, one of the most expensive towns in the country. We had invested our savings in a cottage in West Wales (above St Dogmael's, overlooking Cardigan Bay) and this would come in handy to buy a property somewhere else. But where?

It was my wife's suggestion that we considered Basingstoke. We had a deep respect and affection for Barney Coombs, the pastor of the Baptist church there and had heard how much the work had developed under his ministry, with a growing number of congregations, a close-knit team of full-time workers and wider links with other fellowships. I enquired whether it might be possible to link up with them when the time came for leaving Guildford and was assured that I could be fitted in.

Months later we went house-hunting in the Basingstoke area and found a house in the village of Sherborne St John, with a garden mostly given over to water, a former watercress bed. It was called 'L'Etang' (French for 'The Pond'), which we resolved to re-name 'Still Waters'. The paint-work was black and the rooms inside bright reds, purples and yellows. Before leaving for an extended visit to New Zealand, we left an offer and a deposit with a friend, with instructions to have the doors and windows painted white if it became ours. On our return we drove straight there and our hearts leapt when we saw shiny white paint everywhere. Windows are the eyes of a house and look blind when the frames are black. A team of young men from the church willingly helped us to tone down the inside and went out of their way to welcome us. We have now been in this house longer than anywhere else. Our children have never lived here with us but we have had a 'family' of livestock – ducks, moorhens, kingfishers, a black swan and assorted fish. Our grandchildren take a tent and food in the little boat and spend time out on an island we have created.

We were welcomed into the church and its leadership as warmly as into our home. I was given opportunities to teach, as well as brotherly support. It all seemed too good to be true. Alas it was. I soon began to be aware of major changes which had taken place since I had first come over from Guildford to preach for them. I blame myself for not having found out much more about them in recent days. For one thing, the church was no longer a Baptist church, having left the Baptist Union. They now called themselves the 'Basingstoke Community Church', but were not independent. They were part of a new international network, focusing on a 'Big Five' in Florida (including the late Derek Prince), though Barney had settled in Vancouver, Canada. To me it was a new denomination in all but name and that would follow later.

The distinguishing feature was what would become known as 'Heavy Shepherding'. Watchman Nee's teaching of absolute obedience to one's 'shepherd' had been adopted. This led to a hierarchical authoritarian structure, with an oppressive control of the sheep. Some were glad to be relieved of the responsibility of following their own conscience or being led by the Spirit. Others were paralysed by the conflict between their own convictions and the counsel of the shepherd. The text 'Rebellion is as the sin of witchcraft' was repeatedly quoted. To be fair, the men at the top of the pyramid were bigger than their teaching and therefore more flexible. It was when the principles were passed on to lesser men that more tensions arose.

At the root of the whole 'system' lay what I would regard as a theological error, namely, too close an identification between the Kingdom and the Church, so that the absolute authority of the one was transferred to the other. It is a common mistake, particularly associated with the word 'Restoration', the belief that the Church will establish the Kingdom of God and rule the nations before the King returns (the technical term is 'Post-millennialism'). Some leaders were reacting against 'Brethren' teaching that the Kingdom is entirely future into a 'Kingdom Now' outlook. Jesus got the balance right, exactly half his 'Kingdom' parables said it was already at work in the world, but the other half said it was to come at the end of the age. Now and not yet. Inaugurated but still to be consummated. A delicate balance, easily upset, with serious consequences.

I was assigned two shepherds, one in the UK and one in the USA. I tried to co-operate but was increasingly uncomfortable in my spirit. This was so contrary to my previous preaching and practice. The crunch came when I was asked to teach on 'The government of God', a phrase which virtually bridged any gap between Kingdom and Church. I could only be true to my understanding of Scripture and share how I understood the relationship between the infallible head of the Church and his fallible body, and how his will is communicated and applied. As we left the session, I remarked to my wife: 'I think I've just killed my pig.' It was the beginning of the end. Shortly after, I tendered my resignation from the network.

Now, two decades later, things have changed for the better. No longer is the shepherding as 'heavy'. Churches have been given a degree of autonomy, though not yet in financial matters. I have even been asked back to speak occasionally. But a broken engagement is not easily recovered, if ever.

We have not moved away, not having had either any

prompting from the Lord to do so or any offer from another fellowship to provide cover or a base for us. We worship in an evangelical parish church, where at first I was welcome to take a weeknight series of studies during Lent and very occasionally preach on Sunday. But I could never be an out-and-out Anglican. Baptisms and bishops are the most obvious stumbling blocks but there are more subtle difficulties like the lack of a defined and disciplined membership. It became clear that I was expected to 'toe the line' doctrinally and keep off subjects dear to my heart. In particular, the vicar took a strong anti-charismatic stance. Pentecost Sundays came and went without any mention of the Holy Spirit. I asked if I could hold a meeting on Ascension Day (which is on a Thursday) and preach about this vital gospel event and creedal item, only to be told I would have to submit everything I was going to say in writing before I spoke, which I did. Since then I have given three talks about the challenge of the Muslim resurgence. I felt I am more trusted to speak about Islam than Christianity!

So I am having to sit quietly in the pew like everybody else and to live without honour in my own country (though it is surprising how many local people devour my tapes, videos and books). I can understand that other leaders find me irritating, if not intimidating. One told me that when I came into a room, the floor tilted in my direction. Another told me people find me scary (that is, until they get to know me, when any awe disappears far too rapidly!).

I have had to ask myself whether I would ever really fit into any church of which I was not the responsible leader – and reluctantly came to the conclusion that it is highly unlikely. In addition to the sharp edges of my personality and temperament, my blunt forthrightness and my tendency to dominate others or withdraw from them, there is one basic barrier which seems insuperable:

My study of Scripture over many years has led me to a combination of deeply held convictions which does not fit into any known school or tradition, even in the evangelical stream of Christians. In a word, I am a very unorthodox evangelical, in my own eyes and other people's. That statement requires a chapter to itself.

16

Unorthodox Evangelical

The dining-room fireplace in my boyhood house bore an embossed copper plate with the Latin words '*Vincit Veritas*' (Truth Conquers). The character in Bunyan's *Pilgrim's Progress* with whom I most readily identify is Mr Valiant for Truth. I have a passion for truth, in particular, the truth of Scripture. In fact, it amounts to a jealousy. I get angry when texts are misquoted, taken out of context or in any way abused, which is far more common than many congregations realise. But I would not have the right to challenge anyone else if I did not first do everything possible to attain my own integrity of interpretation.

We are all prone to read the Bible through our own cultural and temperamental spectacles, finding what we are looking for, reading into Scripture what isn't there (this is called 'eisegesis' from the Greek word *eis*, meaning 'into') instead of reading out of Scripture what is there (this is called 'exegesis', from the Greek word *ex*, meaning 'out of'). Not only internal factors can prejudice our understanding. The tradition in which we were nurtured can play a significant role, blinding us to other possible views.

I have sometimes been asked who has most influenced my preaching. I have usually said my wife, who is my most ardent fan and severest critic. But the question usually means what other preachers. I think I can point to two. Unconsciously, the influence of my father must have played a large part. He went for the heart, in order to capture the will. It was difficult to listen to him without being moved, in the deepest sense. His two preaching 'heroes' had been J.H. Jowett (the 'prince of preachers') and Samuel Chadwick (principal of Cliff College), my pulpit grandfathers, though I never knew either.

Consciously, I have only regarded one as a 'model' to emulate. Bob Morley was a fellow lay-pastor in the Shetland Islands in 1950. I bless the Lord that our paths crossed so early in my ministry. He captivated all of us, though he never became widely known, perhaps because of his genuine humility. His preaching was shot through with two outstanding characteristics. One was his clarity. There was never any doubt about what he was saying. He made everything simple and straightforward enough for everyone to grasp, which came across as Christ-like. It was a joy to listen to such clear speaking. But I realised this was the fruit of clear thinking, especially when I lived with him for a time and appreciated how much time he spent in his study, wrestling with issues until they were crystal clear for himself first. I resolved to be the same and would like to think my hearers find me as clear as I found him.

The other great quality was his honesty, especially in handling Scripture. He never ducked 'difficult' texts, tackling the most perplexing passage head on. Nor did he toe any party line, fit texts into a theological system or tradition. In a word, he told it as it was, without fear or favour. He was a servant of the Word, never using it to serve him. It never occurred to him to ask if it fitted in with his own ideas, or anyone else's for that matter (perhaps that is another reason he never became famous). He took the biblical text in its simplest sense, then shared it with everybody else, regardless of cost or consequence. Again, I resolved to do the same, to be as honest with myself and others about my understanding of Scripture as he was.

But there is a downside to such intellectual integrity, a price to pay. It is to run the risk of becoming a doctrinal misfit, isolated from contemporary traditions, suspected of heterodoxy, if not heresy. It has been a constant eye-opener to me to discover how many traditions, springing from figures in church history rather than the apostolic Scriptures, have influenced today's preachers, even those claiming the Bible to be their final, even 'sole', authority in all matters of belief and behaviour.

I am willing to carry the label 'evangelical' if by that is meant someone whose decisive appeal is to the divine revelation in the sixty-six books in the canon of Scripture called the Bible. I have spent a lifetime teaching it and no one could ever quote me as expressing any doubts about its divine source. Whatever else I may or may not be remembered for, I will be known as a Bible teacher, which means that a great proportion of my life has been given to Bible study.

However, I came to Scripture with an open mind, as free as possible from all prejudice (which 'pre-judges') picked up from others. Ever since Jesus' day, human tradition has contaminated divine truth, and I wanted the truth pure and simple. Knowing his warning about popularity, I consciously threw away any thoughts of reputation. I would study the Scriptures to the very best of my ability, coming to my own conclusions, reaching my own convictions, and teach them to others with clarity and confidence, without thought of cost or consequences. In this spirit I offered to be a mouthpiece for the Lord.

This does not mean that I regarded myself as an infallible interpreter of Scripture. I once told a Roman Catholic priest that I admired his denomination for having only one infallible spokesman, adding that we Protestants have thousands (springing from the Reformation belief in the 'right of private interpretation', originally intended to counter the official church monopoly). Nor does it mean that I ignore the interpretations of others. My bookshelves are stacked with commentaries and I have made a point of buying and reading books of contrary opinions. I get worried if I find myself in a minority and even more if my view appears to be unique. But if, after double and triple checking my 'case' with others, I remain convinced that my insight is correct, I have the courage to stand by my convictions. Mind you, I have trembled when I read the letter of James, which says that teachers will be 'judged more strictly', presumably because they have led or misled others. Better a millstone round the neck and be hurled into the sea.

Nevertheless, I have found that my study of Scripture, as honest as I can make it, has led me to a whole bunch of convictions at variance with the majority of my fellow evangelicals. Hence the title of this chapter and the sub-title of the whole book (the publisher's choice). I am an 'unorthodox evangelical'. I don't fit the norm, though I would prefer to say I'm not the average, which is rather different.

For those whose curiosity has been aroused ('What are David's peculiar views?'), I need to give some examples. I can only briefly state what they are but cannot here justify them. I have done that in various books. Two of them I have already expanded in earlier chapters, because of their significant role in my ministry.

I was one of the early ones to embrace the charismatic renewal and did so because I was convinced it was recovering New Testament dimensions. But most evangelicals then believed such things had died out with the apostles, the Spirit's activity now enshrined in Scripture. We were regarded with suspicion. I was the very first 'charismatic' to address the Evangelical Alliance annual assembly on this subject, thanks to the courage and confidence of its then General Secretary, Gilbert Kirby, and felt like the proverbial lion in a den of Daniels. The situation was already changing, especially among young people, when John Wimber came. He believed he could persuade evangelicals to accept the supernatural gifts of the Spirit if the 'Pentecostal' teaching on baptism in the Spirit and speaking in tongues was quietly dropped, and largely succeeded in establishing this compromise. So I am no longer unusual in espousing the gifts, though my views on 'the baptism' are still different from many evangelicals and even most Pentecostals, being in between both (they are fully laid out in the book *Jesus Baptises in One Holy Spirit*).

I am very much in a minority, among British Christians, in believing that the Jews are still God's chosen people, that he has kept his promises to preserve them as a nation 'as long as the sun, moon and stars shine and the sea waves roar' (Jer. 31:35-6) and to bring them back from exile to their own land for 'a second time'. The majority of clergy here teach that the Church has 'replaced' Israel in God's affection and purposes. Sympathy lies with the 'occupied' Palestinians in the contemporary Middle East crisis (I have even heard Jesus called 'a Palestinian'), alongside growing links between Christians and Muslims (and a growing number of people who say that Allah and the God of the Bible are one and the same).

So as a charismatic and a Zionist I differ from most other evangelicals. But there are many other issues, some directly involving the subject of salvation itself. Basically, I see it as a process, rather than an instantaneous event, covering three phases – from the penalty of sin (justification), the power of sin (sanctification) and the presence of sin (glorification). Most evangelicals agree with this in theory but in practice persist in using the verb 'save' in the past tense ('I was saved x years ago' and 'we had x people saved last Sunday'), when the New Testament uses past, present and future tenses ('we have been saved', 'are being saved', 'will be saved') with the majority of references future. My 'unusual' views are how that process starts and how it continues.

It seems to me right that in the New Testament four elements were essential for entry into the Kingdom: repentance towards

God, faith in the Lord Jesus Christ, baptism in water and reception of the Holy Spirit. In my book I have called this composite initiation 'The Normal Christian Birth'. But it is far from the average. Many have been 'badly birthed'. One, two, or even three steps have been neglected, yet they have been told they are now Christians, have been born again and are heading for heaven. Little wonder many prove to be weak and sickly babies, with a high ratio of infant mortality. Pastors and evangelists putting my teaching into practice have testified to a great improvement in the quality of converts, but most stay with the simplistic pattern of nineteenth-century American revivalism, with its altar calls and sinners' prayer, no demand for deeds of repentance, no baptism, no experienced reception of the Spirit.

It is surprising that baptism has disappeared from evangelism and been relegated to a church rite, almost certainly because of the very different traditions of teaching and practice that have arisen over the centuries. To discuss it is a threat to unity and there seems to be an agreement, even a conspiracy, not to mention it in connection with mission, virtually dismissing it as a 'secondary' matter, in spite of its prominence in Jesus' 'great commission'. I have already shared my own 'enlightenment' on this. While I believe total immersion is the right method, combining, as it does so vividly, both a bath and a burial, my reservation about baby baptism, whether by sprinkling, pouring or even immersion, is that it loses the biblical meaning of the act, which can only apply to a penitent believer. And therefore it ceases to be an effective sacrament and becomes an empty symbol, an acted rather than an actual event. The New Testament speaks of baptism as achieving what it signifies, given true repentance and faith.

However, the main question about salvation where I differ from most evangelicals is whether the process, having started, can be interrupted (they would probably agree) or even be terminated (they would certainly disagree). My Bible studies, mainly in Matthew and Revelation, have convinced me that 'once saved always saved' is an unbiblical idea, as well as an unbiblical phrase, going back through Calvin to Augustine, but no further. Over eighty exhortations and warnings in apostolic writings point in a very different direction (I have listed and expounded these in my book *Once Saved, Always Saved?*). It is significant that the cliché uses the verb 'saved' in the past tense, as if it's all over and done with. I have shocked congregations by announcing that I'm not saved yet! But I'm on 'The Way' (of salvation). I'm being saved and look forward to being fully, completely saved from all my sins, every one of them, of being perfectly restored to the image of God and the likeness of Christ and able to enter that new universe, in which righteousness dwells, without polluting it. Now that's salvation and why Mary's son was called Jesus. Forgiveness without holiness would not be enough. One day my wife's husband will be perfect. She tells me that if she based her faith on experience, she couldn't believe it, but I urge her to base it on Scripture, as I have to for her!

When it comes to our future salvation, that is not just an individual hope, but tied up with the redemption of the world, including creation itself. Few things divide evangelicals so sharply as what they believe about the finale of history (which Greeks called the *eschaton*, from which we get the word 'eschatology'). What we believe about the 'end-times' has a profound effect on our present outlook and behaviour. I came to my own understanding quite early and have not seen reason to change, though I have studied alternative views as conscientiously as I can. I am what is called a 'classic pre-millennialist'. All evangelicals believe that Jesus will make a second visit to planet earth but differ deeply over his purpose for doing so and how long he will stay to complete it. Some think it is only to collect all his people on earth and whisk them all off to heaven, which would only take a minute or two. Others, from reciting creeds in church, think he will stay long enough to 'judge the living and the dead', assigning everyone to their eternal destiny in heaven or hell. But in my Bible that Judgement only takes place after our universe has disappeared. I believe that he is coming back to rule and reign over the world for an extended period, often referred to as the 'Millennium', after the six references to 'a thousand years' in Revelation. The King of Kings is coming back to establish his Kingdom 'on earth as in heaven', as we pray every time we use 'the Lord's Prayer'. I do not believe we are already in that 'Millennium' (the so-called 'A-millennial' view) or that the Church will one day rule the world for a thousand years before Jesus returns (the so-called 'Post-millennial' view). Nor do I believe that Jesus is coming back twice, the first time secretly to 'rapture' the Church away before the 'Big Trouble' and the second time publicly (the 'Dispensational' view originating among the Brethren, picked up by the Pentecostals and almost universal among American evangelicals). So I find myself in a tiny minority, but do not hesitate to proclaim what I believe is the 'blessed hope' of the New Testament, that one day Jesus will rule this world in righteousness, bringing the peace that flows from justice. Otherwise, all the prophetic promises for the world in both Old and New Testaments, must be transferred to another world, leaving Satan to have the last word on this. I have outlined the various views and given the arguments for what seems to have been the consensus of the early Church in my book *When Jesus Returns*.

To those who regard me as a 'radical', on the left wing of theology, it has come as a surprise that in some doctrines I am a 'reactionary', on the right wing, more conservative than many of my contemporaries. I mention two by way of illustration. The first is that I have openly upheld the traditional view of hell as the place where the dead are 'tormented day and night for ever and ever', to quote Jesus' own words (Rev. 20:10), which I take at face value. It came as a shock when leading evangelicals, mainly Anglicans, embraced 'annihilationism', that hell is oblivion, the ultimate extinction of sinners. Since 'dreamless sleep' does not seem all that terrible a fate, it is not surprising that annihilationists do not preach their views. Since almost all we know about hell comes from the lips of Jesus, rather than the prophets or apostles, I cannot but believe and preach what he taught. But readers of my book, *The Road to Hell*, were shocked when I pointed out that all but two of his warnings were addressed to his own disciples and apostles, already 'born of God' (the two exceptions were to Pharisees). This was one of the major factors leading me to question 'once saved always saved'. I was deeply moved by letters of thanks for my book, many of which simply said it had 'restored the fear of the Lord'. When Jesus sent his apostles out on a mission, he told them not to be afraid of those who might kill them but 'I will show you whom you should fear: Fear him who, after the killing of the body, has power to throw you into hell' (Luke 12:5).

My second 'reactionary' belief is of male leadership, in the church and the home. I believe it is a God-given role and responsibility, not a question of superiority at all. God made us male and female, with distinct and complementary functions. The current trend to blur and even obliterate the distinction, both inside and outside the church, owes more to the spirit of the secular age than the Holy Spirit. Of course, the whole question came to a head over the ordination of women. But I tell folk I am as unhappy about the ordination of men, if that divides the body of Christ into clergy and laity, professional and amateur Christians, especially if the church is thought of as the former. My book *Leadership is Male* (a title chosen by the publisher from my list of six suggestions) was probably the best known and least read of 1988. One bookshop sold it from under the counter in plain brown paper bags. There was a feminist demonstration outside another that displayed it in the window. I have a file full of letters of thanks for the book, all from women! Deep down, most women want to see men taking their responsibilities, able to be relied upon for provision and protection. I first gave the material of the book to hundreds of women at a European conference in Düsseldorf, Germany. Afterwards, one said to me: 'We've heard the truth from you, but we've seen it in your wife.' But a leading Anglican bishop said in his review:

> In searching the scriptures, he can find only patriarchy, or male leadership as the model for relationship between the sexes, and he is absolutely right. That's what the Bible says, along with a lot of other stuff we have long since discarded. Mr Pawson's difficulty is tragic. He is a good and kindly man and a fine Christian leader, but he is absolutely hung up on a fundamentalist method of scriptural interpretation. It makes him consistent, or as consistent as Scripture, but he believes in doing what he thinks the Bible tells him to do . . .

I couldn't have put it better myself. Apart from his pejorative use of the term 'fundamentalist', he has accurately summed up my life and work.

I also have some peculiar beliefs in the area of ethics, all the fruit of my Bible study. For example, I do not think Gentile believers should be put under the Mosaic law of giving a tenth of their money or a seventh of their time to the Lord, though many churches teach (depend on?) tithing and Sunday observance. They avoid or ignore the Mosaic curses on those who fail to keep them up.

My most unpopular teaching is that though Jesus allowed divorce on the ground of sexual infidelity, he called all re-marriage adultery. Even if he made just one exception, very few today would qualify. Yet changing partners is becoming as common inside the church as outside (and Britain has the highest record in Europe, second only to America), even in the evangelical stream. This stand has created real tension for me, even among my own friends and relatives.

I cannot end this chapter without a few concluding remarks to set the record straight.

First, in many, if not most, major doctrines of the faith, I am a thoroughly orthodox evangelical. The full humanity and divinity of Jesus, his physical incarnation, crucifixion, resurrection, ascension, return; the personality of the Holy Spirit; the holy Trinity of the Godhead. Those who know my teaching will not need any reassurance about my firm hold on such fundamentals of the faith.

Second, I have never claimed to have the last word on any interpretation of Scripture. Many have heard me urge my hearers to check me out in their own Bible and tell them if they cannot find what they have heard for themselves, to forget it, before it does any harm.

Third, holding these views privately would not have adversely affected my ministry. Teaching them openly has carried a cost, particularly since I have travelled. Few pastors are secure enough to allow their flock to be challenged to think for themselves by hearing another interpretation (to be fair I don't think I was). Many doors have been closed to me. To give one example, I was once asked to speak in Canterbury Cathedral to a large representative gathering of Anglicans and readily agreed. Two weeks before the event, the sponsor telephoned to say his committee were now demanding a promise from me not to mention baptism. I told him that I had not intended to do so but that I never preached anywhere I was told what to say or not to say, so they would have to look for another speaker. The demand revealed a lack of trust, though I fully understood that my reputation for forthrightness probably justified it. I don't hide my convictions.

Fourth, my differences have meant a degree of isolation and loneliness. I have often felt like a voice crying in the wilderness and have wished I could simply assent to what others believe and be accepted by one or other traditions. But I cannot deny my intellectual integrity, to search the Scriptures for myself. In particular, what others call my 'Arminian' views of salvation have cut me off from the widespread 'Calvinist' approach of 'Reformed' theology, which dominates current evangelicalism. I simply cannot find their 'Five Points' in my Bible (Total depravity, Unconditional election, Limited atonement, Irresistible grace and Perseverance, better 'preservation', of saints). These doctrines would leave me with a God who does not 'want all men to be saved', as well as using his power to force the minority he wants to save, without any co-operation on their part. This is simply not the God I have come to know in Christ. But to be in a minority is always painful. I rejoice in those who respect my convictions, even when they cannot share them, and much more in the limited number who are willing to maintain a bond of fellowship, in spite of our differences.

Finally, I feel I must justify imposing on my readers such a theological chapter, which is unusual in an autobiography, even of a preacher. But I cannot think of myself apart from my convictions. They are part of me. I live for them. Take away the things I hold so passionately and there's not all that much left. I am never so much myself as when I am sharing my convictions with others, whether singly or with crowds. Others have observed that I 'come alive' when I do so. That's when I feel really me. The words 'true' and 'real' are the same in both the Hebrew and Greek languages. When handling truth I am most in touch with reality.

All this explains why a former head of the Evangelical Alliance, Morgan Derham, called me (in print) 'the Enoch Powell of the evangelical world'. Quite an astute comparison!

17

Burdens, Books and Bible

At seventy-five, I guess I have entered the final phase of my ministry. However, the Lord has had so many surprising changes for me over the years that I dare not assume there are no more. I have now been a travelling preacher for twenty-five years and this has inevitably changed the style and content of my preaching.

For one thing, I preach longer these days. My visits are usually quite short, so to say anything worthwhile and to justify the time and expense involved, I tend to give full measure, 'pressed down, shaken together and running over'. I speak for ninety minutes on average so don't fit into Sunday services, particularly of the morning 'Family' variety. Mind you, I still stop speaking when an audience stops listening, namely at the first signs of fidgeting. But the Lord seems to give special grace to them and me, usually enabling me to share all that's on my heart.

The big difference is that I can no longer give consecutive expositions of Scripture, which was my first love and some said my forte. I miss this terribly. It was so rewarding to meet regularly with the same congregation, who had become adapted to my style and therefore derived more and more from it. The cumulative effect of a series was noticeable.

Nowadays I am often a stranger among strangers, both I and they wondering how we'll get on with each other. Rapport must be established quickly to make communication possible. That is not helped when chairmen introduce me as 'controversial', which is invariably the case, adding an extra hurdle of suspicion to get over. Actually, many come to me afterwards, still puzzled by the chairman's adjective.

Itinerating adds two uncertainties to the task, which I have not found easy, namely where and what to preach. I could not possibly accept all the invitations I get, so have to make constant choices, examining my motives along the way. Of course it helps to know as much as possible about the background to the invitation, the situation prompting it and so on. I try to make direct and indirect enquiries. I never accept or decline over the phone but insist on a letter for my files. And my main principle has been to go where I'm needed rather than where I'm wanted.

I'm getting better at discernment but still make mistakes. When I do, I usually know before I get up to speak, which is not easy to handle. Sometimes I have begun by asking for forgiveness, from the congregation and the Lord, and for his mercy to bless the meeting nevertheless. Sometimes I have left a conference after my first session (which on one occasion bore more fruit than taking the others would have done). Once I was due to speak three times in one day at a national gathering. The previous evening I met with the sponsoring committee and told them the Lord had forbidden me to speak the next day. Two elderly, saintly ladies burst out laughing – with relief, I discovered. Two days previously the Lord had told them I wasn't to speak and they had been in anguish, wondering how on earth to tell me! I soon discovered a hidden hypocrisy in the whole situation, which was grieving the Holy Spirit. The Lord did allow me to give a very brief word (on 'obedience') at the final session, which later led to a fresh start under fresh leadership. I must write a book some day on 'How to lose friends and influence people'.

Most invitations I have accepted have proved to be of the Lord, but that has still left the larger question of what to preach. Since I am only in a place for a day or two, this has meant a return to 'topical' preaching, though the content is still thoroughly biblical, while rarely based on one text or even one passage. But what topic, theme or subject?

I apply the same principle to 'what' as to 'where', namely, to say what is needed rather than what is wanted. It may partly explain why I have the reputation of being 'controversial'. But I see little point in telling people what they already know and believe. I want to enlarge their understanding and experience.

Occasionally my knowledge of a specific situation guides me to what is needed. More often I am aware of more general needs which apply to many situations. In pastoral ministry, it is easy to make the mistake of projecting the local scene on to the wider canvas. If the local church is lively and growing, it is thought that revival is just round the corner. If it is struggling, it is thought that the great falling away in the last days has come. The advantage of travelling is to get a more accurate knowledge of the whole situation. For example, while there are some exciting exceptions, the general picture of the Church in the United Kingdom is one of serious decline, to the point of fatal haemorrhage (by 2040 if the latest report on trends is to be believed).

So as I have travelled around, my heart has become heavy with what I can only describe as 'burdens'. These were of two sorts: things present in the Church that shouldn't be there and things absent that should be. I began to address both issues, bringing my biblical knowledge to bear on them. Whenever I got the opportunity to share these burdens with church leaders, I seized it with both hands, knowing that shepherds are responsible for the state of the flock and that would not change until they did.

ith my ministry, through tapes and
urdens' I have shared, from casual
we and reverence?) to superficial
to repentance and baptism?). The
on of leadership (in church and
(encouraged by teaching 'once
ing standards (re-marriage after
ord and Spirit (which had nearly
), contrast between devotion of
the detriment of the former) and,
ading among evangelicals (hell no
d the cross no longer punishment
emed to lie behind all these: the
Lord, in turn due to the loss of
emphasis on his righteousness, both as Saviour and Judge.

I was not saying much that was new, either to me or to my
hearers, but my preaching certainly had a sharper edge to it. I
began to attract the label 'prophet'. I do not call myself that,
though I would not hesitate to do so if I believed that was my
gift and calling. But I have said I have changed from being a
'pastoral teacher' to a 'prophetic teacher'. The noun, which is
greater, has not changed, but the adjective, which is lesser, has.
Prophets in Scripture were also called 'seers'; they saw people
and situations as God saw them, which they then addressed with
his word. To a degree, I have found myself doing the same.

But hawking such burdens around from meeting to meeting
became a burden in itself. I was enabled to develop it,
incorporating feedback received. But the message could not
remain fresh indefinitely and I would drop it as soon as it ceased
to live for me. That happened after only having reached a limited
number of situations that needed to hear it. True, tapes could
take it further, but not far enough. I asked the Lord to show me
another way to reach his people. To my surprise he replied
through a text (a method of guidance I neither practise nor
encourage, since so often a meaning is read into verses that was

not originally there). My Bible had fallen open at Jeremiah 30:2 ('Write in a book all the words I have spoken to you'). I have written the date in the margin: 18.4.85.

A publisher had pressed me for years to submit a manuscript for publication, but I had persistently refused. I had no desire or ambition to be an author. If truth were known, I was probably shrinking from all the extra work that would be involved. Laziness, I suppose. Eventually, I had relented to the extent of allowing one series of sermons to be transcribed and revised. My 'ghost writer' would be David Winter, then heading up the BBC Religious Department. The result was *Truth to Tell*, which the Lord has used to help many into the Christian faith, including Gerald Williams, the TV sports commentator. But I decided that was to be my first and last book, however fruitful it proved to be.

Now here was the Lord telling me to become a writer as well as a preacher. I dare not refuse any more. But this was totally new territory. I did not even know if I could write. I already knew that transcripts of my recorded speech were far from adequate for publication. Many had tried and quickly realised that my spoken style simply would not translate in this way, perhaps because I have never written a sermon or talk but spoken freely from notes. 'Cold' print lacks tone of voice, facial expression and gestures and needs compensating factors to bring it 'alive'.

However, if the Lord wanted it, it was his responsibility to give me the ability. The sales of about twenty books seem to confirm that he did. Most of them have had to be reprinted. So my burdens became books and carried my messages much further and more quickly than my feet could ever have done.

I prepare to write a book in much the same way as I prepare to preach a sermon, as I have already previously described. The final stage is a pile of paper containing full notes, though in this case much more of it. Then I sit down and write it straight through, if possible continuously, apart from eating and sleeping.

Otherwise I tend to forget what I have already written and start repeating myself. I have never used a typewriter or word-processor, much less a computer. My fountain pen and my brain seem to operate at exactly the same speed. Occasionally I cross out a word, phrase, sentence or paragraph but never make major revisions. Nor do my publishers' copy-editors, though this book may be an exception. It has certainly been the most difficult and the slowest to write.

The two most important books I have written are the first (*The Normal Christian Birth*, on how to become a Christian in the New Testament way) and the latest (*Unlocking the Bible*). The latter is a story in itself, which I must now tell.

I have mentioned my sadness, even frustration, at losing the opportunity to be a regular Bible teacher. But the Lord had planned a special surprise for me, which was to be the climax of my ministry and the project for which I shall probably be most widely known and best remembered. Yet it all began in a way that gave little indication of its ultimate significance, both for me and many others all over the world.

The pastors of two churches in the historic town of Wallingford, on the River Thames, invited me to give some talks to their people, with the objective of encouraging them in personal study of the Bible. We arranged a series of four monthly Sunday evenings, each to last three hours, with a coffee break in the middle. On each, I would introduce them to one book of the Bible. My aim was twofold: to get them so interested in that book that they could hardly wait to read it and to give them enough help to understand it so that when they did they would be excited with what they were discovering. I also suggested that individuals attending committed themselves to reading the whole book through, both before and after my visit, that sermons during the following month were based on it and that house groups discussed it. Thus, after each month, all were familiar with and hopefully enjoying one book in the Bible.

Results exceeded all expectations. So I was asked to extend

the series for the next six years, so that we could get to know all sixty-six books! I laughed and said I might be in heaven by then. But they were serious, so I had to be. I agreed to continue as long as I could and, in fact, completed the course.

It was as exciting for me as for them. Studying Scripture book by book was new for all of us. I had done many books chapter by chapter, but this was different. I had always said that God never intended or inspired the division of his Word into chapters and verses, but he did give it to us in books. The Bible is not a book but a library (*Biblia* is a plural word in Greek and Latin). It yields its best treasures to those who read and study it book by book. The worst way to treat it is as a box full of independent texts, to be selected and combined according to the readers' own presuppositions and prejudices. Immersing myself in one book each month yielded a flood of fresh insights, which kept me excited, as well as my hearers. I realised that the key which unlocked the whole Bible was to ask of each book: 'Why was this one written?' I got many different answers, but added together they revealed the manifold wisdom of God, his heart as well as his mind and, supremely, his overall will for his creation and his creatures. It was an 'eye-opener', which is another word for revelation.

Audio recordings of each session began to circulate far and wide, but these prompted a steady stream of complaints in return. I had used visual aids to stimulate interest – outline charts, maps, photos and models. Verbal reference to these on the tapes were irritating and frustrating listeners, understandably. I was urged to produce a video version.

This would involve repeating the entire series again. I shrank from the task. I remember thinking that, if this were of the Lord, it would guarantee me a few more years on earth. It was and it did! We booked High Leigh Conference Centre in Hertfordshire for three days at a time, hired television cameras and floodlights and turned their main hall into a studio. We had an invited audience of about a hundred, since I need an audience to speak to. There were six programmes made each day. It was heavy going for those attending and I remember one late afternoon session when an entire row fell fast asleep from sheer exhaustion and the cameraman at the front discreetly shot those who were still awake. Afterwards I thought it would have been great fun to include a shot of the sleepers. Fortunately, no snores got onto the soundtrack.

I heaved a sigh of relief when this second run had been completed, assuming the whole project was behind me. Far from it! To my chagrin, I was approached by James Catford, then Religious Editor of HarperCollins. He wanted to publish the whole series in book form. He said it would be my 'legacy to the body of Christ' (I think he will prove to be right). I told him it was out of the question to commit myself for the time required to write such a massive amount of material, but that if he could find someone willing and able to work from the audio and video recordings I would gladly make them available for the purpose. Andy Peck, already an accomplished Christian journalist, proved ideal and could not have done a better job. His costs were covered but I refused any advance on royalties. In fact, there were to be none. The cost of the original eight volumes came to over sixty pounds sterling, which was far too much for the market, limiting purchase to my most ardent fans. The publisher was left some thousands of pounds out of pocket.

I was convinced that a cheaper one-volume paperback would sell much better and believed its contents were needed and wanted. James left to head up the Bible Society and was replaced by my cousin's grandson, which I thought might give me a bit of leverage! He was sympathetic, but it took some time before he was persuaded to take the risk of re-publishing what had been a commercial failure. Eventually he did and it has been a runaway best-seller (for religious books of this sort) – over thirteen hundred pages for under ten pounds. The company has recovered its losses and I have had my first royalties. But the real joy is the knowledge that many Christians are getting into their

Bibles again, delighting in doing so and finding that love for his Word is enhancing their love for the Lord.

Meanwhile the audio and video versions have been widely used on radio and television, both in this country and overseas. I can honestly say that when these recordings are being made I have no conscious thoughts of them reaching a wider audience. So I thank the Lord I can forget them while I'm speaking. But when I'm not I thank him for the privilege of teaching the truth twenty-four hours a day, around the world, to the largest congregation I have ever had or ever dreamed of having. Only he could have made this possible.

18

Both in Love with the Same Man

Some readers may be feeling rather frustrated by now. I have made only passing references to my wife and even fewer to my children. I'm sure that some of you are bursting with curiosity about them. I could have asked them to write this chapter but the truth is I wouldn't dare. They know too much and are all frank and honest. But I will ask them to approve what I write before it goes to the publisher.

I had a number of girlfriends during my teens and twenties but by the time I went to Cambridge I was in the minority of students without a fiancée. When a Salvation Army lassie whom I had recently come to know came to visit me there, the other students decorated my study-bedroom with photographs of all their brides-to-be, hinting that I was being a bit too slow to commit myself, which I probably was. My bachelor status continued right through and after college, until I became a caravan missioner in South Yorkshire.

I fell in love with my mother-in-law before I met her

daughter. My colleague and I were conducting a mission in the Humberside village of Gunness, down the hill from the steel town of Scunthorpe. We cooked our own breakfast, but members of the Methodist chapel, which was our base, gave us other meals in their homes. Mrs Pepperdine was a good cook, but it was her sweet nature, reflected in her face, which attracted me. One of her daughters was already married and serving as a Baptist missionary in Angola, Africa. The other was still single, a doctor's secretary on a mobile X-ray unit, seeking to eliminate tuberculosis in the county. I thought to myself: 'If she's anything like her mother I'm interested.' She was and I was.

Her father was a council officer, of retiring disposition but strong socialistic convictions inspired by Keir Hardie. He had a shock of pure white hair, the result of medical service in World War I. He had been on the *Britannic*, sister ship to the *Titanic*, when it was sunk by enemy action on its way to Gallipoli to pick up the many wounded soldiers. Years later we met up with a Professor of Law in the Christian 'Pepperdine University' in Malibu, California. He showed us a painting of its founder and benefactor, who had made a fortune selling spare parts for the Ford model 'T', the 'Tin Lizzie'. It might have been a portrait of my father-in-law, so similar was the likeness.

When I heard that their daughter Enid was coming home for the weekend, I was eager to meet her. I learned later that others in the church, knowing I was eligible, also had hopes for the encounter. After the morning service, at which I had preached, she asked me if I could spare the time to answer a question that was troubling her. Could I?! After all others had left, we adjourned to the caravan parked in a nearby field. So what was the problem? To my astonishment it was baptism. She was attending a Baptist church in Lincoln, from which her sister had gone out as a missionary. Witnessing believers' baptisms by immersion had brought doubts about her christening as a baby. I found myself confessing that I couldn't really give her an answer since I shared her perplexity, even though, as a Methodist minister, I was committed to 'doing' babies, by moistening their foreheads. So a mutual uncertainty drew us together but we soon found we shared other more positive links. All who met Enid, including my parents, approved of our relationship and encouraged us to get engaged, which we did a few months later.

That our first conversation was about baptism proved to be prophetic. After we had produced three children, all of whom were 'dedicated' rather than christened and after I had been baptised as a believer and transferred to the Baptist ministry, Enid became the first person I ever baptised by immersion, along with Reg, a new convert, head of finance for what was then BOAC (British Overseas Airways), now British Airways. It was special for all three of us.

To backtrack a bit, our engagement was announced at a final rally in Doncaster to complete the year of caravan missioning and we celebrated it by joining a Methodist party touring the Norwegian Fjords, a romantic setting if ever there was one. If our engagement was quick, we expected it to be long. I knew by then that RAF officers had to build up 'points' for a married quarter over many months. Then came the surprise that I could have one straight away, but they could only hold it for six weeks. So we had a 'shotgun' wedding, but not for the usual reason. We chose Epworth as the venue, because of its association with John Wesley (he was born and brought up in the vicarage there, famously rescued 'as a brand plucked from the burning' when it burnt down). We both admired him and owed him a great deal for our Methodist upbringing. The RAF gave us a few days' 'compassionate' leave for the honeymoon, though I had not served long enough to merit any, which we spent in Dovedale, Derbyshire.

The life of an officer's wife was as different for Enid as that of an officer was for me. She had to make courtesy calls on the wives of the Air Commodore, Group Captains and other senior officers, leaving visiting cards. At the other end of the scale she heated up many tins of baked beans for boy entrants. But one great advantage was that we 'marched' into a fully furnished home with everything provided, down to the last teaspoon. It was all taken away a few months later when I was posted to Aden. She followed me out into the blistering heat and humidity, prepared to live in an apartment I had found, which would have been called a 'slum' back home. What we will do for love! By then she was pregnant with our first child. We soon had three, so close together that they were almost like triplets. They would grow up as good friends, crossing the same milestones of life at almost the same time. Later they all left home within a short time of each other, for jobs or college. Oh, and our collie dog, Trixie, had to be put down just then! So the nest emptied again.

In a sense, I have already told the rest of Enid's life story, since she has shared mine all the way. Quite simply, I could not have done all I have been able to do without her loyal and patient support. She sacrificed her own life for mine and has paid a price for that. Six different homes in the first five years of marriage is not every bride's dream.

As with most couples Enid and I are alike in some ways and unlike in others. We have similar tastes – furniture and furnishing, 'autumn' colour clothes, music and art – but dissimilar temperaments. I am sentimental, she is sensible. I am romantic, she is realistic. This has been very good for me.

The greatest tension between us can be summed up in one word – clutter. We are both squirrels, hoarding things that may some day come in useful, but I am ten times worse than she is. That is only partly because I do so much of my work at home. My papers (all in a patented piling system!) overflow from my study into other rooms. I have never been able to keep on top of constant correspondence. I dabble in many interests and hobbies – photography, painting, conjuring, model cars and trains, etc. I inherited a love of gadgets from my mother. And as for books, they fill two rooms in the house and a shed in the garden. Enid's mother kept an extremely tidy house in which evidence of her father's activities was largely confined to a desk and the garage. It has been a sore trial for my wife to be married to such an untidy and disorganised husband. Now she is anxious not to lumber herself or the children with the task of clearing up after I've gone.

She nearly went first. Back in 1975 she came within sight of her grave. She'd always had an unsightly blemish in her left eye. In that year it began to be sore and irritating. An optician, testing her sight for spectacles, said she ought to get it looked at. The local hospital gave her an appointment three months ahead. Had she waited till then, it would have been far too late. As it 'happened' a missionary friend was returning to his work in Kenya and called at our front door to say goodbye. He 'happened' to be an eye surgeon, so I asked him to look at Enid's eye. He took one look, came in, went straight to the telephone and booked a bed in East Grinstead Hospital (where the famous surgeon 'Archie' McIndoe rebuilt the burnt faces of Spitfire pilots during the Battle of Britain). After examining her, the ophthalmic surgeon was kind enough to tell me the worst. It was a virulent melanoma. It might already be too late. In his previous case like this, he had had to remove half a face. I confess I felt I'd rather she was in heaven with a whole face than on earth with half of one. He suggested I take her home for two days, build up her morale and bring her back for surgery.

On the way home she wanted to know the whole truth. After I'd told her, an astonishing peace came over her. There was no panic. We didn't mobilise prayer, though many decided to pray. Nor did we contact anyone with a healing ministry, though we knew quite a few. I took her back to the hospital and came home to wrestle with the problem of what to preach about the following Sunday. The Spirit directed me to Psalm 121 ('I will lift up my eyes . . .'). To my surprise, I discovered every verse was about eyes, human or divine ('keeper' in Hebrew means 'eyelid'). I took a tape with me on my next visit, so that it could be passed round the ward, all the patients in it having problems with their sight.

I found Enid sitting up in bed looking at me. She had come through the operation with a graft implanted in her eye. We shall always be grateful to the person who donated it when they died, whoever it was. But more than that happened. A young New Zealand nurse, only two months old as a Christian, had come to her bed in an agitated state and blurted out: 'The devil is trying to destroy you; may I pray for you?' Enid calmed her down and said she'd rather have 'elders' present as well. Into the ward came the hospital chaplain and a dental surgeon, both filled with the Spirit. The four of them went to the chapel for a time of 'ministry'. The nurse gave Enid a piece of paper on which she had written: 'You will lift up your eyes to the hills.'

To cut a long story short, after a second operation and another graft, I drove her away without even a bandage on. We went to Canada and visited the Rocky Mountains, so she could 'lift up her eyes to the hills'. At the first check-up after our return, the surgeon who had assisted at the operation, a Jew, could not find any trace of their work, even with a binocular microscope. He finally asked Enid which eye it had been! Then he put his hands together, looked up to the ceiling and simply said: 'I join you.' We already knew the Lord's hand had been with them, but it was good to know he felt the same. The main surgeon made a film of his surgery and her remarkable recovery to show his fellows at conferences.

There has been no sign of any recurrence for thirty years, so we can safely say she was cured of the cancer. She is still with me and expects to die of something quite different.

Some years after all this, she came with me to New Zealand, where a number of funny things happened, one of which explains the title of this chapter. She was introduced to one group as 'Enid Pawson, formerly Enid Blyton'. We never knew whether this was a joke or our host's device for remembering her Christian name (she often gets called 'Edna'). However, the bush telegraph in that country is so efficient that within a day or two the national press were on the telephone demanding an interview with the famous children's authoress. I was upset that anyone should think I would marry her!

I was speaking in a large, unheated hall and Enid is very susceptible to draught, giving her heavy colds and sinus problems. When I got up to speak she would pull a scarf over her head, knowing she'd be sitting still for an hour or more. The rumour went countrywide that I taught that wives should cover their heads when their husbands are speaking in public!

It was while there that I came across a statement by a wife who said that the secret of her happy marriage was that she and her husband were both in love with the same man – him. When I drew this to Enid's attention, her immediate and spontaneous response was: 'That's us'! Every time I have quoted it since as the secret of our own marriage, my audience has taken it as a reference to Jesus. I enjoy enlightening them, even though their laughter is against myself. That explains the title to this chapter.

Some may be a little surprised that Enid has not taken more part in public ministry with me. There are two main reasons for this. First, she is naturally modest and hates drawing attention to herself. It was only with extreme reluctance that she has permitted me to write this chapter or even this book. Second, she made a conscious choice to see her calling in the Lord as a good wife and mother, my helpmeet rather than my co-worker. And she has been just that quite superbly. But she has had a ministry, particularly in counselling, at which she is excellent, never finishing a session without telling someone a practical step they can take to help themselves, which they must take before she will see them again.

Those who assume the author of a book like *Leadership is Male* must have a meek and submissive wife could not be more mistaken. She can be surprisingly strong-minded and strong-willed when she wants to be. But I was only able to write what I did because she genuinely shared my convictions. On the few occasions she has spoken in public, she has astonished her audience with her clarity and confidence (and she didn't get that from me).

If the Lord leaves those who live in the public eye to get their reward from men and concentrates on the services done in secret for him, then she's going to be way ahead of me in the queue for rewards in heaven.

And that's enough about her. Far too much in her opinion!

We have three children, as I've already said, one in heaven and two on earth. I shall say more about our eldest daughter, no longer with us, than the others, whose right to privacy I must respect. We have not lost her but, sadly and inevitably, we have lost contact with her. She will never live with us again, but we look forward to living with her again.

Deborah has that special place in our hearts that belongs to the first-born. She was born in the Middle East. Enid's contractions began on the morning I was due to fly out for a tour of stations up the Arabian coast, so I rushed her to the military hospital and did not expect to see her for days. But a careless truck driver backed his vehicle into the plane's propeller, so I could stay around. 'It always happens to David'!

As a baby 'Debbie' wore nothing but nappies in that blistering climate, which saved on baby clothes. But we flew back to England in freezing fog and we shall never forget her pinched, miserable face peering out of the bundle of blankets.

She grew up to be a fine young lady, choosing teaching as her career, having inherited her mother's ability with children. All who knew her became very fond of her.

She was the first to come to faith and ask for baptism, so when she went for training at the King Alfred College in Winchester she was soon taking a leading role in the Christian Union there. She did the same in every evangelical church she later attended, most of them Anglican.

She met and married a church youth leader in one of these, eventually settling in Yately, where they became part of what the *Daily Telegraph* described as 'the best parish church in England'. Soon, their first child was on the way. Her husband got a very lucrative post with a top bank in the City and he joined the ranks of commuters to London. All seemed well – lovely home; good job; marvellous church; family on the way. But there are subtle pressures and temptations in the City, and he began to stay overnight up there, which should have been a warning. Three months after his daughter Rebecca was born, he left home for good, leaving a parting letter. He said there was no one else, but the eventual divorce was on the ground of his adultery.

For the next seven years Deborah lived the life of a single mother, yet retained her infectious enthusiasm for life, maintaining and even increasing all her Christian activities. Indeed, it was only after she died that we found out how much she had been doing, partly from her meticulous accounts (supporting an orphan in Haiti and a missionary in New Guinea, for example). She never gave in to self-pity; she was too busy helping others (just like her grandmother did in her home for the retired, until she fell and broke her pelvis at ninety-eight).

Then the blow struck. She had been feeling unwell for a few months, but the doctor had simply prescribed tonics to pick her up. But she was actually suffering from a dangerous form of leukaemia. I was with Enid in Windermere, where I was speaking at meetings in a hotel ballroom. Deborah telephoned us to say she had asked for a second opinion from another doctor and had been given just two hours to find somewhere her daughter could stay and be admitted to hospital. We realised straight away how very serious it must be. I felt I must be alone with the Lord and went out to walk by the lake. I remembered saying out loud: 'Lord, you know the end from the beginning; is this fatal?' Somehow, deep in my spirit, I sensed that it was. I wrestled with the pain of that until I came to a measure of acceptance and then I asked him to keep the days of her suffering as short as possible. Jesus said his Father could do this (read Matthew 24 if you doubt me). This prayer was answered.

The prognosis was in terms of a few months but she left us in less than one.

Knowing she was now in good hands, I finished my engagements and then we rushed back. Rebecca was with a friendly family and Deborah had her own room in a hospital, already receiving treatment. 'Get well' cards plastered the walls. The nurses were clearly fond of her. Not a word of self-pity or complaint ever escaped her lips. Her church had set up a country-wide chain of prayer for her and the elders came to anoint her with oil. She corresponded with the television star Roy Castle, now a member of our former church in Chalfont St Peter, who was also dying of cancer at the same time.

Her church's concern and attention led to one difficult crisis. Shortly after she was transferred to the intensive care unit, a lady came to visit her, only to find the room and bed empty. Enquiring of a nurse where she was, she received the ambiguous information: 'Oh, she went at nine o'clock' (meaning to another department). The visitor went home and telephoned the prayer chain with the 'news' that Deborah had died. Next morning, the vicar phoned to commiserate with us and was shocked to learn it was not true. To our horror we realised Rebecca may have been told and drove like fury to her school (I recall passing a policeman with a speed camera, but I sent up a little prayer and we never heard anything). But we were too late. The headmistress had taken her out of class and a staff member was looking after her. As we took Rebecca away, she told us that children in the playground had taunted her with 'Your mummy's dead.' But she had replied: 'Look into my eyes. I'd be crying if she was dead.' So we went straight to the hospital for a visit.

Only those who have watched their nearest and dearest fighting a losing battle with a fatal disease can really understand the agony. After each visit I had to find somewhere quiet where I could shed my tears. Enid was a tower of strength. To see our 'Debbie' lying there, hooked up to machines and screens with more tubes and wires than we could count, was so contrary to her normal liveliness that at moments we could hardly believe it was our daughter. She developed septicaemia and her body was poisoning itself. She had already had two distressing heart attacks and the doctors, having done all they could for her, decided not to attempt to revive her if she had a third. We asked them to take her off the life support systems before that happened. She lay in complete peace for some hours, then quietly slipped away to be with the Lord she had loved and served.

The hardest thing I have ever had to do was to tell her seven-year-old daughter the news. I took Rebecca into a room where we could be alone, sat her on my knee and told her that Jesus had decided he could look after her mummy better in heaven than even the dedicated staff at the hospital. Then we just wept together.

We buried Deborah on a sunny morning, in a cemetery surrounded by heathery woodland, and held the funeral service in the afternoon, free from a coffin and waiting pall-bearers. The church was packed. My son read a psalm he had skilfully personalised for the occasion, Enid read some of Deborah's compositions and I preached – on the text 'In everything give thanks'. I told the congregation I was glad it said 'in' and not 'for' and then listed many items of gratitude in our hearts, not least that she had died in Christ. It must be dreadful for Christian parents where offspring pass away without the promising future he alone makes possible. I shared with them that I had told the Lord I was proud of my daughter and dared to ask for his opinion of her. I got an astonishing reply. The words came clearly into my mind: 'She's one of my successes.' They are now on her gravestone: 'One of the Lord's successes.' Even in her death, her influence continued. There were conversions at the funeral service and through the tape-recording of it.

But further sorrow was to follow. Her ex-husband had been in the porch listening but left because he felt it was 'going on too long'. He telephoned that very evening to say he was coming to collect his daughter the next day. She had seen so little of him, especially when he had been posted overseas and the thought of her being taken from all her friends so soon after losing her mother was more than we could bear. Deborah in her will had nominated a lovely Christian couple with two girls as guardians in case anything happened to her. So they took Rebecca with them to a Christian holiday camp the next week.

The day after the funeral we took our granddaughter to Bournemouth, hoping the sea and sand would help to heal. On the drive home she was very quiet and thoughtful, finally coming out with: 'We didn't need to cry yesterday afternoon, only yesterday morning.' When asked why, she said: 'Because the morning was the end of Mummy's old life [the burial] and the afternoon the beginning of her new life' (the service had been a celebration). While she was at camp we went to court and obtained a restraint order forbidding her being taken from us for three months. In the event she stayed for a year with her 'guardians' but then her father claimed and obtained custody and she went to live with his second wife (who was a kind stepmother) and their baby son. Alas, he left her too and went to Singapore, taking a new German girlfriend and my granddaughter with him.

Rebecca is now a fine young lady of nineteen, driving her own car. It doesn't seem possible. But she is still clearly influenced quite deeply by the memory of her mother. Wasn't it a Roman Catholic cardinal who said: 'Give me a child up to the age of seven and you can do what you like with them after that'?

Deborah was thirty-six when she died (the same age as my younger sister had been). It was only half the allotted span but she had done more for the Kingdom in that time than many who are granted the whole. For my part, my faith had to be stretched to comprehend both the wonders of my wife's healing and the mystery of my daughter's passing. Both had a profound effect on me, as others have noticed.

Our son, Richard Wesley (born on the same day of the week

and at the exact time when John Wesley was born again in 1738), has successfully pursued his chosen career in information technology, gaining on the way a doctorate from Trinity College, Dublin, where he is currently re-organising the computerised welfare records of the Irish government.

He married Ann, an Indian girl from Malaysia, whom he met in the church they both attended. She is most attractive, intelligent, artistic and, above all, a keen Christian. They have given us two delightful grandchildren, Guy and Aruna, and together are a happy and relaxed family.

Yet we did not feel able to attend their wedding, which was very painful for them and us. They have nobly said they have no problem if I share our reasons, of which there were two.

The primary one was that she had already been married but had separated from what had been an unhappy relationship and divorce proceedings were under way. But my understanding of Scripture is that a woman in such circumstances has only two options. 'But if she does [separate from her husband], she must remain unmarried or else be reconciled to her husband' (Paul, quoting Jesus himself, in 1 Cor. 7:11). However, the pastor of their fellowship and the leaders of the network to which it related took the line that if attempts at restoring the marriage failed (which they did in this case), the woman was free to remarry. I had already been speaking out against the declining standards in the churches on this very issue and felt that my authority to continue doing so would be compromised if I was known to make exceptions for my own family. It was the most acute test of my convictions I have ever had.

The secondary one was a further complication, even if Ann had been single and totally free to marry. In a word I feared that she would find herself in an 'unequal yoke' with an unbeliever. Richard had genuinely held Christian beliefs at the time of his adult baptism and made a sincere profession of faith. But I was already aware he was wrestling with serious doubts. These began with disillusioning encounters with inconsistencies in the evangelicals and charismatics he was meeting. But they progressed to intellectual questions about the faith itself through exposure to the scepticism of others, by reading and acquaintance. He freely admits he no longer believes that Jesus is the Son of God or that the Bible is the Word of God. He does not claim to be 'Christian' but calls himself a 'God-fearer', using the New Testament term for synagogue adherents.

Over the years I have consistently refused to take part in a wedding between a believer and an unbeliever, as contrary to Scripture, though I have been prepared to marry two unbelievers, in the name of God who recognises all valid marriages, not just Christian ones.

Enid loyally stood with me and on the day itself we drove far away to a quiet place where we could share our sadness. One of the worst aspects was that others could think we were being racist, but that would also be a contradiction of apostolic teaching that 'From one man he made every nation of men' (some translations have 'from one blood'). We had to run the risk of this gross misunderstanding.

Once the marriage was a 'fait accompli' and our position known, we have felt it right to accept the situation and normalise relationships as far as possible, not least for the sake of their children. I have worked with Richard to build a large deck for their American home when his work took him there and on the plans for their present home near Henley, just forty minutes away from us. He has copy-edited this very book for me.

The whole family attend a lively fellowship nearby. Ann is a member, taking a leading role in Alpha courses, but Richard is not, by his own choice. Nevertheless, he supports the work financially and takes a keen interest in the pastor's philanthropic work in Liberia.

Ann has been everything a good daughter-in-law could be, while Richard has shown himself a good husband and a better father than I. So we have much to be thankful for, though wounds can take a long time to heal.

Angela Ruth (the second name came from my younger sister), our youngest, was a shy little girl but she has developed a remarkable gift for relating to people (in this she is more like her mother than me). Beginning her career as a secretary in Shell's London headquarters, she soon transferred to the all-male exploration department, where she was teased but gave as good as she got. The work took her out to oil rigs in the North Sea and she had to practise escaping from sunken helicopters. Having been promoted as high as she could get without a degree, she applied to Birkbeck College, London and attended a course in geology in her spare time.

She got more than a degree. She is now married to one of her lecturers, Dr Neil Harbury, who has a most interesting background as well as a charming personality. Descended from the chief rabbi of Manchester and with a Czech mother, he was sent to a Methodist boarding school founded by John Wesley, at Kingswood, near Bristol. (One of his best friends there is now responsible for BBC TV's programme *Songs of Praise*.) But he emerged without either a Jewish or a Christian faith.

Since 'Angie' has not yet professed faith or requested baptism, I asked them not to have a church wedding. However, after the registry office formalities, I did conduct a brief ceremony, at their request, in the hotel before the reception, in which I reminded them that God was a witness to their union and their vows to each other (which they had composed themselves and have conscientiously kept).

Life has been good to them. They have two fascinating children, Evie (short for Evangeline!) and Daniel. They have their own business, training geologists for small and large oil companies, with staff on both sides of the Atlantic. They also have interests in the Czech Republic, having opened a hotel in the medieval square in Tabor (famed for the Reformer, Jan Huss, who predated Martin Luther and was burned at the stake; his museum is adjacent to their property).

Though Angie does not yet share my faith, I have been

touched by her respect for me and my ministry. One of her carefully chosen birthday cards to me contained the following words:

He's wisdom and integrity
    that links the heritage of the past
    to the lessons of today.
He's courage that allows him to stand tall
    and defend the things that he believes.
He's strength that enables him to know
    when gentleness and caring
    are the strongest inspiration he can give.
He's pride that allows his children
    to walk in his shadow
    and gives them hope for the dreams of the future.

That tribute tells you more about her than me.

When our three children were small, they were proud to be mentioned in my sermons. Family life can provide so many illustrations. But there came a day when this made them self-conscious and embarrassed among the other young people. They were beginning to suffer 'PK' (Preacher's Kids) disease and gave me an ultimatum: 'Stop telling the church about us or we'll start telling the church about you.' You can actually date this from my tape recordings! I have asked their permission for what I have said about them here.

As readers will have realised by now, Enid and I have run the gamut of situations faced by Christian parents in contemporary society. At least it has given us sympathy with them. For myself I wish I had been as devoted a husband and father as I have been a preacher. The fact that Billy Graham has recently expressed similar sentiments does not ease my conscience but only reinforces regret. The family have paid their own price for my ministry to others. May the Lord reward them and forgive me.

19

'Usually in the Flesh'

'It's nice to meet you in the flesh' is the most common greeting I receive when face to face with those who have listened to tapes, watched videos or read books. My invariable response is: 'I'm usually in the flesh.' This disconcerting repartee is not original (I overheard a famous preacher use it), but it opens up some interesting conversations, sometimes about 'out of body' experiences, which I cannot claim to have had.

By the same token, I react quite negatively to people who apologise for not being able to come and hear me preach but assure me they'll 'be with me in spirit'. I tell them I much prefer preaching to those who are with me in flesh. I derive no inspiration from empty seats.

Then there was the Australian visitor who finally came to see me preach after years of listening to my tapes. When I asked for her reaction she said, 'I think I prefer the tapes.' It is surprising how many have imagined a tall dark and handsome physique behind the voice. I share their disappointment. My confident tone is not derived from my physical attributes.

All of which brings me to the subject of this chapter – my body. This may seem an unusual ingredient in an autobiography but my body and I have been together for three-quarters of a century, mutually influencing each other, for better for worse, in sickness and in health, till death us do part. In this life, I am an embodied spirit.

Our bodies provide us with two indispensable features of being a person. First, they give us our own identity. The mirror confirms our unique appearance, making us different from all others on earth. Mention of a name switches on a picture in the memory. Second, they enable us to communicate with others. Relationships depend on physical contact, on sight, hearing and touch. They are totally disrupted by the death of a body.

It is Greek thinking that separates human beings into bodies and 'souls', devaluing the former and exalting the latter. In Hebrew thinking a 'living soul' is a breathing body, applied to animals in Genesis 1 and humans in Genesis 2. The emergency call for help, 'SOS', is thoroughly biblical, 'save our souls' meaning 'keep our bodies alive'. The Old and New Testaments are both concerned with whole people, keeping body and soul together, in both time and eternity.

So I have scriptural as well as personal reasons for writing this chapter. The state of my body is integral to the story of my life.

Jesus assumed that we love ourselves and Paul assumed that 'no one ever hated his own body'. While it is generally true that we feed and care for our bodies, there are often one or more features that we dislike intensely, especially if they present a social or physical handicap. In my case it is my feet. They are very flat and rather big, both of which have affected me quite deeply.

The Almighty must have had a temporary shortage of arches when fashioning my extremities. All attempts to correct this minor deformity failed. As a child I was forbidden to stand on bare feet for a whole year, wearing only specially built-up shoes, but it did no good. The result is that I am not much good at running. I came to hate most sports because of the humiliation I suffered. I well remember the 'whole school' race on sports day, when I was so far behind everybody else that the physical training teacher pulled me out of the contest, in full view of staff, parents and pupils. From then on I did my best to avoid all physical activities that involved chasing after balls, leading to a total disinterest in rugby, soccer or even cricket.

The size of my feet was not a handicap: more an embarrassment and a disappointment. A lady missionary, visiting our home when I was a little boy, observed them and told my parents I was going to be tall. That remark stayed in my memory but never materialised, probably due to a combination of the aforementioned allergy to sport and the sparse wartime rationing of food during my growing teenage years. All my life I have wrestled with envy of those who have a more 'commanding' presence, noticing that leaders in most walks of life tend to be above average height. It has not helped to know that I should and could have been taller than I am. But the Lord has made it clear that anxiety cannot add one cubit to our stature. I was comforted to find that the only 'tradition' we have of Jesus' physical appearance put him at about 5 feet 9 inches. That gave me a new perspective on my 5 feet 8½ inches (the ½ inch was very important but I have now lost it in my old age!).

And I have had to change my opinion about my feet quite radically. In the Lord's eyes, feet that bring good news are beautiful and mine have carried the Word right round the world. So thank you, Lord, for my beautiful, big, flat feet! They've served both of us well. Actually, they're beginning to protest when I stand on them for too long, so I'm thinking of imitating rabbis by sitting to preach.

As far as the rest of my body goes, I can live with it. Indeed, I have no choice. Short of cosmetic surgery, we are limited in altering our appearance. Men are able to adjust their cranial and facial hair. Like many young men I grew a moustache as soon as I could, primarily to look more like a man and less like a boy.

We eventually became so mutually attached that I kept it. Decades later I went on a canal boating holiday and, in true naval tradition, let my beard grow. But I looked too much like Esau, who was 'an hairy man', so as a compromise I settled for my present 'goatee' style, only later realising, from family photographs, that I was emulating both my grandfathers.

I have had my share of hospitals. One of my earliest recollections is of being incarcerated in the 'Isolation Hospital' in the middle of Newcastle's Town Moor, which allowed no visitors. To this day I have no idea what dangerous disease I was carrying.

One Christmas Day I was rushed off in an ambulance with suspected meningitis and my 'present' that year was a lumbar puncture. At seven I lost my appendix but have not missed it. Working on farms after leaving school gave my health a real lift, as well as giving me a permanent rosy, almost ruddy complexion. This survives even through illness, reducing sympathy and tempting me to elicit more by talking about my trials: which I will now proceed to do by sharing two hilarious experiences in hospital.

While serving as a Royal Air Force chaplain in Arabia, I failed to drink the recommended thirteen pints of liquid each day (not taking alcohol made this a pain rather than a pleasure). The result was a painful kidney stone and I was flown back to England as a 'Casevac' (Casualty Evacuee), which made me feel a fraudulent hero! I found myself in the officers' ward of a hospital near Lincoln, presided over by a most attractive Sister, about to be married, to the great disappointment of some patients. She came round each evening to tuck us up. The day after my operation, which seemed to have cut me in half, I was in such pain I asked her for help to sleep and she gave me two small yellow torpedoes to swallow. The next thing I knew was two nurses slapping my face to wake me up – at noon the next day! So that night I asked for just one of the deadly pills. This time I woke in the middle of the night to see the illuminated and disembodied face of a beautiful blonde girl, hovering over my bed, smiling at me but holding a finger over her lips in a hushing gesture. I whispered, 'Have we met?', but she shook her head and said, 'I'm Muriel.' At that point a look of horror came over her face, she vanished and I went back to sleep. In the morning I could vividly recall the encounter, but was far from sure if it was real or a dream. I foolishly told the officer in the next bed about it and he commented, 'So even chaplains have dreams like that!' – and spread the word. That evening every officer in the ward asked for one yellow pill to help him sleep, smiling in anticipation of a visit from 'Muriel'.

Months later I was preaching in a Baptist church in Lincoln and, as is my custom, shaking hands with members of the congregation afterwards at the church door. To my astonishment I found myself facing a blonde girl and gasped: 'You're Muriel! Did you visit me in hospital during the night?' She explained that she was a nurse on another ward and had been told I was there. Since she was forbidden to visit the officers, she had waited till our night nurse went for a coffee break and then crept in with a torch. But she had barely introduced herself when she heard the nurse returning and fled. So it had all really happened. Years later I met a man who had been in the same hospital long after me and when I praised the staff's care and skill, he qualified it by telling me that 'some funny things happen there' and proceeded to tell me about a chaplain who took pills to get girls in the middle of the night. So I became a legend in my own lifetime!

The second incident was the result of another stone in the other kidney. The two scars almost met around my middle, making me look like a conjurer's trick gone badly wrong. This time the excruciating pain struck me while preaching in Burton on Trent. I was rushed to hospital immediately afterwards and a surgeon told me it was so urgent that he was willing to operate at midnight. I was put in a single room to be 'prepared'. I dislike one aspect of this even more than the surgery (when I am unconscious of what is happening) – namely, being shaved, especially in the nether regions. As I lay, dreading this humiliation, the door opened and in came a teenage West Indian girl, with disposable razors in one hand and a tin of talcum powder in the other. Incredulous, I asked if she was going to do it and, being assured that she was, I shut my eyes to control my embarrassment, tore off my underwear and urged her to get on with it. Her reaction was a peal of laughter and a cry of 'Jesus! He's doing a striptease!' I thought I had reached the bottom of a pit of embarrassment, but worse was to come. As she pursued her vocation, she cheerfully asked me, 'And what's your job?' I was sorely tempted to tell a white lie and say 'teacher' (without 'Bible'), but gritted my teeth and murmured 'preacher'. At which point she looked horror-struck, shrieked, went into hysterics and fled the room. I heard her cries fading down the corridor. So I picked up where she had left off and tried to complete the task, unsuccessfully. Eventually she crept back in, looking utterly crestfallen. She confessed: 'Will I ever be forgiven for what I said, you being a preacher?' So we began to chat. She had been a regular churchgoer in Jamaica ('three times a Sunday but I never understood what it was all about'), but lapsed on coming here. Eventually, I suggested that we both got on with our respective callings and I preached while she shaved. Scripture tells us to 'preach the Word in season and out of season', but this was as far 'out of season' as I would wish. When I later told Enid about it, she had the last word: 'Do you realise she'll never be able to give her testimony?'

To be able to laugh at situations and at self is, I believe, a saving grace, though it is always easier in retrospect than at the time. But I went through one crisis which afforded no humour, either then or since. I think this chapter, highlighting my weakness, is the most appropriate context in which to share it, even though it was not primarily concerned with my body, its cause being only partly physical, likewise its effect (the loss of natural sleep).

In a word, I suffered a serious 'breakdown'. Many words are used to describe such, from adjectives like 'nervous' to nouns like 'burn-out'. It was in the late seventies, towards the end of my time in Guildford. In sharing it, I hope that others who have experienced similar problems will draw hope and encouragement. At the time I thought my ministry had come to an end, yet now it is richer, fuller and wider than ever before.

Looking back, I can see why it happened but at the time I didn't see it coming, nor did anyone else. The work at the Millmead Centre in Guildford had reached a 'high', with large 'celebrations', five 'area' congregations and many 'house group' cells all over town. We had a full-time staff but I was still taking far too much on my own shoulders, mainly because I am not good at delegating responsibility to others, preferring to get on and do it myself, perhaps thinking I could do as well, if not better, than anyone else. Pride goes before a fall.

As well as this build-up, I was already embarking on occasional overseas ministry tours, which enriched both me and the congregation with a wider vision. One of these was to prove the 'last straw'. I travelled alone to the heart of Africa, flying in a small plane from Kenya to Upper Congo, where a missionary doctor connected with our church was working. Lithe and athletic, he took me for long treks through the scrub. After some days I flew on to Kinshasa and was driven to Lower Congo where my wife's sister and her husband worked among Angolan refugees. By then I had discovered, to my horror, what appeared to be suppurating ulcers in my groin and feared that I had somehow picked up a horrible, even sexually associated disease. Preaching and teaching with this possibility dominating my mind was a nightmare. Eventually I found a doctor I could consult and was relieved to be told that the 'blisters' were the result of tramping the tropics in tight underpants. I returned home in a state of nervous exhaustion only to find that one of my associates had been discovered having an unhealthy though not immoral relationship with a girl in the youth group (he subsequently left his disabled wife and married her). On my first Sunday back, a man whose 'prophecies' I had questioned 'threatened' me with a 'black cloud' over my future.

It was all too much. I simply could not face the resumption of all my responsibilities. The elders were understanding and astonishingly generous. My wife and I were packed off to Madeira for a fortnight but it would take much more and much longer than that for a full recovery. I came to know depression and even despair, wondering if my life's work was over, in my forties. I even consulted a Christian psychiatrist, whose marriage I had conducted years before. He assured me I was not mentally ill and told me he was convinced I would learn things from all this that would give me a more effective ministry in the future. I knew he was not trying to give a 'patient' reassurance. It was the first glimmer of hope. Later a church member gave me a text from Scripture she felt was for me – Acts 16:28: 'Don't harm yourself! We are all here!' That released my first smile for months.

It was a Chinese doctor from Borneo, a dynamic Christian evangelist, who got me back to work. One Sunday afternoon he took me for a walk in the Surrey countryside and persuaded me to get back into the pulpit that very evening. It was Pentecost and I spoke on Ezekiel's valley of dry bones brought back miraculously to life and battle. I was addressing myself as much as anyone else.

From then on I learned to live and serve within my gift and calling, allowing others to do the same. Members took up many pastoral tasks, including weddings and even funerals. In the services, worship was led by others, while I concentrated on my teaching gift, which has since developed in some unexpected and more effective ways. Many commented on a new sensitivity and mellowness, even though my preaching is sharper and more challenging than ever.

So I can now thank the Lord for allowing it to happen, for making it work together for my good, for the patience of a church prepared to wait for my recovery and most of all for a loyal wife who faithfully supported myself and the children throughout that empty and negative time. The nightmare is over, though never forgotten. It does seem a long time ago, in my 'Middle Ages'.

Now old age beckons. I am into what I call 'injury time' and others 'borrowed time', after the biblical allotment of three score years and ten. We become more aware of our bodies, taking more notice when they go wrong than when they were working properly. Are the increasing problems God's way of loosening our ties with and affection for our bodies, preparing us to part with them? Having been good servants they become bad masters, telling us things we are no longer free to do, making us increasingly dependent on others, causing fresh aches and pains and generally fulfilling the scriptural description: 'this body of our humiliation'. I said to our family doctor recently: 'I'm beginning to suffer from old age.' His laconic reply was: 'There's an awful lot of it about'!

I am grateful for keeping most of my hair and many of my teeth (the dentist recently told me I'd still have some when I was 150 years old). Cataract removal is already 'in sight'. I have recently had the 'wee' problem common to old men. The prostatectomy was in the hands of a Muslim surgeon from Iran, so I did not give him my book on Islam until after I came round from the anaesthetic!

The resurgence of Islam is indelibly associated in my memory with my first, and so far only, stroke. I had had a strong premonition (prophetic revelation?) that this second-largest and fastest-growing religion would become the dominant and domineering faith in the United Kingdom and had arranged to record an extended message on the significance of this for Christians before an invited audience. Shortly before, I had been in Holland for a Pentecost camp of 35,000 believers, where I picked up a nasty virus. I should have taken to my bed but had to go straight on to Kansas City in America, where I spoke for up to six hours a day at a national conference. A three-plane journey brought me home exhausted, but I relaxed and rested for a few days. After one afternoon nap, I rose a little unsteadily, looked in the mirror and hardly recognised the stranger with a twisted face who stared back at me.

I knew at once I had had a stroke, though the family doctor at first suspected Bell's palsy, since only my face seemed to be affected. But many tests, including a brain scan, confirmed that the stroke had affected cranial nerves to throat, tongue and lips, slurring my speech. Yet the results of all blood tests were within normal range (pressure, flow, sugar and cholesterol). A friend put the news on the Internet and hundreds prayed that I would have enough speech and strength to record that vital message on Islam. In the event I spoke for five and a half hours, but finished standing on one leg with a useless left side in spasm. Three men in the front row told me afterwards they were on the edge of their seats, ready to catch me.

Talking has remained a conscious effort, particularly in personal conversation. But this eases and I am thankful that audiences are often unaware of the handicap. It takes a great deal to shut me up!

These reminders of mortality are good for us, reminding us to number our days and get a heart of wisdom. New questions assail the mind. How and when will I die? Will my body or my brain give up first? I find myself echoing John Wesley's (answered) prayer: 'Lord, let me not live to be useless.'

Death is the point at which the eschatological becomes existential. What a preacher has expounded about the future is experienced in the present. Convictions become reality.

I have long believed that we pass through three phases of existence: first, as embodied spirits; second, as disembodied spirits; third, as re-embodied spirits. Jesus went through all three within one week. Our transitions will be more spaced out. The New Testament puts most emphasis on the final phase but questions about the intermediate are inevitable.

I look forward with genuine curiosity to life in the 'middle room'. True, I will have lost contact with family and friends on earth but I will have regained communion with so many more already in heaven, including my daughter. For I am convinced that I will be fully conscious and able to communicate, just as Jesus was between his death and resurrection, preaching the gospel to those drowned in Noah's flood. I have never been convinced that our spirits 'fall asleep' when our bodies do or that we remain in a somnolent state until the resurrection. I just cannot imagine an activist like Paul believing it was far better to depart and be with Christ if he would be totally unconscious of where he was or whom he was with. Of course he admitted that he would be incomplete, but would rather be 'at home with the Lord' even if it meant being 'away from the body'. And I'm sure that even now he is looking forward to getting his new body, free from that 'thorn in the flesh' that so irritated and frustrated him.

And I do, too. If my new body is going to be 'like his glorious' body. I dare to believe and preach that I shall be thirty-three years old, in my physical and mental prime, able to enjoy life in a recycled universe to the full. And no more birthdays, those annual reminders of more years behind and fewer ahead. No Christian creed has ever included the immortality of the soul, but only the resurrection of the body, that supernatural event in which my mortal soul is clothed with an immortal body.

That is why I share the early Christian preference for burial, rather than the general practice, then and now, of burning dead bodies. I have often been asked what I think about cremation. I do not think it affects the deceased in any way. God is as able to raise ashes as well as dust. Indeed, he needs none of the old body to create the new; he made the whole physical universe *ex nihilo*, from nothing. Nagasaki was the most Christian city in Japan and many believers were totally vaporised when the second atomic bomb was dropped, but they will be raised in the last day.

But it can affect the bereaved, in that they have taken some responsibility in hastening the decomposition of a loved one's body, instead of leaving the natural process to take its course. Cremation has led to more cases of chronic grief because it conveys a sense of bringing about a more complete 'end' to a life, whereas burial speaks more of planting in the soil with the hope of seeing something similar appearing as a result, as every farmer and gardener knows. Anyway, there's a lovely little cemetery in the village where I live and I already have my eye on it, every time I walk past it to the post office.

Meanwhile, I can wholeheartedly echo the poet Robert Browning:

> Grow old along with me,
> The best is yet to be.

Epilogue:
'Not as Bad as the Truth'

Re-living my life in this way has been an unusual experience, leading to considerable introspection. In particular, I have constantly faced three questions.

First, what do I think of myself? Such self-examination was bound to result from an overview of three-quarters of a century on planet earth. What is there of any lasting value in all I have said and done?

I would certainly not want to exchange my life for anyone else's, so I do not have any feelings of envy. I could not have had a more interesting time. But I would want to have made changes in my own life, so I do have feelings of regret, even remorse.

As I have pondered over all the advantages I have had and all that has been invested in me by other persons, both human and divine, the phrase 'unprofitable servant' has repeatedly popped into my mind. The gap between what has gone into my life and what has come out is clear to me, if to no one else.

That is not mock modesty, which is an inverted form of pride. While outwardly appearing quite self-confident in public, I suffer inwardly from a lack of self-esteem and have a constant need of reassurance, as those closest to me know.

In letting this 'hang out', I trust that others may be encouraged. If God can use an insecure, even dysfunctional personality such as I, there must be hope for anyone! Earthen vessels can contain heavenly treasure.

Second, what will others think of me? I have had the reputation of being a rather private person, as Jennifer has noted in her Foreword. That has probably come from the basic instinct of self-preservation, which acts in relation to social rejection as much as physical danger. We put up shields of protection, lest people find out what we're really like.

As I have bared my soul (and my body) in these pages, I have battled with the fear of disappointing and disillusioning readers who have looked up to me. As a friend of mine used to say: 'When people get to know me, all awe and wonder rapidly disappear; I wouldn't mind so much if they left me a tiny little pedestal I could still stand on!'

I have had to run the risk of readers thinking: 'I didn't know he was like that.' More than one who has seen parts of the manuscript accurately summed me up as 'ordinary', but their tone of surprise troubles me, as if I have robbed them of something they cherished. To be totally honest, I have felt I have robbed myself as well!

For years I said I would never write my autobiography, considering it an egotistical exercise of self-importance, based as it is on an assumption that others would want to read it. Pressure from friends and publishers made me change my mind. Yet my consent may also be an act of self-protection. It will forestall any other biographer probing into my private affairs. At least I am still in control of what is said about me!

However, in the last analysis, what I think about myself and what others think of me is relatively unimportant. Which brings me to the crucial question, which has kept recurring as I have put pen to paper:

Third, what will the Lord think of me? He will have the last word, on me and on all of us. It is to him that we shall have to give account for the use of the time and talents he gave us. Each of us will stand before him alone, without the support of family and friends, or the accusations of our foes.

I have the advantage, perhaps unique, of having had more than a hint of the verdict. Some years ago I was the target of rumours which were totally untrue. I later tracked them down to a source in Wales and was able to stop them. But at the time they were both painful and damaging. Speaking engagements began to be cancelled (evasive apologies simply said: 'Arrangements for your visit have fallen through'). I had no idea why until three elders from Cardiff drove all the way to Surrey to tell me what was being said and ask whether any of the accusations were true. I told them it was not for me to say. Scripture orders that any accusations against a Christian leader must be accompanied by the testimony of two or three first-hand witnesses of the offence, which they could not provide in this case. However, I took pity on them for making the effort to come and see me, so told them there was no truth at all in what they had heard (among others, that I no longer read my Bible but only listened to the Spirit and that I believed that all Jews would go to heaven without believing in the Saviour).

After they had gone I turned to the Lord and complained bitterly about both the personal pain and the damage to my ministry. I have rarely known him speak to me as clearly as he did then. His reply was this: 'The worst they can say about you is not as bad as the truth.' I burst out laughing, both at the unexpectedness of it (the heart of most humour) and with relief that my enemies didn't know as much as the Lord did. Later, when I told my wife, she had the same reaction. It has cured me of sensitivity to hostile criticism. I immediately thank the Lord they don't know the whole truth.

I ought to add what the Lord added to this surprising statement: 'but I know the worst and I still love and use you.' My laughter mixed with tears at that point (and my eyes fill up again as I write this). I realised what incredible grace he had shown to, in and through me.

My tale is told. To God be the credit.

Appendix I:
Names Dropped

I have tried to keep the irritating habit of name-dropping, which can leave the wrong impression, to an absolute minimum in the main body of this book. Nevertheless, it has been my privilege to know personally many well-known servants of the Lord, each of whom has left an imprint on my spirit and inspired me to pursue my own calling. I list them in alphabetical order.

'Brother' Andrew

Ian Andrews

Gordon Bailey

John Barr

Alex Buchanan

Ken Burnett

Clive Calver

Michael Cassidy

Larry Christensen

Gerald Coates

Barney Coombs

Nick Cuthbert

Morgan Derham

Don Double

Edward England

Joni Erickson-Tada

Roger Forster

Bob Gordon

Billy Graham

Lynn Green

Michael Green

Harry Greenwood

Michael Griffiths

Michael Harper

Greg Haslam
Tony Higton
Chris Hill
Clifford Hill
Jan Willem van der Hoeven
Tom Houston
Benson Idahosa
Bryn Jones
'R.T.' Kendall
Graham Kendrick
Gilbert Kirby
Lance Lambert
Martyn Lloyd-Jones
George (Lord) MacLeod
John Noble
Ian Petit
Derek Prince
Jackie Pullinger
Mike Pusey
David Pytches
Alan Redpath
Tom Rees

Will Sangster
Francis Schaeffer
Ian Smale (Ishmael)
Donald (Lord) Soper
Mark Stibbe
John Stott
Bill Subritsky
(Cardinal) Suenens
George Thomas (Lord Tonypandy)
Colin Urquhart
George Verwer
Terry Virgo
Phil Vogel
Arthur Wallis
David Watson
Leslie Weatherhead
Andrew White
Gerald Williams
John Wright
Richard Wurmbrand
Pastor Yun ('Heavenly Man')

Appendix II:
Books Written

Truth to Tell
Hodder and Stoughton, 1977 (now Bethel)

Leadership Is Male
Highland, 1988 (then Eagle, now Bethel)

The Normal Christian Birth
Hodder and Stoughton, 1989

The Road to Hell
Hodder and Stoughton, 1992

Explaining Water Baptism
Sovereign World, 1992

Explaining the Resurrection
Sovereign World, 1993

Explaining the Second Coming
Sovereign World, 1993

Fourth Wave (now *Word and Spirit Together*)
Hodder and Stoughton, 1993

When Jesus Returns
Hodder and Stoughton, 1995

Is the Blessing Biblical?
Hodder and Stoughton, 1995

Once Saved, Always Saved?
Hodder and Stoughton, 1996

Jesus Baptises in One Holy Spirit
Hodder and Stoughton, 1997 (now Terra Nova)

Where is Jesus Now?
Kingsway, 2001

Unlocking the Bible
HarperCollins –8 volume edition, 1999–2001;
Omnibus edition, 2003

The Challenge of Islam to Christians
Hodder and Stoughton, 2003